The International Jewish Cook Book

Other books by Nina Froud

French Cooking for Everyone
The Home Book of Russian Cookery
Cooking the Chinese Way
Cooking the Japanese Way
The World Book of Meat Dishes
The World Book of Poultry and Game Dishes
The World Book of Sweets and Desserts

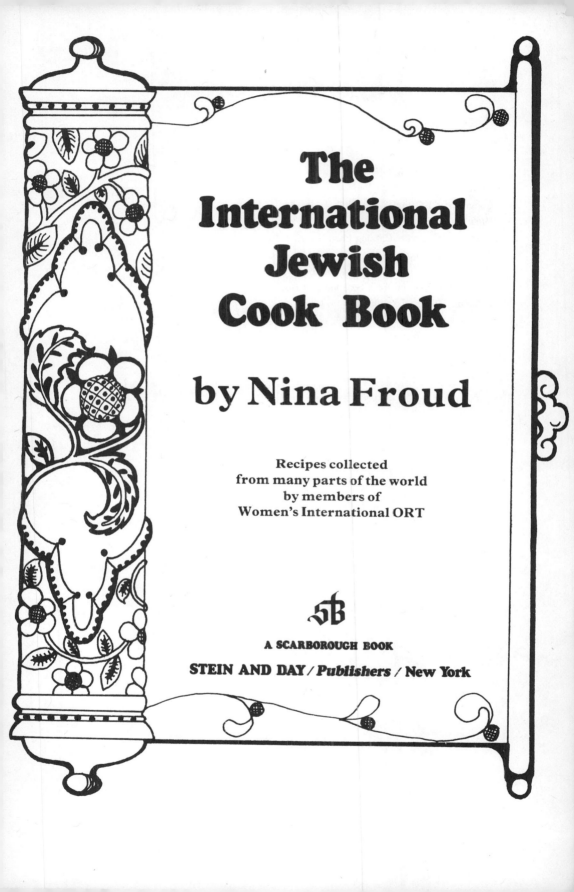

The International Jewish Cook Book

by Nina Froud

Recipes collected
from many parts of the world
by members of
Women's International ORT

ᔕᖯ

A SCARBOROUGH BOOK

STEIN AND DAY / *Publishers* / New York

A SCARBOROUGH BOOK

First published in 1972

Copyright © 1972 by World ORT Union as

Some of Our Best Recipes Are Jewish

Library of Congress Catalog Card No. 72-82215

All rights reserved

Printed in the United States of America

Stein and Day/*Publishers*/Scarborough House

Briarcliff Manor, N.Y. 10510

This book is dedicated to the memory of Mrs Melanie Horn, the late President of Women's Israel ORT, who was tragically killed in the Swiss Air Disaster and without whose continual encouragement this book would not have been published.

Acknowledgements

There are many people in many countries whose help and generosity made the appearance of this book possible. I should like to express particular gratitude to the following members and supporters of ORT who have kindly contributed recipes from their countries for this collection: Madame D. Aboulker, France; Mrs Eva Alfert, Great Britain; Madame B. Virmaux-Auroy, Principal of ORT School, Val d'Anga, Morocco; Mrs Bea Beham, Israel; Mrs Eunice Braude, Switzerland; Mrs Sarah Chinks, Canada; Mrs Gwen Davidner, Winnipeg Women's ORT; Mrs L. Geis, Israel; Miss Elisabeth Hausmann, Women's International ORT, Geneva; the late Mrs M. Horn, Israel; Chef Hans Jebsen, Norway; Mrs E. King, Israel; Mrs Pearl Lee, Great Britain; Mrs D. Loewenthal, Israel; Mrs Malewski, Canada; Mrs Valda Norwitz, ORT South Africa; Mrs S. Racine, Israel; Miss Alida Reuben and Miss Sadie Reuben, Great Britain; Mrs Lynn Rosenfield, Winnipeg Women's ORT; Mrs Sarah Sachs, Tel-Aviv, Israel; Mrs Nathan Silver, President of Women's ORT, Toronto, Canada; Mrs Roslyn Snyder, Canada; Mrs Cissie Solomons, Great Britain; Mrs Rosaline Stotland, Montreal Women's ORT, Canada; Mrs Toby Veinish, Canada; Mrs Esther Vilnay, Israel.

I should also like to thank contributors, whose names are not known to me, and who have sent recipes from Argentina, Belgium, Denmark, India, Iran, Italy, Mexico, and Peru. My thanks are due to Mrs Eunice Braude, Mr Bert Cantor, and Harold and June Sterne, for their constructive criticism and helpful suggestions for improvements of the book, to Gila Michaeli for checking Hebrew words and names, to Penny Jones, the typographical designer, and last but not least to Miss Kathleen Tranmar for typing so many versions of the manuscript.

London   NINA FROUD

Foreword by the President of Women's International ORT, Mrs H. H. Wingate

For an experienced chef a cookery book is a *guide* to the art of cooking and not a *roadmap*. Knowledge allows the trained person to concentrate on the aesthetics of food – the touches of flavour and the flourishes of presentation – that change a meal from a drab and necessary function to a warm and rewarding experience for family and friends to enjoy.

In a way we can compare the work of our organization – ORT, the Organization for Rehabilitation through Training – to an experienced cook working comfortably in her kitchen. Now in its tenth decade of service in vocational training, ORT has experienced just about every kind of problem and surmounted just about every kind of challenge that has arisen in this field. Technical assistance? ORT has been involved in technical assistance since its foundation in Russia in 1880 when a small group of dedicated men banded together to offer training, tools, and opportunity to their less fortunate co-religionists. True, the term 'technical assistance' had not yet been coined, but when it came into vogue in the post World War II years, the experienced and skilled ORT staff could say: 'Oh yes, this is familiar to us – it is what we have always done – a variation on the recipe and a new application of our expertise will do the necessary job.'

Similarly ORT has adapted to the retraining of refugees (one million Jews have been in movement since World War II, and that movement continues today), the long-term training of young people, and the upgrading and retraining of workers faced with the rapid, and sometimes terrifying, changes in technology.

During the next ten years, ORT will train an average of 60,000 students each year in its 1,000 schools and training units in twenty-two countries around the world. These schools will be staffed by 3,000 teachers and workshop instructors, many trained at ORTs own Teacher Training Institute at Anières near Geneva. As trades develop and change to follow industrial needs, ORT will no doubt add to the more than seventy skills which are already taught in its schools.

Perhaps best of all is our realization that the training, that these boys and girls and men and women will receive from ORT, will allow them to add spice and relish to life as well as supplying the skills for useful work.

I would like to express my thanks, and the thanks of ORT women around the world, to Nina Froud for what is a most exciting guide to new and interesting meals, and again express my thanks to the women in our organization who have submitted treasured recipes for the rest of us to share.

H. H. WINGATE

Introduction

When I was asked to work on this book, I hesitated. Briefly. Just long enough to declare the fact that I was not Jewish. I liked the idea of associating with ORT, in however small a way, and found the truly international project too exciting to resist.

What attracts me in this collection of recipes is its essential Jewishness, which lends it a special glamour. After all, not many cuisines can claim recipes which are thousands of years old and still viable! The climate of ancient tradition, the link with the Bible is fascinating.

Yet this is not meant to be just another Jewish cookery book, for its aim is to show the international character of ORT. This book presents a selection of recipes from sixteen countries in which ORT is active: Argentina, Belgium, Canada, Denmark, France, Great Britain, India, Iran, Israel, Italy, Morocco, Mexico, Norway, Peru, South Africa, and Switzerland.

It is interesting to see how the cooking traditions of each country, in which the Jews have lived throughout the centuries, are reflected in Jewish cooking. Polish, Russian, German, Hungarian, French, Italian, Spanish, Arab, etc. dishes have been adapted by Jewish cooks and made their own. The modifications often shifted the emphasis and changed the personality of the dish, reflecting the nuances both from the East and the West. Thus an Israeli version of a Polish dish may offer a subtle transformation, due to use of Mediterranean produce, which was not available in Eastern Europe.

In spite of drawing on so many sources for culinary inspiration in over two thousand years of the dispersion all over the world, the Jews have succeeded in giving a definite unity to their cooking. This stemmed from biblical symbolism and religious and traditional requirements.

The ancient heritage and the additions to the Jewish menus in the last two thousand years, have been enriched still further in modern times. Many new foods, demanding new treatment, have come into Jewish cooking since Israel has transformed deserts and stony hills into a fertile land. Fulfilling the biblical promise that the desert shall blossom as the rose (*Isaiah* 35.1), Israel's orchards and vineyards produce an abundance of fruit.

So much so, that there is a story that in El Al 'planes an extra notice to the

Introduction

passengers has been added. The El Al inscription is reputed to read:
>NO SMOKING
>FASTEN YOUR SAFETY BELTS
>EAT FRUIT

To the Jewish housewife this book, with contributions from many countries, in addition to traditional Jewish recipes, offers a wider scope and greater variety of culinary repertoire, without in any way departing from the requirements of the Dietary Laws.

The Israelis have an ice-cream which contains no dairy products. It is, therefore, equally possible to reproduce a Greek moussaka, omitting cheese and using breadcrumbs and a sprinkling of oil to make the gratin surface.

To anticipate protests against inclusion of several classical recipes in this book, I must plead the universal borrowing of dishes by many countries from each other. Even the French, who could be forgiven for thinking that they don't need to borrow anything from anyone, gastronomically speaking, include in their cookery books oriental pilaffs, Italian ravioli, Russian coulibiacs. The British practically claim curry as an English speciality. Small wonder then that the Jews, who have lived in Italy since the Roman times, should have adopted and adapted some Italian dishes.

Because of the specific purpose of this book, I have restricted the amount of general information to the minimum, but no preparation is indicated unless a recipe for it is included in one of the sections.

Nor would I attempt to outline the Dietary Laws, although in all recipes all the rules have been observed. I presume that all orthodox readers will know everything about it. Such data as is included in the text is given for its poetic quality for the benefit of non-Jewish readers. Should any of them be interested to learn more about the subject, I recommend Rabbi Seymour Siegel's book *Jewish Dietary Laws*, which is clear and easy to read.

This book does not pretend to be comprehensive – the area is too vast, covering four continents and thousands of years. It is hoped that this cross-section of recipes gives a glimpse of ethnic and cultural cross-pollination of North and South, East and West, old and new.

Contents

Decorative scrolls all derived from Megillahs in the Jewish Museum, London

Abbreviations

Measurements

Oven temperatures

Metric equivalents

Abbreviations

fl oz	–	fluid ounce
oz	–	ounce
lb	–	pound
g	–	gramme
kg	–	kilogramme
ml	–	millilitre
dl	–	decilitre
tbs	–	tablespoon
tsp	–	teaspoon

Measurements

The ingredients are given in Continental, English, and American weights
and measures. These are not always straight conversions from the English
measures, but suitable adjustments. Where, for the sake of convenience,
1 oz is shown as 30 grammes, instead of 28·35, amounts of all ingredients
have been proportionally scaled up or down. The cups, tablespoons, and
teaspoons are American Standard.

Oven temperatures

Oven temperatures are given in all recipes in °C, °F, and Gas Mark.
Allowances, however, have to be made for variations of settings on
different models of electric cookers and it is advisable to consult the
instructions supplied with the cookers.

Approximate metric equivalents

Mass			Capacity			Length		
$\frac{1}{4}$ oz	=	7g	1 fl oz	=	25 ml	$\frac{1}{8}$ inch	=	3 mm
$\frac{1}{2}$ oz	=	15g	$\frac{1}{4}$ gill	=	30 ml	$\frac{1}{4}$ inch	=	5 mm
1 oz	=	30g	1 gill	=	125 ml	$\frac{1}{2}$ inch	=	1 cm
16 oz	=	480g or 500g	1 pint	=	500 ml	1 inch	=	2·5 cm
2 lb	=	1kg	1 quart	=	1 litre			
10 lb	=	5kg	10 dl	=	1 litre			

Starters

Herring

Herring is the basis of many *hors-d'oeuvre* dishes. Herring can be salted, marinated or pickled. The flesh is quite delicate and responds harmoniously to the flavours of various dressings and garnishes, examples below:

Chopped herring

6 Servings

2 salt herrings, soaked in water for 2 hours
1 slice, crustless white bread
2 tablespoons vinegar
1 tablespoon finely chopped onion
1 large, grated apple
pinch freshly ground black pepper
2 tablespoons oil
small pinch sugar (optional)
6 lettuce shells
2 hard-boiled chopped eggs

Rinse herring, bone, and chop. Soak bread in vinegar, mash with a fork, and mix with herring. Add onion, apple, pepper, oil, and sugar. Mix well, arrange on lettuce shells, sprinkle with chopped egg, and serve cold.

Salted herring in sour cream

4 Servings

4 salted herring fillets
strained tea
100ml (4fl oz or $\frac{1}{2}$ cup) sour cream
1 teaspoon fresh chopped dill (or parsley)
$\frac{1}{4}$ teaspoon cracked black pepper
juice of 1 clove of garlic
watercress for garnish

Soak the herring fillets in strained cold tea for a few hours, or preferably overnight. Drain well and slice. Mix sour cream with dill, pepper, and garlic juice. Add herring slices, mix well, and chill. Garnish with watercress and serve with thin slices of rye bread.

Starters

Salt herring with cream cheese and chives

3–4 Servings

2 filleted salt herrings
milk
pepper
dried dill
chopped onion
2 tablespoons sugar
1·25dl (1 gill or ½ cup) vinegar
2 cooking apples
90g (3oz or 6 tablespoons) cream cheese
1·25dl (1 gill or ½ cup) cream
1 tablespoon lemon juice
1 tablespoon chopped chives

Soak the herring fillets in milk overnight. Grate the pepper coarsely, mix with dill, onion, sugar, and vinegar. Pour this mixture over the herrings (having first removed from milk and rinsed) and leave for five to six hours. Drain the fillets and put in a dish on a foundation of coarsely grated apples. Blend cream cheese, cream, and lemon juice, pour this dressing over the herrings, and sprinkle with chives.

Marinated herring

These keep well for two or three weeks and are excellent standbys, so it is a good idea to marinate more than you need for one occasion, especially as, by changing the dressing, you can completely transform the *hors-d'oeuvre*.

6 plump herrings
60g (2oz or 4 tablespoons) kitchen salt
0·5 litre (1 pint or 2 cups) water
0·25 litre (½ pint or 1 cup) vinegar
0·25 litre (½ pint or 1 cup) wine
2 large, sliced onions
2 sliced lemons
2 teaspoons peppercorns
2 bay leaves
1–2 red chillies
1–2 tablespoons sugar

Starters

Clean, bone, and fillet the herrings. Reserve soft roes. Mix salt and water and put the herring fillets in a shallow dish, cover with vinegar, and leave to stand for two to three hours. Keeping all the vinegar, drain the fillets and roll up. Put the rolled fillets into a pickling jar, in layers, covering each layer with sliced onion, lemon, and sprinkling with peppercorns. Add bay leaves and chillies.

Pour the vinegar in which the herrings were soaked into a saucepan. Add wine and sugar. You should have enough marinating liquid to cover the fillets in the jar completely. Therefore, if necessary, add water. Bring the marinade to the boil, cook for two minutes, and remove from heat. Allow to cool.

Pound the soft roes to a paste, dilute with a little of the marinade, then stir the mixture into the cold marinade. Pour the marinade over the fillets, cover jars, and store in a cool place.

You can serve a whole fillet per portion, or slice the fillets and arrange in an *hors-d'eouvre* dish with cream cheese and chives; sliced tomatoes and fresh or pickled cucumber; onion rings and olives; with apple slices and horseradish cream; with hard boiled eggs and mayonnaise; potato salad and mustard or tartare sauce; with salad dressing (pages 253–5) with a little sugar, chopped onion, and sour cream added to it.

Rollmops

Use marinated and strongly spiced fillets of herring. Stuff with a small gherkin, roll up, and secure with a cocktail stick. Serve in an *hors-d'oeuvre* dish decorated with thin onion rings.

Starters

Blini with smoked salmon or kippers

6 Servings

1 yeast cake
2·5dl ($\frac{1}{2}$ pint or 1 cup) lukewarm water
0·5 litre (1 pint or 2 cups) lukewarm milk
240g ($\frac{1}{2}$lb or 2 cups) buckwheat flour
4 egg yolks
$\frac{1}{2}$ teaspoon salt
2 teaspoons sugar
2 tablespoons melted butter
4 egg whites
360g (12oz) smoked salmon or 2 plump smoked kippers*
butter
sour cream

Dissolve yeast in water and 1dl (1 gill or $\frac{1}{2}$ cup) milk. Add half the flour and mix well. Cover the mixing bowl with a tea towel and leave in a warm place for three hours.

Beat egg yolks with salt and sugar, add the rest of the lukewarm milk, mix, add melted butter, mix again, and add to the yeast mixture, stirring thoroughly. Incorporate the rest of the flour. Beat the whites until stiff, fold into the batter, cover, and allow to stand for forty-five to fifty minutes without disturbing the batter, which should have the consistency of thick cream.

I use special cast iron pancake frying pans about 7 to 8cm (3 inches) in diameter, but blini can be baked in any good lightly greased frying pan or on a griddle. Take care to measure out the correct amount of batter to keep the blini of uniform size, brown on both sides, stack on a dish, and keep warm until all batter is used up.

Slice the smoked salmon thinly and arrange on a dish. (If using kippers, do not cook in any way at all, just carefully remove the bone, and slice thinly as for smoked salmon.)

* This delectable variation on a Russian theme, using kippers, was invented, as far as I am aware, by my late father-in-law, collaborator in cookery, and friend, George Froud. Being an engineer by profession, an artist at heart, and often impecunious, he was determined to serve blini with fish but could not afford smoked salmon. The result of his famous experiment was so wonderfully good that it was adopted into our regular repertoire.

Starters

Serve the salmon (or kippers) and the blini together with melted butter and sour cream handed in separate sauce-boats. Let your guests spread their blini with melted butter, put a slice of salmon or kipper over it, top with a spoonful of sour cream, and double the pancake or not, as they please.

Gefilte fish, Polish style

6 Servings

1·25kg (2½lb) mixed fish: haddock, bream, cod, hake*
0·75 litre (1½ pints or 5 cups) water
2 sliced carrots
2 chopped onions
2 stalks chopped celery (optional)
1 tablespoon ground almonds
1 tablespoon chopped parsley (optional)
salt and pepper
2 beaten eggs
2–3 tablespoons medium matzo meal
small pinch sugar

Trim and fillet the fish. Cook the skins, bones, heads, etc. in the water with one sliced carrot, celery (if used), and seasoning, to make fish stock. Bring to boil, skim carefully, cover, simmer for one hour, and strain. Chop the fish, put in a mixing bowl, add onions, parsley, sugar, almonds, and seasoning. Put the whole mixture through a mincer, add eggs, blend well, then add enough matzo meal to bind the mixture.
Shape into balls or quenelles and simmer in the prepared fish stock with the remaining sliced carrot for two hours. Lift the fish out of the stock with a perforated spoon, put on a serving dish, decorate each with a slice of carrot. Cook down the stock to reduce and concentrate it, taste for seasoning, spoon a little over the gefilte fish, leave to set, and serve cold.

* Various kinds of fish may be included in the mixture, but haddock gives the gefilte fish its firm texture.

Starters

Gefilte fish, Russian style

The varieties of sea fish indicated take into consideration the supplies available to the majority of readers of this book. In the past, when mainly fresh water fish was available to the Polish or Russian Jewish communities, gefilte fish was traditionally made of such fish as carp and pike. In fact, as the name 'gefilte' i.e. 'stuffed' implies, originally the preparation described in these recipes was intended as stuffing either for carp or pike. Broadly speaking, this should include fish with three qualities of flesh: flaky, dry, and fat.

6 Servings

1·25kg (2½lb) assorted fish, as in preceding recipe
0·75litre (1½ pints or 5 cups) water
salt
white pepper
1 finely chopped onion
3 chopped celery stalks
2 tablespoons medium matzo meal or equivalent amount of white bread
2 eggs
2 sliced onions
1–2 sliced carrots

Trim and fillet the fish. Use bones, heads, and skins for making fish stock, well seasoned with salt and pepper. Put the fish, chopped onion, celery, and matzo meal through a mincer. Season, stir in eggs. Shape the mixture into balls.

Line a fish kettle with sliced onions. Strain fish stock into it. Add carrots and gently put in fish balls. Slowly bring to the boil and simmer for two hours. Finish off as described in the previous recipe.

Cod roe pâté

This Mediterranean *hors-d'oeuvre* is delicious. Serve it with hot Arab bread. See pita (page 185):

4 Servings

120g (4oz) pressed salt cod roe
2 slices white bread

Starters

1 tablespoon grated onion
1 clove crushed garlic (optional)
150ml (6fl oz or ¾ cup) olive oil
juice of 1 lemon
1 tablespoon finely chopped parsley
black olives for garnish

Soak the roe in cold water for a few minutes to remove excess salt. Cut crusts off bread slices and soak bread in water. Squeeze out surplus water from roe and bread and put together into a mortar. Pound into a paste. Add onion and garlic and continue to pound until the paste is smooth, or pass the mixture through a blender. Gradually, as for mayonnaise (page 250), stir in alternately little amounts of oil and lemon juice. Stir until the pâté is smooth, light, and well blended. Spoon into an *hors-d'oeuvre* dish, sprinkle with parsley, garnish with olives, and serve.

Bagels mit lox

History does not record the name of the genius who invented this delectable combination, which has become a Sunday morning favourite among the American Jews. I would give him a medal any day. If you've never had a home-made bagel, cut in half, buttered, spread generously with cream cheese, topped with a slice of smoked salmon, and covered with its own lid – you haven't lived!

4 Servings

12 home-made bagels (pages 190–1)
sweet butter
240g (8oz or 1 cup) cream cheese
240g (8oz) smoked salmon
watercress

If the bagels were not baked on the morning on which you mean to serve them, warm them in a gentle oven, 121°C (250°F or Gas Mark ½). Split the bagels without severing completely, butter, spread with cream cheese. Put slices of smoked salmon on top of cream cheese, garnish with watercress, and serve.

Starters

Salami omelette

4 Servings

4 eggs
1 tablespoon cold water
salt and pepper
1 tablespoon oil
12 thin slices salami

Break the eggs one by one into a bowl, beat with a fork until they become runny and start to froth. Add water, season with salt and pepper, and mix.

Heat oil in a frying pan, put in salami, brown lightly, and turn to brown the other side.

Pour in beaten eggs over salami, cook, lifting the edges to allow raw egg to flow underneath. As soon as the underside is done, turn the omelette over without folding it, cook for a few seconds to set the other side, and serve at once.

Falafel

Falafel, along with humous and tehina, must be among the most popular *hors-d'oeuvre* throughout the Mediterranean area. It is sold as a street snack, a pita (page 185) sandwich, served as a first course in restaurants of all categories and as 'dig-dag' or a 'palate teaser' at cocktail parties. The *sabras* claim it as part of their oriental heritage and in Israel falafel is an ingredient of many dishes.

6 Servings

240g (8oz or $1\frac{1}{8}$ cups) chick-peas
$\frac{1}{4}$ teaspoon coriander
2 cloves garlic
1 teaspoon cumin
$\frac{1}{4}$ teaspoon red chilli pepper
$1-1\frac{1}{4}$ teaspoon salt
2–3 tablespoons cracked, wheat flour
1 lightly beaten egg
oil for deep frying

Starters

Soak chick-peas overnight, then skin and cook as described in recipe for humous below. Drain, mash, and mince.

Pound coriander, garlic, cumin, and chilli and add to chick-pea purée. Season with salt, sprinkle in flour, bind with egg, and mix thoroughly. Taking a spoonful of the mixture at a time, roll into balls about 2·5cm (1 inch) in diameter.

Heat the oil and deep fry the falafel until they are uniformly brown. Drain and serve hot with tehina, or humous and a salad.

Humous

4 Servings

180g (6oz or $\frac{7}{8}$ cup) chick-peas
1 teaspoon bicarbonate of soda
salt
135g ($4\frac{1}{2}$oz or $\frac{1}{2}$ cup) tehina (page 10)
1 clove pounded garlic
juice of 1 lemon
chilli pepper or zhug (page 252)

Garnish
2 tablespoons olive oil
pinch paprika
1 tablespoon chopped parsley
2–3 tablespoons olives

Soak the chick-peas overnight in water with bicarbonate of soda. This helps to loosen the skins. Drain, rub well to remove skins, rinse, put in a pan of cold water, and bring to the boil. Boil gently but steadily for one and a half to two hours. Season with salt to taste and continue to simmer until tender.

Put tehina and garlic, with a pinch of salt and lemon juice, through a blender. (Or pound the garlic finely, then mix with the other ingredients to make a smooth paste.) Drain the chick-peas, mash well to make a purée and while it is still hot, blend in the tehina and garlic mixture. Mix well, arrange on a dish as described in recipe for tehina (page 10). Trickle on olive oil, sprinkle with chopped parsley and paprika, garnish with olives, and serve.

Starters

Tehina

Tehina, a preparation which can best be described as a sesame seed butter, is used in Arab countries as a dip for bread. In Greece it is used as a lenten soup and in Israel it is a favourite *hors-d'oeuvre*. It is also a vital ingredient for making humous.

4 Servings

120g (4oz or $\frac{3}{4}$ cup) sesame seeds
1–2 cloves crushed garlic
salt
150ml (6fl oz or $\frac{3}{4}$ cup) cold water
juice of 1–1$\frac{1}{2}$ lemons
pinch cayenne pepper or zhug (page 252)
2 chopped, hard-boiled eggs (optional)
2 tablespoons olive oil
pinch paprika
1 tablespoon chopped parsley
2 tablespoons black or green olives for garnish

Reduce the sesame seeds with garlic, salt, and water to a paste in a blender. (If you don't possess a blender, then do as 99 per cent of Middle Eastern housewives do – pound the sesame seeds and garlic in a mortar, adding water gradually to obtain a thick butter-like paste.)

Transfer to a bowl and, little by little, as for mayonnaise, stir in lemon juice. Season with cayenne pepper or zhug and the tehina is ready if you are going to use it as an ingredient for another dish.

If served as an independent *hors-d'oeuvre*, add chopped egg, arrange on a serving dish, flattening the surface evenly, then make a few shallow channels with the back of a spoon. Trickle olive oil into these channels, sprinkle the surface with a small pinch of paprika, decorate with parsley, garnish with olives, and serve.

Salat chatzilim (aubergine (egg-plant) salad)

4–6 Servings

2 large aubergines
1 small, finely chopped onion

Starters

2 tablespoons olive oil
salt and pepper
2 teaspoons wine vinegar
2 tablespoons lemon juice
1 seeded green pepper, cut in thin rings
2–3 peeled, sliced tomatoes
1 tablespoon olives
1 tablespoon chopped parsley

Bake or grill the aubergines until the outside is burnt and the inside soft. Heat oil and lightly fry the onion.

Peel the aubergines, chop finely or mash with a fork. Add to onion, fry together for five minutes, stirring constantly. Remove from heat, transfer to a bowl, season, add vinegar and lemon juice, and mix well.

Spread the aubergine, which should have the consistency of thick homogenous paste, on a serving dish. Garnish with pepper rings and tomato slices, put an olive in the centre of each tomato slice, sprinkle with parsley, and serve cold.

Chatzilim im tehina (aubergine with tehina)

6 Servings

2 large aubergines
1 small, finely chopped onion
2 tablespoons olive oil
salt and pepper
2 teaspoons vinegar
2 tablespoons lemon juice
tehina (page 10)
1–2 chopped cloves garlic
1 tablespoon chopped parsley

Prepare aubergine salad as described above. Mix with equal amount of tehina, add garlic, mix well, spread on a dish, sprinkle with parsley, and serve cold.

Starters

Aubergine (egg-plant) and cheese soufflé

Traditional dish of Balkan Jewish communities. In countries of origin a mixture of hard local cheese and cream cheese is used:

6 Servings

2–3 aubergines (egg-plants)
2–3 tablespoons margarine or butter
180g (6oz or 1½ cups) grated cheese (Cheddar, Gruyère or Parmesan, or any combination of these)
300g (10oz or 1¼ cups) cream cheese
salt and pepper
3 eggs

Scorch aubergines under a grill or over a stove burner, allow to cool, and peel. While the aubergines are cooling, pre-heat oven to 205°C (400°F or Gas Mark 5). Grease a *soufflé* mould with a little margarine. Put the peeled aubergines in a bowl and mash thoroughly with a fork. Reserve two to three tablespoons grated cheese, add the rest to aubergines with all of the cream cheese. Season with salt and pepper to taste. Separate eggs and stir the yolks into the aubergine mixture. Beat the whites until very stiff, fold into the mixture, and pour into the *soufflé* mould. Sprinkle the top with remaining grated cheese, dot with small pieces of margarine or butter, and bake for eight to twenty minutes. Serve at once.

Salat pilpel (stuffed pepper salad)

4–8 Servings

1 medium-sized aubergine
salt and pepper
100ml (4fl oz or ½ cup) olive oil
1 medium-sized, finely chopped onion
4 large green peppers
180g (6oz or ¾ cup) humous (page 9)

If serving as an *hors-d'oeuvre*, the above quantity will make eight portions; if as a main course, four portions.

Peel and dice the aubergine. Sprinkle with salt and allow to stand for fifteen to twenty minutes, then drain off all liquid. Heat oil, fry aubergine

Starters

until uniformly brown. Remove from pan and in the same oil lightly fry the onion. Allow to cool. Cut the peppers into quarters, remove seeds. Keep half the pepper quarters and shred the rest.

Mix shredded pepper with aubergine and onion. Add humous, season to taste, mix well, and chill this stuffing. Fill reserved pepper shells with the stuffing, piling it into domes. Serve cold.

Salat gezer b'klipat tapuzim (carrot salad in orange shells)

6 Servings

480g (1lb or 1⅓ cups) carrots
3 oranges
pinch salt
pinch sugar
1 tablespoon chopped, fresh ginger
2 tablespoons lemon juice
6 peeled orange slices

Peel and shred the carrots. Put in a bowl. Cut oranges in half, squeeze out all juice but do not break the orange shells.

Season carrots with salt and sugar, sprinkle in ginger and lemon juice, and pour on orange juice. Stir and chill for several hours.

Drain the carrot salad. (The marinating dressing can be strained and kept to be used again.) Spoon the salad into orange shells, top with a slice of orange, and serve.

Starters

Leeks with olives

4 Servings

6 leeks
3 tablespoons olive oil
2 tablespoons lemon juice
salt and pepper
tomato fondue (page 260)
2 dozen ripe black olives

Wash the leeks, cut into bite-sized chunks, put in an oven-proof dish with olive oil, lemon juice, and salt and pepper to taste. Cook in the oven pre-heated to 205°C (400°F Gas Mark 5) until tender. Dress with tomato fondue, garnish with olives, and put back in the oven for a few minutes.

Serve hot or cold.

French liver pâté with grapes

4 Servings

8 slices fresh goose liver (*foie gras*)
flour
60g (2oz or 4 tablespoons) chicken fat
salt and pepper
4 slices white, crustless bread
2 tablespoons brandy
2 tablespoons stock or water
1 bunch seedless grapes

Dip the liver slices in flour and fry lightly in half the chicken fat. Allow one and a half minutes each side. Season to taste.

In another pan at the same time fry the bread in the chicken fat. Arrange two slices of liver on each slice of bread and keep hot. Dilute the pan juices left from cooking the liver with brandy and stock, add grapes, simmer for a few minutes. Whisk in a little chicken fat (or margarine) adding it in small pieces, pour the sauce and the grapes over the liver, and serve.

Starters

Iraqi hors-d'oeuvre sarmi

8 Servings

500g (1 pint) jar vine leaves
240g (8oz or 1¼ cup) uncooked rice
75g (2½oz or ½ cup) shelled pine kernels
30g (1oz or ½ cup) chopped parsley
30g (1oz or ½ cup) chopped mint
30g (1oz or ½ cup) chopped spring onions
100ml (4fl oz or ½ cup) olive oil
salt and pepper
pinch cinnamon
150g (5oz or 1 cup) peeled, chopped tomatoes
2–3 cloves garlic
juice of 2 lemons
2·5dl (½ pint or 1 cup) water

Drain and rinse vine leaves. Wash rice and mix with pine kernels, parsley, mint, spring onions, and oil. Season with salt, pepper, and cinnamon. Use this mixture for stuffing the vine leaves as described (pages 146–7).

Line a *sauté* pan with tomatoes, add garlic. Pack the stuffed vine leaves in layers on this foundation, sprinkle in lemon juice, add water, cover with a plate, and simmer for one hour. Remove from heat. Leave in the pan to cool, then chill overnight and serve cold in their own sauce.

Salat perot b' avocado (avocado pears with fruit)

4 Servings

2 avocado pears
lemon juice
2 peeled oranges, in segments
a few strawberries
castor sugar

Halve the avocados, remove stones, and sprinkle with a little lemon juice to prevent discoloration. Fill with orange segments, decorate with strawberries, sprinkle with sugar, chill, and serve.

Starters

Anavim b' avocado (avocado with grapes)

4 Servings

2 medium-sized avocado pears
1 tablespoon lemon juice
salt and pinch sugar
480g (1lb) red grapes, peeled and seeded
4 tablespoons shredded celery
4 tablespoons fresh lime juice
1·25dl (1 gill or ½ cup) red wine
fresh mint leaves

Cut avocados in half lengthwise, remove stones, brush with lemon juice to prevent discoloration, season with salt. Combine grapes with celery, spoon into halved avocado pears. Mix lime juice, wine, and sugar, pour over avocados, chill. Garnish with mint leaves and serve. If fresh lime juice is not available, use lemon juice but not bottled lime juice.

Loks b' avocado (avocado with smoked salmon)

4 Servings

carrot salad (page 13)
2 avocado pears
120g (4oz) smoked salmon

Prepare and chill the salad as described. Drain. Halve the avocado pears. Fill with salad. Cut the salmon into strips, arrange on the carrot salad in a lattice pattern, and serve.

Chopped liver (international Jewish hors-d'oeuvre)

6 Servings

1 large, sliced Spanish onion
chicken fat or oil
500g (1lb) chicken livers (or ox livers – or a combination of both)
2 hard-boiled eggs
¼ teaspoon sugar
salt and pepper

Starters

Fry onion in fat until transparent. Slice and fry livers until very brown on both sides. Mince livers, onion, egg whites (reserving yolks) twice. Add sugar and seasoning to taste. Moisten with a little melted chicken fat. Spread evenly on a flat plate. Mash egg yolks and sprinkle over liver.

Israeli hot olive hors-d'oeuvre

Olives are a staple food throughout the Middle East. All Jewish communities appear to like olives, even those who could have known them only as an imported article. In Israel the *kibbutzniks* are as likely to go to work on a salad of cream cheese and green olives as on an egg.

This hot *hors-d'oeuvre* makes a good accompaniment to plain poultry dishes:

6 Servings

50ml (2fl oz or 4 tablespoons) olive oil
2 crushed cloves garlic
1–2 seeded, shredded, sweet red peppers
0·5kg (1lb) pitted green olives
salt and pepper
150ml (6fl oz or ¾ cup) water
2 tablespoons lemon juice
6 peeled, thin lemon slices
1 tablespoon chopped parsley

Heat oil and fry garlic for two to three minutes. Add peppers and olives. Season to taste, pour in water, bring to the boil, then reduce heat to the minimum and simmer for thirty-five to forty minutes, by which time most of the liquid should be absorbed. Sprinkle with lemon juice, simmer for two to three minutes, and transfer to a heated serving dish. Garnish with lemon slices, sprinkle with chopped parsley, and serve.

Starters

Israeli leek and beef croquettes

4 Servings

480g (1lb) cooked leeks
120g (4oz) minced beef
1 chopped, hard-boiled egg
salt and pepper
1 beaten egg
matzo meal or breadcrumbs
oil for deep frying

Chop leeks, beef, and hard-boiled egg together or put all through a mincer.
Season to taste, mix well, and bind with beaten egg. Taking a little of the
mixture at a time shape into balls the size of a walnut. Lightly roll in
matzo meal or breadcrumbs. Heat oil, deep fry the croquettes, drain on
kitchen paper, and serve.

Israeli melon with anchovies

6 Servings

1 large melon
2 small tins anchovy fillets
parsley
lemon juice

Cut melon in half and discard seeds. With a ball scoop, scoop out the flesh.
Keep the shells. Taking a ball of melon flesh and a small sprig of parsley
at a time, encircle them with an anchovy fillet. Quite often the texture of the
anchovy 'ribbon' will hold each melon ball and parsley sprig securely; if
you have any difficulty, pin with a cocktail stick. Put the wrapped melon
balls back into shells, sprinkle with a dash of lemon juice, chill, and serve.

Cucumber and cream cheese mousse

4 Servings

cucumbers
1 tablespoon gelatine
1 tablespoon chopped chives
360g (12oz or 1½ cups) cream cheese

Starters

salt and white pepper
lettuce

Peel, seed, and grate enough cucumbers to make 2½ decilitres (½ pint or
1 cup) pulp. Drain off the juice and soften gelatine in it for five minutes,
then dissolve completely over hot water, cool, and add to cucumber. Add
chives, stir, and chill the mixture until it starts to thicken. Beat the cheese
until smooth and add to cucumber mixture. Blend well, season to taste,
pour into a mould rinsed in cold water, and chill. Unmould the mousse
onto a chilled dish and serve on lettuce leaves garnished with cucumber
slices.

Peppers in oil with cheese

This dish of Balkan origin makes an interesting salad or a light snack:

4 Servings

8 sweet red peppers
salt
75ml (3fl oz or 6 tablespoons) olive oil
1 tablespoon lemon juice
1 crushed clove garlic
pinch paprika
240g (8oz or 1½ cups) cubed cheese
black olives for garnish
1 tablespoon chopped parsley

Wash peppers, dry on a cloth; take care to keep stalks on. Scorch under the
grill or over a stove burner until the skin becomes dark and begins to split.
Lay peppers out on a shallow dish, sprinkle with salt, and leave to cool off.
Dip fingers in cold water and peel off the charred skin, but leave the stalks
intact. Carefully scrape out seeds. Put in a shallow bowl. Mix oil, lemon
juice, garlic, and paprika. Add a good pinch of salt, and pour this dressing
over peppers. Tilt bowl and spoon the dressing over them to make sure all
are well coated.

Chill for several hours, turning the peppers or basting with their dressing
from time to time. Arrange peppers on individual plates, spoon some of the
dressing over them. Garnish with cubes of cheese and olives, sprinkle with
parsley, and serve.

Soups

Decoration on lower panels from a seventeenth century German Megillah in the Jewish Museum, London

Meat and vegetable soups

Chicken soup

Two words of great evocative power, full of comfort and mother love and theatrical inspiration. Chicken soup with noodles, kreplach, farfel, meat or liver balls, soup nuts or matzo meal dumplings, is traditionally served on Friday nights and for festival meals.

6–8 Servings

noodle paste (page 126)
1 boiling fowl
2·5 litres (5 pints or 10 cups) water
salt and pepper
1–2 medium-sized onions, quartered
3 stalks celery, shredded
1 peeled, quartered parsnip
2 peeled, quartered carrots
1 tablespoon chopped dill or parsley

Roll out the paste on a floured board into very thin sheets and leave on a cloth to dry for an hour. Fold the dough lightly and with a sharp knife cut into strips. Shake the noodles lightly to separate them and leave on a cloth to dry until hard. Home-made noodles can be made in advance and stored in air-tight jars.

Wash the chicken thoroughly, joint, and chop carcass into pieces. Wash all giblets, scald and peel gizzard.

Put chicken, giblets, and carcass into a saucepan with water, bring to the boil, skim until the surface is clear. Season, add vegetables, cover, and simmer on low heat for two and a half to three hours.

Strain, leave until cold then remove surface fat. Bring the soup to the boil, add noodles, cook for ten minutes. Sprinkle with chopped dill and serve.

The chicken and the vegetables used for making the broth can be used for croquettes.

Meat and vegetable soups

Chicken soup with kreplach

Prepare broth as before, strain, add kreplach (page 129) instead of
noodles. Finish cooking and garnish as described.

Marak auf mi teiman (yemeni chicken and marrow soup)

6 Servings

1 jointed chicken
1·5 litres (1½ quarts) water
0·5kg (1lb) young marrows (courgettes or zucchini)
2 medium-sized tomatoes
4–5 spring onions
salt
pinch hawayij (page 252)

Put the chicken in a pan of water, bring to the boil, skim off all the scum
which rises to the surface until the liquid is clear. Cover and simmer for
one hour.

Meat and vegetable soups

Wash and dry the marrow. If young, leave unpeeled, cut in half and then slice. If the marrow is past its prime, peel and remove seeds.

Drop tomatoes into boiling water for a few seconds to loosen skins. Peel and slice tomatoes. Add marrows and tomatoes to soup. Continue to simmer for twenty minutes.

Chop spring onions. Add to soup. Season to taste with salt and hawayij and serve piping hot.

Krupnik

This is Polish barley soup, a substantial one, and has frequently served as a meal in itself. The only adaptation this has needed to make it a staple and favourite item in the menu of the Jews in Poland was the omission of the final topping of sour cream:

6 Servings

90g (3oz or 1 cup) pearl barley
cold water
2 litres (2 quarts) meat stock
2 tablespoons oil
2 sliced onions
2 diced carrots
1 diced parsnip
3 stalks shredded celery
2–3 diced potatoes
60g (2oz or ¾ cup) diced, fresh mushrooms (or 7–8 dried mushrooms)
1 bay leaf
salt and pepper
chopped dill

Soak barley in water overnight. Drain. Cook in 0·5 litre (1 pint or two cups) stock for one and a half hours.

In a big pan heat oil and lightly fry onion, add barley and the liquid in which it has been simmering, the rest of the stock, carrots, parsnip, celery, potatoes, mushrooms, and bay leaf. Cover and simmer for thirty minutes. Season to taste with salt and pepper. Serve garnished with chopped dill. If fresh dill is not available, use parsley.

Meat and vegetable soups

Marak shkedim mi paras (Persian almond soup)

6 Servings

1 kilo (2lb) lean veal
2 litres (2 quarts) cold water
1 medium-sized onion
1–2 stalks celery
1 bay leaf
4–5 white peppercorns
1–1½ teaspoons salt
rind and juice of 1 lemon
240g (8oz or 2⅔ cups) ground almonds
6 hard-boiled eggs, shelled
6 bitter almonds, blanched
pinch verbena salt

Put the veal in a saucepan, add water, bring to the boil. Skim any scum which rises to the surface. Cover and simmer for one hour.

Chop onion and shred celery, add to stock, together with bay leaf, peppercorns, and salt. Cook for one and a half hours.

Chop the lemon rind finely. Add half of it and all the lemon juice to the stock. Continue to simmer for another hour. Strain the stock, leave until cold, then remove all surface fat. Put the ground almonds into a mortar. Halve hard-boiled eggs, remove yolks, and add to almonds, together with bitter almonds. (Keep the whites of egg and use for another dish, as stuffing or garnish.)

Season the almonds in the mortar with verbena salt, add remaining chopped lemon rind, and pound to a paste. Dilute with a cupful of stock, adding it little by little. Bring the rest of the stock to the boil. Add pounded almond mixture, blend thoroughly, simmer for ten minutes, and serve.

Meat borsch

Borsch quite deservedly is classed in the gastronomical world with about a dozen really great soups and this is a classical example of a Russian national speciality being adapted to kosher needs. The only omission is the final topping of sour cream. Serve with potato and kasha pirozhki (page 133).

Meat and vegetable soups

It is a good plan to make double the amount of borsch required, for it is one of those soups which taste even better on the second day. To enhance the colour, add some fresh beetroot as described.

8 Servings

720g (1½lb) stewing beef
2·5 litres (2¼ quarts) water
0·5kg (1lb) white cabbage
3–4 beetroots
2 carrots
1 parsnip
2 stalks celery
1 large onion
4 tablespoons tomato purée
1 tablespoon red wine vinegar
1 tablespoon sugar
1–2 bay leaves
1½ teaspoons salt
½ teaspoon ground black pepper
4–5 whole allspice seeds
1 tablespoon lemon juice
1 tablespoon chopped dill
1 tablespoon chopped parsley

Wash and dry the meat, trim off surplus fat, cut into pieces, and put in a saucepan with water. Bring to the boil, skim off any scum which rises to the surface, reduce heat, cover, and simmer for forty-five minutes.

Reserve one beetroot. Shred the cabbage and cut all root vegetables, first into slices then into 'matchsticks'. Quarter the onion and slice thinly. Add all vegetables to stock and continue to simmer for twenty to twenty-five minutes. Add tomato purée, vinegar, sugar, bay leaf, salt, pepper, and allspice. Cook for fifteen minutes on low heat, check seasoning, sharpen with lemon juice, sprinkle with chopped dill and parsley, and serve piping hot. To ensure the characteristic attractive rich colour of borsch, keep one beetroot for last minute use. Grate it finely, put in a small pan with a cupful of stock, simmer for five minutes, and strain into the borsch.

Meat and vegetable soups

Sour cream borsch (cold)

8 Servings

This version of borsch is served cold and, because no meat is used in the recipe, it has a dressing of sour cream, which is added just before serving. Leftover borsch should be poured into a screw top jar and kept in the refrigerator.

3–4 large beetroots
2·5 litres (2½ quarts) water
2 carrots
½ parsnip
2 stalks celery
2 large onions
1 finely chopped clove garlic
480g (1lb or 2 cups) peeled, fresh or tinned tomatoes
1 tablespoon sugar
1½–2 teaspoons salt
1 tablespoon wine vinegar
1 bay leaf
¼ teaspoon ground black pepper
5–6 whole allspice seeds
3 tablespoons dry white wine
2·5dl (½ pint or 1 cup) sour cream
lemon or cucumber slices for garnish

Scrub, peel and cut up beetroot, reserving one for subsequent colouring. Put in a saucepan with water, bring to the boil, cover, and simmer for one hour. Meanwhile, cut up all the other vegetables and add to pan with sugar, salt, vinegar, bay leaf, pepper, and allspice. Cook for a further forty-five to sixty minutes, until beetroot is tender. Put the vegetables with a cup of the soup through a blender until smooth, or rub through a sieve. Strain the soup into a bowl, add the blended vegetables to it, check seasoning, and colour. If necessary, add some of the reserved beetroot, as described in the previous recipe. Add wine, stir, cover, and allow to cool completely, then chill, preferably overnight.

Serve in individual soup bowls, topped with a dollop of sour cream, and garnished with a slice of lemon or a few thin slices of fresh cucumber.

Meat and vegetable soups

Rassolnik (Russian kidney and dill pickle soup)

6 Servings

1·5 litres (3 pints or 6 cups) stock
0·5kg (1lb) veal or lamb kidney
1 parsnip
2 stalks celery
3 medium-sized potatoes
240g (8oz) dill cucumbers (pages 270–1)
2 tablespoons margarine
1 chopped onion
1 bay leaf
120g (4oz) sorrel or lettuce
1·5dl (4fl oz or ½ cup) brine in which cucumbers were pickled
salt and freshly ground black pepper
2 tablespoons chopped fresh dill or parsley

Strain stock, remove all surface fat.
Trim kidneys, remove all fat and membranes, cut each kidney in three to four pieces, and wash thoroughly. Put in a saucepan, cover with cold water, bring to the boil. Drain, rinse, put in fresh cold water, and simmer for one hour.

Peel and cut parsnip into matchsticks. Shred celery, peel and dice potatoes. Slice the cucumbers.

The best cucumbers for this soup are home-pickled in brine with dill for three days, but there are quite good dill cucumbers sold in delicatessen shops which do very well. Just make sure that they are pickled in brine and not in vinegar. Heat margarine in large saucepan and gently fry onion, parsnip, and celery, to soften, but do not allow to brown. Add cucumbers, potatoes, stock, and bay leaf Bring to the boil, simmer for fifteen minutes.

Shred sorrel and add to soup. Pour in cucumber brine. Drain the kidneys, slice, and add to soup. Check seasoning, add more salt if necessary, grind in pepper to taste. Sprinkle with dill and serve piping hot with kasha croûtons (page 48).

Meat and vegetable soups

Hungarian goulash soup

6 Servings

1 tablespoon margarine or oil
240g (8oz or 1½ cups) chopped onion
1½ teaspoons paprika
½ teaspoon caraway seed
pinch marjoram
1 crushed clove garlic
2 litres (4 pints or 8 cups) beef stock
0·5kg (1lb or 2 cups) beef, cut in cubes
300g (10oz or 2 cups) peeled, chopped tomatoes
salt
360g (12oz or 1¾ cups) peeled, diced potatoes
30g (1oz or 4 tablespoons) flour
150ml (6fl oz or ¾ cup) water
2–3 tablespoons diced salami
lemon juice

In a large pot heat margarine, put in onion, and fry until golden.
Add paprika, caraway seed, marjoram, and garlic. Stir well and cook for two minutes. Add stock, beef, tomatoes, and salt to taste. Bring to the boil, simmer for thirty minutes. Add potatoes and cook until they are done.

Mix flour with water and stir into the soup. Simmer until soup thickens. Add salami, simmer for two minutes. Check seasoning, squeeze a dash of lemon juice into the soup, and serve.

Italian soup with noodles and chicken livers

This is a delicious soup, easy and quick to make, but you must have all ingredients ready and perform three simple operations simultaneously:

4 Servings

100g (3½oz or ⅞ cup) fine noodles
240g (8oz or 1½ cups) tender young peas, shelled
salt and pepper
water
1 litre (2 pints or 4 cups) chicken broth
240g (8oz or 1 cup) sliced chicken livers

Meat and vegetable soups

1½ tablespoons margarine
1 tablespoon chopped, fresh basil

Cook noodles and peas in salted boiling water for five to six minutes and drain. While the noodles are cooking, bring broth to the boil and fry chicken livers in margarine. Season to taste with salt and pepper. Combine broth with noodles, peas, chicken livers, and their pan juices. Reheat to boiling point and serve with a sprinkling of basil.

Cream of mushroom soup

4 Servings

360g (12oz) mushrooms
2 chopped onions
90g (3oz or 6 tablespoons) butter or margarine
2 tablespoons flour
0·5 litre (1 pint or 2 cups) milk
salt and pepper
100ml (4fl oz or ½ cup) cream

Reserve 120g (4oz) mushroom caps, chop the rest. Fry chopped mushrooms and onion in half the butter and rub through a sieve or purée in a blender. Slice reserved mushroom caps and fry in remaining butter until soft. Sprinkle in flour, cook, stirring for two minutes, without allowing the mixture to brown. Dilute with milk, stirring it in a little at a time. Simmer for five minutes stirring, add mushroom and onion purée, and season to taste. Remove from heat, blend in cream, and serve at once.

Green pea soup

6 Servings

720g (1½lb or 3 cups) fresh or frozen green peas
1 litre (1 quart) scalded milk
salt and pepper
100ml (4fl oz or ½ cup) cream

Cook the peas in minimum of salted boiling water until just tender. Strain and rub through a sieve or purée in a blender. Dilute with milk, re-heat, season to taste, and just before serving blend in cream.

Meat and vegetable soups

Lentil soup I

6 Servings

0·5 litre (1 pint or 2 cups) lentils
2 litres (2 quarts) pickled beef (corn beef) liquor (page 78)
1 large, grated onion
1–2 crushed cloves garlic
salt and pepper
60g (2oz or 4 tablespoons) diced salami
1 tablespoon chopped dill or parsley

Soak lentils in enough water to cover overnight. Drain, put in a saucepan with pickled beef liquor (or stock), bring to the boil, cover, reduce heat, and simmer for one hour. Add onion and garlic and cook for a further thirty minutes or until the lentils are tender.

Rub through a sieve or purée in a blender. Re-heat, taste for seasoning (you may not need any salt if the pickled beef liquor is salty enough), grate a little pepper over the soup. Add salami, simmer for five minutes. Sprinkle with dill and serve.

Lentil soup II

Soak lentils overnight and cook in lightly salted water until tender. Then strain, purée, and dilute with milk and cream as described in recipe for green pea soup (page 29).

Yemenite yoghourt soup

This is reputed by the Yemenites to be a health-giving summer soup. It is certainly a refreshing one and has an added advantage – it requires no cooking. A similar soup is also eaten by European Jews, who substitute dill for mint:

4 Servings

240g (8oz or 1 cup) peeled, diced cucumber
1 clove garlic
1 tablespoon vinegar

Meat and vegetable soups

0·5 litre (1 pint or 2 cups) yoghourt
salt
1 tablespoon olive oil
1 tablespoon fresh, chopped mint

Put the cucumbers in a dish, sprinkle with salt, and leave for thirty
minutes. Slice garlic and rub with it a bowl big enough to take all the
ingredients. Sprinkle in vinegar and rinse the bowl with it. Spoon yoghourt
into this vinegar and garlic flavoured bowl and stir to thin down, adding
two to three tablespoons of water, if necessary.
Drain cucumbers, add to yoghourt, mix, and chill. Blend in olive oil, a few
drops at a time, sprinkle with mint, and serve.

Sephardic garlic soup

6 Servings

3 tablespoons oil
4 cloves garlic
180g (6oz) stale bread
pinch paprika
1·5 litres (1½ quarts) salted water
2–3 tablespoons milk

Heat oil and fry garlic until golden. Cut bread into very thin slices, fry
with the garlic, remove, and put in an oven-proof tureen.

Stir paprika into oil, remove from heat as soon as it is blended in. Bring
salted water to the boil, pour over bread slices, cover, and leave to stand for
five minutes. Remove garlic and discard. Mix garlic-flavoured oil with a
little milk, add to soup, stir well. Put in a hot oven for five to six minutes, to
give the bread which floats up to the surface a nice, crusty, brown top.

Sephardic garlic soup with poached eggs

6 Servings

Prepare garlic soup as described. Just before serving, add a lightly
poached, trimmed egg to each plate.

Meat and vegetable soups

Sephardic mint soup

6 Servings

30g (1oz or 2 tablespoons) olive oil
1 chopped onion
2 large, peeled, chopped tomatoes
180g (6oz) bread
1·25 litres (1¼ quarts) hot water
salt
a handful fresh mint leaves

Heat oil in saucepan and fry onion and tomatoes. Cut bread in chunks and add to onions and tomatoes. Stir once or twice to impregnate bread with the pan juices. Pour in water, season to taste with salt. Add mint, simmer for one hour, and serve.

Marak avocado (avocado soup)

This soup originates in Latin America. Because of the extensive cultivation of avocado pears in Israel, this dish has become naturalized. It can be served hot or cold. If the rest of the menu does not preclude the use of cream, and the soup is based on a light vegetable stock, this soup looks and tastes delightful with lightly whipped cream or sour cream, floated on the surface through a perforated spoon.

4 Servings

1 litre (1 quart or 4 cups) strained stock
1 large avocado pear
salt and pepper
pinch nutmeg
2 tablespoons lemon juice
1 glass dry white wine or sherry
fresh mint leaves

Bring the stock to the boil. Peel, stone, and dice the avocado and add to stock. Simmer for one minute. Season with salt and pepper. Add nutmeg and lemon juice to taste. Rub through a fine sieve or pass the soup through a blender.

If you are going to serve the soup cold, transfer to a tureen, add wine, cool, then chill.

Meat and vegetable soups

If the soup is to be eaten hot, return the sieved mixture to pan, add wine, reheat without allowing it to boil, and serve garnished with fresh mint leaves.

Avocado gazpacho

This is another cold avocado soup, with mixed vegetables. It makes a delicious and refreshing summer starter and is a speciality of the Sheraton Hotel in Tel-Aviv:

6 Servings

480g (1lb or 2 cups) avocado flesh
2 sliced, medium-sized onions
200ml (8fl oz or 1 cup) dry white wine
juice of 1 lemon
200ml (8fl oz or 1 cup) iced water
1 teaspoon sugar
1 teaspoon salt
black pepper

Garnish
60g (2oz or ¼ cup) peeled, diced tomatoes
60g (2oz or ¼ cup) seeded, diced green pepper
60g (2oz or ¼ cup) diced cucumber

Pass the avocado and onions through a blender with wine, lemon juice, and water. Add sugar, season to taste with salt and pepper, transfer to a bowl, and chill.

Make sure tomatoes, peppers, and cucumber are cut in uniform small dice. Mix this garnish and chill.

Serve the gazpacho iced, in individual bowls, topped with a portion of mixed, diced vegetables.

Meat and vegetable soups

Schav (sorrel soup)

These summer soups are popular in the Baltic countries, in Russia, Poland, Ukraine, and Rumania. They can be made with meat or chicken stock, or the liquid can be a mixture of milk and water.

If meat stock is used, garnish with chopped hard-boiled eggs only; if milk and water, stir in sour cream before serving. These soups can be served hot or cold. Schav traditionally is part of the *Shavuot* menu, when it is served cold.

6 Servings

240g (8oz) fresh sorrel leaves
15g ($\frac{1}{2}$oz 4 tablespoons) parsley
2 tablespoons butter
1 litre (1 quart) water
3–4 potatoes
salt and pepper
pinch sugar
0·5 litre (1 pint or 2 cups) milk
1–2 yolks
1–2 tablespoons lemon juice
1 carton sour cream

Wash and chop sorrel and parsley. Heat butter in a pan large enough to to take all ingredients. Add sorrel and parsley and cook on low heat, stirring for ten minutes. Add water, stir, and simmer for five minutes. Peel and dice potatoes, add to sorrel soup, season to taste with salt and pepper, add sugar, bring to the boil, cover, reduce heat, and simmer on low heat for twenty-five minutes. Strain and keep the soup stock.

Rub the sorrel and potatoes through a sieve or pass through a blender, with half the milk, to make a smooth purée. Reheat stock, add sorrel purée, simmer for a few minutes to heat through.

Dilute yolks with remaining milk and blend into the soup. Reheat, without allowing the soup to boil, check seasoning, remove from heat, sharpen with lemon juice to taste, and serve with a tablespoon of sour cream for each helping.

Milk soups

Milk soups are very nourishing, extremely simple to make, and popular in the nursery. They should be cooked on a low heat, in a saucepan with a thick bottom.

You can vary them by changing the garnishes. The following are recommended:

matzo meal dumplings (page 45), cheese quenelles (page 47), rice, fine vermicelli, soup nuts (page 45), almond dumplings (page 46), farfel (page 47).

See also individual recipes for milk soups.

Russian milk soup with noodles

6 Servings

120g (4oz) home-made noodles (page 21)
1 litre (2 pints or 4 cups) milk
½ teaspoon salt
1 teaspoon sugar
1 tablespoon butter

Prepare the noodles. Bring milk to the boil, add noodles, salt, and sugar. Simmer for fifteen minutes. Before serving add butter. This soup is also very good made with vermicelli.

Milk soup with potato dumplings

6 Servings

1 litre (2 pints or 4 cups) milk
potato dumplings (page 47)
salt
1 tablespoon butter

Bring milk to the boil. Drop dumplings into hot milk. Simmer on the lowest possible heat for ten minutes, season with salt to taste, add a little butter, and serve.

Milk soups can also be made with almond dumplings (page 46) or soup nuts (page 45).

Milk soups

Belgian chicory milk soup

6 Servings

0·5kg (1lb or 2 cups) finely chopped chicory
2 finely chopped leeks, white portion only
3 peeled, thinly sliced potatoes
6 tablespoons butter
1·5 litres (3 pints or 6 cups) scalded milk
salt and pepper

In a big saucepan lightly fry chicory, leeks, and potatoes in butter without allowing the vegetables to brown. Add milk, season to taste, simmer very gently for thirty-five to forty minutes. Serve with dry toast.

Baltic dill soup

The liquid for this soup is a mixture of sour cream and potato water. The potatoes themselves can be mashed and used for another dish:

4 Servings

480g (1lb or 2½ cups) raw, diced potatoes
salt and pepper
water
1½ tablespoons flour
375ml (¾ pint or 1½ cups) scalded sour cream
1 large bunch dill
2 raw yolks
dash nutmeg

Cook potatoes in boiling salted water to give you 0·5 litre (1 pint or 2 cups) potato water. Simmer potatoes until tender and drain off potato water into a saucepan. Heat gently.

Dilute flour with three tablespoons cold water. Stir a third of the sour cream into soup, followed by a tablespoon of water and flour mixture. Continue until 250ml (2 pint or 1 cup) of sour cream and all the flour and water have been blended in.

Wash dill, reserve a few sprigs for garnishing, and chop the rest finely or put through a mill. Add to soup, bring to the boil, simmer for three to four minutes.

Milk soups

Beat yolks with remaining scalded sour cream and stir into the soup.
Bring to the boil, season to taste with salt and pepper, add nutmeg, stir,
and remove from heat. Cool, then chill. Serve in individual *consommé* cups
garnished with little sprigs of dill.

Brussels sprouts soup

4 Servings

0·5kg (1lb) brussels sprouts
0·5kg (1lb or 2½ cups) peeled, thinly sliced potatoes
2 chopped onions
0·5 litre (1 pint or 2 cups) water
salt and pepper
30g (1oz or 2 tablespoons) butter
0·5 litre (1 pint or 2 cups) scalded milk

Trim, wash, and drain sprouts. Cook sprouts, potatoes, and onions in
salted water for twenty minutes, or until tender, then rub through a sieve
or purée in a blender. Put the purée back in the pan, reheat, incorporate
butter, blending it in small pieces. Stir in milk, season to taste with salt
and pepper, and serve.

Fruit soups

Marak peyrot (fruit soup)

Fruit soups of all kinds are popular throughout Israel – some are indigenous, some originated in Southern Russia and Bessarabia, many are common to all Middle Eastern countries. These soups make ideal starting courses for summer and any fruit in season can be used: apples, pears, grapes, peaches, apricots, red and black currants, melons, strawberries, cherries, plums, etc. You can also use a mixture of fresh and dried fruit.

Mixed fruit soup

6 Servings

2 apples
2 pears
juice of 1 lemon
1 peach
150g (5oz or about 1 cup) hulled strawberries
750ml ($\frac{3}{4}$ quart or $3\frac{1}{4}$ cups) water
2 tablespoons sugar
500ml (1 pint or 2 cups) orange juice
$1\frac{1}{2}$ tablespoons cornflour
100ml (4fl oz or $\frac{1}{2}$ cup) dry white wine
small carton soured cream
fresh mint

Peel and core apples and pears and dip in lemon juice to prevent discoloration. Dip peach into boiling water for a few seconds, skin it, and remove stone. Dice apples, pears, and peach. Leave small strawberries whole, slice large ones. Put water and sugar to boil, add fruit, and simmer for four to five minutes. Add orange juice.

Dilute cornflour with two tablespoons cold water and whatever is left of the lemon juice, and stir into the soup. Simmer, stirring gently for a couple of minutes, and remove from heat. Allow to cool, then chill.

Just before serving, add wine. Serve in individual bowls, with a dollop of sour cream on top, and decorated with fresh mint.

Fruit soups

Danish elderberry soup

6 Servings

720g (1½lb or 3 cups) ripe elderberries
1·5 litres (3 pints or 6 cups) water
sugar
grated rind of ½ lemon
pinch of cinnamon
1½ tablespoons cornflour

De-stalk the berries, wash, drain, put in a pan with water. Bring to the boil, simmer gently until the berries become soft and yield up their juices. Press through a fine sieve. Return elderberry purée and all liquid to pan with lemon rind, cinnamon, and sugar to taste. Dissolve cornflour in three tablespoons cold water, blend into the soup, simmer stirring until the soup thickens, and serve.

Scandinavian blueberry soup with almond dumplings

6 Servings

1kg (2lb or 4 cups) blueberries
2 litres (2 quarts) water
90g (3oz or 6 tablespoons) sugar
3 tablespoons cornflour
almond dumplings (page 46)

Cook the blueberries in water until soft. Strain, rub through a sieve or pass through a blender. Return to pan, heat, add sugar, and simmer on low heat until it dissolves. Dissolve cornflour with three tablespoons cold water, stir into the pan, simmer until the soup thickens.

Poach the dumplings separately. Drain, add to blueberry soup, and serve.

Cold blueberry soup

Follow above recipe, omit dumplings. Chill the soup and serve with a topping of whipped cream.

Fruit soups

Marak melon (melon soup)

6 Servings

1 melon
1 litre (1 quart) chicken stock
½ bottle dry white wine
salt and pepper
pinch mace

Cut the melon, discard seeds, scoop out some of the flesh with a ball
scoop, and reserve a dozen and a half of these for garnish. Keep them in a
refrigerator.

Dice the rest of the melon, keeping all the juice which flows out.

Heat the stock with the wine, add seasoning, bring to the boil. Put in diced
melon flesh and its juice, cook over gentle heat for twenty minutes. Pass
the whole of the soup through a sieve, or a blender, cool, and chill. Garnish
with melon balls and serve.

Marak dubduvanim (hot cherry soup)

6–8 Servings

500g (1 ¼lb or 3 cups) stoned, sweet cherries
2 litre (2 quarts) water
1 stick cinnamon
1 lemon, thinly sliced

Fruit soups

120g (4oz or ½ cup) sugar
100ml (4fl oz or ½ cup) sweet white wine
1½ tablespoons cornflour
rusks

Put half the cherries with water into a pan, bring to the boil, and simmer until tender. Strain into another pan, rubbing the cherry flesh through. Put back to heat. Add cinnamon, lemon slices, and the rest of the cherries. Simmer for five minutes. Sprinkle in sugar, add wine, simmer until sugar is dissolved.

Dilute cornflour with two tablespoons water and stir into the soup. As soon as the soup thickens slightly, remove from heat.

Serve rusks separately.

Norwegian rhubarb soup

This soup can be served hot or cold. In Norway it is usually served hot, with rusks:

6 Servings

1kg (2lb) rhubarb
2 litres (2 quarts) water
1 stick cinnamon
2–3 slices lemon
240g (8oz or 1 cup) sugar
2 tablespoons cornflour
1 raw yolk
100ml (4fl oz or ½ cup) double cream

Wash rhubarb, strip off any strings, cut, and simmer in water until tender. Rub through a sieve with all its liquid, or pass through a blender. Return to saucepan, add cinnamon, lemon, and sugar. Stir to dissolve sugar completely, simmer for seven to eight minutes. Remove cinnamon and lemon.

Dilute cornflour with three tablespoons cold water and blend into the hot soup. Simmer, stirring, for three to four minutes, until the soup thickens. Remove from heat. Whisk yolk with cream, stir into the soup, and serve.

Fruit soups

Israeli apple and red wine soup

4 Servings

1kg (2lb or 6 medium-sized) cooking apples
60g (2oz or 4 tablespoons) butter
100ml (4fl oz or ½ cup) water
pinch nutmeg
½ teaspoon lemon rind
lemon juice
1 bottle red wine (not too dry)
100ml (4fl oz or ½ cup) sour cream

Peel, core, and slice the apples. Melt butter in a pan, add apples, cook gently, then add water and simmer until apples are quite soft. Add nutmeg, lemon rind, and a dash of lemon juice, rub through a sieve or pass through a blender for perfect smoothness and cool.

Dilute with red wine, add two to three tablespoons lemon juice to sharpen the soup.

If you are going to serve it hot, re-heat, stir in sour cream, and serve. If it is to be served cold, stir in sour cream without re-heating, chill.

Russian cranberry and apple soup

6 Servings

360g (12oz or 3 cups) cranberries
1 litre (1 quart) boiling water
480g (1lb) cooking apples
4–6 tablespoons sugar (or to taste)
1 tablespoon cornflour
3 tablespoons cold water
100ml (4fl oz or ½ cup) sour cream

Wash and mash cranberries in a saucepan. Pour in boiling water, stir, cover, and leave to stand for fifteen minutes. Strain into a saucepan, pressing out all the juice. Add sugar and stir to dissolve. Peel, core, and slice apples. Add to cranberry juice, gently bring to the boil. Simmer for two to three minutes. Mix cornflour with cold water and stir into the soup. Remove from heat, chill, and serve with sour cream.

Fruit soups

Scandinavian prune soup

6 Servings

2 litres (2 quarts) water
6 tablespoons sago
240g (8oz or 1 cup) stoned prunes
pinch cinnamon
250ml ($\frac{1}{2}$ pint or 1 cup) cranberry or other red fruit juice
sugar to taste
3 tablespoons slivered almonds

Cook the sago in boiling water, stirring, for five minutes. Add prunes and simmer until they are soft. Add cinnamon, fruit juice, and sugar to taste. Simmer for thirty minutes. Sprinkle in almonds and serve hot or cold.

Canadian chilled orange and tomato soup

4 Servings

0.5 litre (1 pint or 2 cups) strained orange juice
0.5 litre (1 pint or 2 cups) tomato juice
100ml (4fl oz or $\frac{1}{2}$ cup) dry white wine
juice of $\frac{1}{2}$ lemon
1 teaspoon sugar
salt
cayenne pepper
1 tablespoon finely chopped parsley

Blend orange juice with tomato juice, wine, and lemon juice. Add sugar, season to taste with salt and cayenne pepper. Chill and serve sprinkled with parsley.

Accompaniments
to soups
and garnishes

Decoration on soup bowl from an eighteenth century Scroll of Esther
in the Jewish Museum, London

Soup nuts

'Nuts' here is used as a 'courtesy title', because the little pellets of dough, baked or deep fried, look like nuts. The Yiddish name for them is *mandeln*, which means almonds:

2 eggs
2 tablespoons oil
180g (6oz or 1½ cups) sifted flour
pinch salt
pinch baking powder
fat for deep frying, if the nuts are to be fried

Beat eggs with oil, add flour, salt, and baking powder, and mix into a soft dough. Chill for thirty minutes. With your hands roll portions of dough into thin little sausages, no more than 1·25 cm (½ inch) thick. Cut into 1-cm (½-inch) pieces. Then either bake or deep fry. To bake, put on a greased baking sheet and cook in the oven preheated to 190°C (375°F or Gas Mark 4), shaking from time to time until the nuts are uniformly golden brown.

To deep fry, heat the fat, drop the pellets of dough into it, cook until they puff up and turn golden brown, drain. Whether you bake or fry the soup nuts, serve them piping hot.

Matzo meal dumplings for soup

180g (6oz or 1½ cups) matzo meal
160ml (6fl oz or ⅔ cup) water
salt and pepper
pinch grated nutmeg
3 eggs
6 tablespoons oil

Mix matzo meal with water, season to taste with salt, pepper, and nutmeg.

Beat the eggs and whisk them into the batter. Blend in oil. Chill the batter for four hours.

Taking a little mixture at a time, shape into balls or quenelles. To cook, drop the dumplings into strained boiling broth a few at a time, allowing boiling to be re-established again before adding more dumplings, simmer for thirty-five to forty minutes.

Accompaniments to soups and garnishes

Almond dumplings for chicken soup

2 eggs
90g (3oz or 1 cup) ground almonds
pinch salt
½ teaspoon grated lemon rind
fat for deep frying

Separate the eggs and mix yolks with almonds. Add salt and lemon rind.

Whisk the egg whites until very stiff and fold into the almond mixture.

Heat fat. Using a coffee spoon, take a little of the mixture at a time, drop into fat, cook as described in recipe for soup nuts (page 45). Drain well and serve at once while the dumplings are still crisp.

Meat balls for soup

180g (6oz or ¾ cup) raw, minced beef
1½ teaspoons finely grated onion
1 teaspoon finely chopped parsley
pinch grated lemon rind
salt and pepper to taste
pinch nutmeg
1 beaten egg

Combine all ingredients, mix well, roll into small balls, and boil them in strained broth for fifteen minutes.

Liver balls for soup

30g (1oz or ⅞ cup) freshly grated breadcrumbs
4–5 tablespoons stock
120g (4oz or ½ cup) minced chicken livers
½ teaspoon grated onion
salt and pepper
1 beaten egg

Mix breadcrumbs with stock, simmer over low heat stirring to amalgamate. Remove from heat, add liver, onion, and seasoning. Bind with egg, shape into balls, and cook in soup for ten to twelve minutes.

Accompaniments to soups and garnishes

Farfel

Using noodle paste (page 126), knead, roll into a ball, and leave for forty-five minutes. Grate on a coarse grater, leave on a cloth or board to dry. Drop into strained boiling broth and cook in the same way as noodles.

Cheese quenelles

120g (4oz or 2 tablespoons) cheese (Cheddar, Dutch or Parmesan)
1 tablespoon butter
2 eggs
60g (2oz) bread, soaked in 6 tablespoons milk
1 tablespoon sour cream
30g (1oz) toasted breadcrumbs

Grate the cheese, add butter, pound together into a smooth mixture, add eggs, bread previously soaked in milk, and sour cream. Mix well, roll into walnut-sized balls, dip in toasted breadcrumbs, and drop into stock. As soon as they float up to the surface, they are ready to serve.

Potato dumplings

3 medium-sized potatoes
750ml (1½ pints or 3 cups) water
1 teaspoon salt
1 tablespoon margarine
2 tablespoons flour
2 raw yolks
2 stiffly beaten whites of egg

Peel, slice, and boil the potatoes in water. After they come to the boil, add salt and continue to simmer fifteen to twenty minutes. Strain and rub through a sieve while still hot. Add margarine, flour, and the yolks. Blend well together, add beaten whites, mix thoroughly. Ten minutes before serving, drop the dumplings into boiling stock, or salted boiling water. Using a teaspoon, dip the spoon into a cup of cold water, scoop up half a teaspoonful of the mixture at a time, and quickly shake it off into the stock. Continue until all the mixture is used up. Cook the dumplings on a low heat. As soon as they float up to the surface – they are done.

Accompaniments to soups and garnishes

Croûtons

To make croûtons cut crustless slices of bread into cubes or into various shapes, triangles, hearts, half-moons, lozenges – or stamp them out with small pastry cutters – and fry in margarine or oil until golden all over.

To make potato croûtons, dice raw potato, fry as above, and drain on absorbent kitchen paper.

Buckwheat croûtons

All buckwheat preparations, croûtons, pirozhki, and just plain kasha are traditional accompaniments to borsch and light clear soups:

6 Servings

180g (6oz or 1 cup) cooked buckwheat (see kasha page 132)
3–4 tablespoons margarine
salt and pepper

Place the cooked buckwheat in a large oblong, straight-sided dish, slightly moistened with water. Press down to a thickness of 1·25cm ($\frac{1}{2}$ inch), cover with another dish rinsed out with cold water, and allow to cool between the two dishes with a light weight on top. Trim off any rough edges, cut into neat slices, and fry in sizzling margarine. Brown on both sides turning carefully. Drain on absorbent paper and serve.

Meat pirozhki

6 Servings

dough or puff pastry (pages 187–8–9)
beef filling (see blini, page 54)
1 beaten egg for glazing
$\frac{1}{2}$ teaspoon salt

Use either dough for knishes or puff pastry made with vegetable margarine. Roll out dough or pastry to a thickness of 5 mm ($\frac{1}{4}$ inch) and cut into circles. Make sure the filling is cold. Put a spoonful of filling on each circle of dough or pastry, fold over into semi-circles, and pinch edges together. Whisk egg with salt and use the mixture for brushing the pirozhki, to give them a beautiful glaze.

Accompaniments to soups and garnishes

If you are using dough, preheat oven to 175°C (350°F or Gas Mark 3). Bake for thirty to thirty-five minutes.

If you are using puff pastry, put the baking tray with the glazed pirozhki in a refrigerator for half an hour. Preheat oven to 230°C (450°F or Gas Mark 7) and bake the pirozhki until golden.

Liver pirozhki or knishes

dough for knishes (page 187–8)
90g (3oz or 6 tablespoons) margarine or chicken fat
2 finely chopped, medium-sized onions
360g (12oz or 1½ cups) chicken or calf's liver
1–2 tablespoons breadcrumbs (day old)
salt and pepper

Have the dough ready for rolling out.
Heat half the margarine or chicken fat, fry onion until soft, and remove. Add the rest of the fat and brown livers for a few minutes keeping them tender.

Using the finest cutter of the mincer, mince livers with onions and breadcrumbs. If a smoother filling is desired, put it through the mincer twice. Season with salt and pepper to taste.

Roll out the dough, cut, fill, shape into pirozhki or knishes, and bake as described.

Both pirozhki and knishes can be served as an accompaniment to clear soups or other dishes, or served on their own as a light meal.

Accompaniments to soups and garnishes

Meat knishes

dough for knishes (pages 187–8)
beef filling (see blini page 54)
1 beaten egg
$\frac{3}{4}$ teaspoon salt

Roll out the dough into thin sheets and cut into circles or squares. Cool the filling, put a spoonful in the middle of each square or round piece of dough, bring the edges together in the middle, and pinch to seal. Brush with beaten egg seasoned with salt. Preheat oven to 175°C (350°F or Gas Mark 4). Bake for thirty to forty-five minutes.

Cabbage pirozhki

These are great favourites. They are particularly delicious. Excellent with meat borsch, or a clear bouillon, served on the side plate and eaten instead of bread:

6 Servings

puff pastry (page 189)
240g (8oz or $\frac{2}{3}$ cup) shredded white cabbage
salt
1 small, chopped onion
2 tablespoons vegetable margarine
2 hard-boiled eggs
pepper
1 beaten egg for gloss

Prepare puff pastry, using vegetable margarine, and keep cold. Sprinkle cabbage with teaspoon salt and leave to stand for twenty minutes. Put in a colander, scald with boiling water, and drain.

Fry onion in margarine until soft and transparent. Squeeze surplus water out of cabbage and add to onion. Fry gently, without allowing it to brown, until soft. Remove from heat and leave until cold.

Chop the hard-boiled eggs, add to cabbage, check for salt, season with pepper.

Roll out pastry, fill pirozhki, brush with beaten egg, and bake as described, in oven preheated to 230°C (450°F or Gas Mark 7).

Accompaniments to soups and garnishes

Rice and egg pirozhki

6 Servings

dough or puff pastry (pages 187–9)
180g (6oz or $\frac{7}{8}$ cup) rice
60g (2oz or 4 tablespoons) margarine
2–3 hard-boiled eggs
30g (1oz or 3 tablespoons) chopped spring onions
1 tablespoon chopped parsley
salt and pepper
1 beaten egg

Have the dough or pastry ready. Boil rice in lightly salted water until done. Drain thoroughly, add half the margarine and chopped eggs, and mix. Heat remaining margarine and fry spring onions and parsley to soften. Add to rice, season to taste with salt and pepper, remove from heat, and cool the filling. Roll out pastry, complete pirozhki as described in earlier recipes, brush with egg beaten with a pinch of salt, and bake.

Sauerkraut pirozhki

480g (1lb) sauerkraut (pages 274–5)
1 finely chopped onion
4 tablespoons butter or margarine
1 tablespoon sugar
dough or pastry (pages 187–9)
1 egg beaten
1 teaspoon water
pinch salt

Drain sauerkraut, taste it, and if it is too salty, rinse with water, then drain thoroughly again.

Fry onion in butter, add sauerkraut, sprinkle with sugar, and cook on low heat for fifteen to twenty minutes, stirring from time to time. Remove from heat and cool. Roll out dough or pastry. Fill, shape, and seal pirozhki as described.

Preheat oven to 205°C (400°F or Gas Mark 5). Mix egg with water and salt, brush the pirozhki with it, and bake in the oven until golden.

Accompaniments to soups and garnishes

Mushroom pirozhki

6 Servings

500g (1lb or 7 cups) fresh, sliced mushrooms
½ teaspoon salt
¼ teaspoon pepper
3 tablespoons chopped spring onions
1 tablespoon dill or parsley
60g (2oz or 4 tablespoons) margarine
1 tablespoon lemon juice
puff pastry (page 189)
1 egg

Put the mushrooms in a saucepan, sprinkle with salt and pepper, spring onions, and dill. Stir and sweat them over low heat for a few minutes. As soon as the mushrooms yield up their juices, add margarine and lemon juice. Simmer gently for ten minutes. Remove and chill before using the filling.

Roll out and cut pastry, fill, and shape pirozhki as described (pages 48–52). Beat egg with a pinch of salt, paint the pirozhki with the mixture to give them a lovely gloss, and place in refrigerator until ready to bake.
Heat oven to 230°C (450°F or Gas Mark 7). Bake as described and serve with *consommé*.

Salmon pirozhki

6 Servings

yeast dough (pages 187–8) or puff pastry (page 189)
240g (8oz) fresh salmon
court bouillon (page 257)
1 finely chopped onion
3 tablespoons butter
3 tablespoons cooked rice
salt and pepper
¼ teaspoon nutmeg
2 eggs
fried parsley for garnish (page 53)

Prepare dough or pastry of your choice.

Accompaniments to soups and garnishes

To make filling, poach salmon in court bouillon until just tender. Do not overcook. Remove fish, skin, bone, and flake.

Fry onion in butter until soft, without browning. Add salmon, fry together for two minutes. Add rice, season to taste with salt, pepper, and nutmeg. Remove from heat. Add one lightly beaten egg, stir, and allow the filling to cool.

Roll out and fill pirozhki. Use the second egg, beaten with a pinch of salt, to brush the pirozhki to give them a gloss.

Bake as described in oven preheated to 230°C (450°F or Gas Mark 7), garnish with fried parsley.

Stuffed eggs

6 eggs
60g (2oz or 4 tablespoons) margarine
1 teaspoon salt
$\frac{1}{4}$ teaspoon pepper
2 tablespoons chopped parsley
2 tablespoons toasted breadcrumbs
1 raw egg

Boil the eggs for seven to eight minutes, plunge in cold water, then cut longways with a sharp knife taking care not to break up the shells. Take out the eggs and chop up finely. Melt three tablespoons margarine in a saucepan, put in eggs for a few seconds, remove from heat, add salt, pepper, parsley, breadcrumbs, and egg. Blend well, fill the shells with the mixture, sprinkle with breadcrumbs, put a piece of margarine on each, and put in the oven or under a grill to brown. Serve with sorrel soup on separate plates, garnished with fried parsley (page 53).

Fried parsley

30–60g (1–2oz) parsley
1 tablespoon melted butter or margarine

Wash the parsley, cut off the long stalks, dip lightly in melted butter or margarine, and put in a hot oven to dry off. Be careful not to burn. To garnish meat dishes use margarine for dipping parsley.

Accompaniments to soups and garnishes

Blini

There are two kinds of blini, the Russian name for pancakes. The small
diameter, thick sort, usually served with smoked fish, melted butter, etc.
and the larger thin ones. These latter rolled pancakes can be served as an
accompaniment to clear soups, or as a course in their own right. The
filling can be of infinite variety. They are delicious with minced chicken,
chicken livers, rice and mushrooms, salmon, veal, chopped hard-boiled
eggs and spring onions, etc.

4 Servings

Batter
120g (4oz or 1 cup) self-raising flour
pinch salt
1 teaspoon sugar
1 lightly beaten egg
2·5dl ($\frac{1}{2}$ pint or 1 cup) warm water
oil or chicken fat

Filling
1 small, finely chopped onion
240g (8oz or 1 cup) fresh, minced beef
2 tablespoons chopped mushrooms
1–2 chopped, hard-boiled eggs
4 tablespoons stock or water
salt and pepper
$\frac{1}{2}$ tablespoon chopped dill or parsley
a little white of egg for sealing pancake rolls

Combine flour, salt, and sugar, stir in egg, and gradually blend in water.
Mix well and leave for twenty-five to thirty minutes. Heat a frying pan,
brush with a little oil or chicken fat, pour a small ladleful of batter into
the pan, and tilt it to spread the batter evenly over the bottom. Do not
pour in more than two and a half tablespoons at a time. If you put in too
much, pour it off. Fry on one side only. As soon as one side is done, turn
the pancake out on to a wooden board and cover with a cloth to keep warm.
Grease the pan again and proceed to fry the rest of the pancakes.

Heat two tablespoons oil or chicken fat and fry onion until soft. Add beef
and brown. Add mushroom, cook together for five minutes, stirring all the
time to prevent sticking and adding more fat if necessary.

Accompaniments to soups and garnishes

Add eggs, stock, seasoning, and dill. Cook, stirring for one to two minutes, remove from heat. Place the pancakes fried side up, put a spoonful of filling at one edge, fold it over, tuck in sides, and roll the pancakes. Brush the edge of the outer flap with egg white to prevent unrolling.

Before serving, fry blini to brown lightly, drain on absorbent kitchen paper, and serve with a clear soup. Alternately, for a posher presentation, you can dip the pancake rolls in lightly beaten egg, coat with fine sieved breadcrumbs, then fry.

Blinchaty pirog

This is a *de luxe* pancake pie which in a Russian menu is classed as an accompaniment to clear soups, but is substantial and interesting enough to be served independently. Served with a vegetable *consommé* it would require only a light dessert, or fruit, to make a complete meal. It is possible to do most of the preparation of this dish well in advance, so that all you will have to do would be to preheat the oven and bake the pie.

6 Servings

pancake batter (pages 4 and 54)
vegetable margarine
mushroom filling (see mushroom pirozhki, page 52)
2·5dl ($\frac{1}{2}$ pint or 1 cup) white sauce (page 248)
cream cheese filling (page 266)
parsley

Fry the pancake on both sides. Grease with margarine a deep soufflé dish to match the pancakes in diameter. Line the bottom with a pancake. Put on a layer of mushroom filling and spread some white sauce over it. Cover with a pancake spread with a layer of cream cheese filling.

Continue in this way, alternating mushroom and white sauce filling with cream cheese, until all is used up. Finish off with a pancake, scatter a few dabs of margarine on top, and bake in a hot oven, preheated to 235°C (450°F or Gas Mark 7), long enough to heat through and brown the top. Turn out on to a heated serving dish, decorate with parsley. To serve cut into wedges, as you would a layer cake. To serve with meat based *consommé*, substitute kasha or other filling for cream cheese.

Fish dishes

Seventeenth century Danish Megillah, silver case
in the Jewish Museum, London

Grilled fish Galilee

This is an old dish dating back to the biblical times. The fish used in the Galilee, then as now, is the John Dory, 'St Peter's Fish', which has, it is said, the marks of St Peter's thumbs on its back, a distinction it shares with haddock. If John Dory is not available, red mullet, small bass, and of course trout, are all good cooked this way. Traditionally the fish should be cooked over glowing charcoal.

4 Servings

4 John Dory, whole, ready for cooking
2 onions
oil
salt and pepper
4 sprigs parsley
4 halved lemon slices and lemon juice

Wash and dry the fish. Cut onions into fairly thick slices. Brush the fish with oil on the inside, season, stuff each with a portion of sliced onion, a sprig of parsley, and two semi-circles of lemon. Oil grill rack and heat grill. Brush fish with oil on the outside and grill for six to seven minutes each side, turning once and basting with lemon juice and oil during cooking.

Potted char, salmon or trout

A recipe which comes, originally, from Norway:

1kg (2lb) char
white wine court-bouillon (page 257)
480g (1lb) clarified butter (page 260)

Clean, wash, and dry the char and poach in court-bouillon, for fifteen minutes. Allow to cool, remove skin and bones, and slice the fish. Put it in an ovenproof dish, baste with plenty of butter, cover, and bake in the oven for fifteen minutes at 190°C (375°F or Gas Mark 5). Remove from oven, allow to cool completely, decant into jars, pour in the rest of the clarified butter so that the fish is completely covered with it, seal, and store in a refrigerator. Char, salmon or trout potted in this way will keep for two weeks. Very useful if you come by more than you need for the day and wish to preserve it for a week or more. Serve with a salad.

Fish dishes

Escabeche (Peruvian soused fish)

4–6 Servings

720g-1kg (1½-2lb) sea bass
2 medium-sized onions
2·5-cm (1-inch) piece fresh ginger
2 cloves garlic
6 tablespoons olive oil
salt and pepper
120g (4oz or 2 cups) mushrooms
1 green pepper
2·5dl (½ pint or 1 cup) good vinegar
125ml (¼ pint or ½ cup) water
1½ tablespoons sugar

Use the fish whole, with the head removed. Wash and dry fish. Cut onions into rings, slice garlic and ginger finely. Heat half the oil, brown the fish on both sides, sprinkle with salt and pepper, and remove from pan. Add remaining oil to pan, fry onions and garlic for five minutes. Add ginger, cook for one minute. Slice mushrooms. Seed and shred green pepper. Add mushrooms and pepper to the onion mixture. Stir and fry for two minutes. Add vinegar, water, and sugar, bring to the boil, then reduce heat to very low, simmer for two to three minutes. Add fish to pan, spoon the hot marinade over it, simmer for five minutes and remove from heat. Allow to cool, chill for twenty-four hours before serving.

Danish buckling or kipper flan (pie)

4 Servings

120g (4oz or 1 cup) flour
120g (4oz or 8 tablespoons) butter or vegetable margarine
iced water
salt and pepper
2–3 skinned, boned bucklings
120g (4oz or ⅔ cup) stoned, black olives
1 small, chopped onion, softened in butter or vegetable margarine
2 beaten eggs
milk (or water)
few tablespoons dried beans (or rice)

Fish dishes

Mix flour with a pinch of salt, cut in butter with a knife, and add enough iced water to bind the pastry, sprinkling the water in a tablespoon at a time, and blending it in evenly. Roll out the pastry, line a 20-cm (8-inch) flan tin, press down gently, to make it fit and prevent formation of bubbles underneath, and crimp edges. Prick the bottom of the flan all over with a fork, cover with a circle of greaseproof paper, cut to fit the bottom, and fill with dried beans or rice. Bake in a hot oven 204°C (400°F or Gas Mark 6) for about thirty minutes or until the flan case becomes lightly browned. Remove beans, which can be used again for a similar operation. Discard paper.

Flake the bucklings, put in the flan case with olives and onion. Season the eggs, add a *little* milk (or water) – bearing in mind that this mixture is to form the custard over the bucklings; it should come up to the rim of the flan case but not spill over. Bake in the oven 190°C (375°F or Gas Mark 4) until the flan sets. Serve hot or cold. Excellent with a green salad.

Baked cod with apple and celery, Danish style

4 Servings

720g (1½lb) cod fillet
120g (4oz or 1 cup) shredded celery
1 finely chopped onion
3 diced cooking apples
salt and pepper
4 tablespoons tomato purée
1 dl (1 gill or ½ cup) milk
2 tablespoons butter

Wash and dry the cod fillets. Lightly butter an ovenproof dish, put in celery, onion, and apples, mix, and spread out evenly and put the fish on this foundation. Season with salt and pepper. Dilute tomato purée with milk, pour over the fillets. Bake in the oven, 233°C (450°F or Gas Mark 7) for thirty minutes. Serve with mashed potatoes or rice.

Fish dishes

Cod, Norwegian style

4 Servings

This recipe was first brought to my attention by a Norwegian professor at a terribly learned international conference. I have since tried it, and it certainly does things for dear old cod:

500–750g (1–1½lb) cod fillets
2 carrots
90g (3oz or ¾ cup) celery
6 slices white bread
120g (4oz or ½ cup) butter
1 medium-sized, chopped onion
3 tablespoons chopped parsley
salt and pepper
3 tablespoons breadcrumbs

Wash and dry cod fillets. Grate the carrot and dice the celery. Cut the crusts off and dice the bread. Melt the butter (reserving a quarter of it for later use) in a bowl, add carrots, celery, diced bread, onion, and parsley, season to taste, and mix well. Put the fish in a well buttered ovenproof dish, season, cover with the mixed vegetables, sprinkle with breadcrumbs, dot with remainder of the butter in tiny pieces, bake in a preheated oven, 235°C (450°F or Gas Mark 7) for thirty minutes.

Carp, Israeli style

4 Servings

1 medium carp
1 small, chopped onion
4 chopped shallots
3·75dl (3 gills or 1½ cups) oil
2 tablespoons flour
2·5dl (½ pint or 1 cup) white wine
salt
cayenne pepper
2 crushed cloves garlic
pinch thyme
¼ bay leaf

Fish dishes

pinch saffron
30g (1oz or 2 tablespoons) blanched, chopped almonds
1 tablespoon chopped parsley

Skin the carp, cut into uniform slices. Heat three tablespoons oil and
gently cook onion and shallots, without browning. Add carp, sprinkle with
flour, stir gently, cover with wine, season with salt and pepper, add garlic,
thyme, and bay leaf, sprinkle with a few tablespoons oil. Bring to the boil,
then simmer on a low heat for twenty minutes. Drain the carp slices and
re-form in the original shape on a long dish. Boil down the liquid in which
the fish was cooked by two-thirds. Away from direct heat, whisk in the
rest of the oil, add saffron and almonds, pour over the carp, and leave to
cool. Sprinkle with parsley and serve.

Ceviche (mackerel, Mexican style)

6–8 Servings

1kg (2lb) mackerel (or other firm fleshed fish)
lemon juice
125ml (1 gill or $\frac{1}{2}$ cup) olive oil
1 medium-sized, chopped onion
2 ripe, large, peeled chopped tomatoes
12–16 chopped green olives
4 tablespoons chopped fresh coriander (or watercress)
1 finely chopped green chili
salt
vinegar
2 medium-sized avocado pears

Skin and bone the fish and cut into uniform 1-cm ($\frac{1}{2}$-inch) cubes.
Put in a deep dish, add enough lemon juice to cover the fish.
Allow to stand for a couple of hours to macerate. This lemon treatment is
all the cooking the fish needs. Pour off surplus liquid. Add oil, onion,
tomatoes, olives, coriander, and chili. Season with salt and vinegar to
taste. Mix carefully.

Peel avocado, slice, and dip immediately in lemon juice, to prevent
discoloration. Garnish the fish with avocado slices, chill, and serve.

Fish dishes

Sinai perch

This is another ancient recipe and is suitable for any fresh water fish. Its distinctive feature is the top dressing of tehina used for the *gratin* surface:

4 Servings

4 medium-size perch
salt and pepper
juice of $\frac{1}{2}$ lemon
oil
1 tablespoon breadcrumbs
2 tablespoons chopped parsley
1 clove chopped garlic
2 sliced onions
180g (6oz or $\frac{1}{4}$ cup) tehina (page 10)

Score both sides of the fish, season, sprinkle with lemon juice. Preheat oven to 205°C (400°F Gas Mark 5). Oil an ovenproof dish. Mix breadcrumbs with one tablespoon chopped parsley and sprinkle the mixture over the inside of the dish. Heat two to three tablespoons oil, gently fry the fish until pale golden on both sides. Carefully remove, without breaking, and put in the prepared dish.

Heat the oil left from cooking the fish. Fry the garlic for one minute. Add onions and fry together. Season. As soon as onions become soft and transparent, spoon them over the fish. Sprinkle in any remaining lemon juice. Spread tehina over the surface and cook in the oven for about fifteen minutes. Sprinkle with parsley and serve.

Sprats in pink cream

4 Servings

720g (1$\frac{1}{2}$lb) fresh sprats
2 tablespoons butter
1 tablespoon breadcrumbs
salt and pepper
2 teaspoons French mustard
2 tablespoons tomato purée
2·5dl (2 gills or 1 cup) cream
1 tablespoon chopped chives

Fish dishes

Open sprats, clean out, and remove bone carefully, without breaking up
the little fish. Wash and pat dry. Butter a pie dish, sprinkle with
breadcrumbs. Blend cream with mustard and whip until stiff. Season
sprats with salt and pepper, spread with cream on the inside, and roll up
like rollmops. Arrange the sprats in the pie dish in neat rows. Blend tomato
purée into the cream, pour over the sprats, sprinkle with chives, dot with
small pieces of butter, and bake in a hot oven, 204°C (400°F or Gas Mark
6) for thirty minutes.

Red mullet with tomatoes, anchovies, and olives (cold)
Mediterranean recipe

4 Servings

4 small mullets
salt and pepper
3 tablespoons olive oil
3 chopped shallots
1 crushed clove garlic
500g (1lb or 3 cups) peeled, chopped tomatoes
12 anchovy fillets
60g (2oz or ⅓ cup) stoned olives

Scale the fish, cut off fins, clean out, but leave the livers. Wash and gently
dab with a cloth to dry. Season on the inside with salt and pepper. Rub
with a little olive oil and grill until done and both sides are uniformly
browned. While the fish is grilling, prepare the sauce. Heat the rest of the
oil and gently fry the shallots with garlic for two to three minutes. Add
tomatoes and increase heat to cook down the sauce to a thick consistency.
Season to taste.

Arrange the fish in a serving dish, pour the sauce over it, and leave until
cold. Decorate the top with anchovies in a crisscross pattern, stud with
olives, and serve.

Fish dishes

Whole baked salmon, Canadian style

This is a relatively new recipe, but I think it is the finest way of cooking whole salmon and salmon trout. After all, however good the liquid in which you poach the fish, some of its flavour goes towards enriching the liquid. Baked slowly this way, the fish preserves all its juices and flavour.

It is impossible to indicate the number of servings – all depends on how big a salmon you catch and on the appetites of your guests.

Cut a piece of kitchen metal foil big enough to enclose the whole fish and allow for overlap. Spread the foil with butter, put the salmon on it, season to taste, wrap up, and put in a baking pan.

Preheat oven to 120°C (250°F or Gas Mark $\frac{1}{2}$) and bake, allowing two hours cooking time for a four-pound salmon and adding fifteen minutes for each additional pound.

Serve hot with its own juices, garnished with cucumber salad, black olives, lemon wedges, and pats of tarragon butter (page 259).

Salmon coulibiac

8–10 Servings

Coulibiac dough
500g (1lb or 4 cups) sifted flour
25g ($\frac{3}{4}$oz or 1$\frac{1}{2}$ cakes) baker's yeast
4 eggs
1 teaspoon sugar
pinch salt
1·25dl (1 gill or $\frac{1}{2}$ cup) warm milk
180g (6oz or $\frac{3}{4}$ cup) softened butter

Filling
720g (1$\frac{1}{2}$lb) fresh salmon
butter
240g ($\frac{1}{2}$lb or 1$\frac{1}{8}$ cups) rice (or buckwheat)
fish stock (optional)
3 4 chopped, hard-boiled eggs
120g (4oz or 2 cups) sliced mushrooms
1 chopped onion

Fish dishes

1 tablespoon chopped parsley
4 tablespoons Madeira
salt and pepper
pinch nutmeg
1 tablespoon chopped chives
sieved breadcrumbs

Firstly, prepare the coulibiac dough. To make leaven, put a quarter of the flour in a circle on the table, put the yeast in the middle, dilute with a little water, mix, moistening from time to time to keep the dough on the soft side. Roll into a ball, make a crossways incision in the top, cover, and leave in a warm place for the leaven to ferment and double its volume.

Put the rest of the flour in a circle on the table, put eggs and two tablespoons of warm water in the middle, moisten the dough with milk, and knead it. Add sugar and salt dissolved in a teaspoon of water and incorporate the softened butter. Mix well, spread the dough on the table, pour the leaven into the middle, blend it in, put the dough in a bowl, cover with a clean cloth, and leave in a warm place to rise – this fermentation process takes five to six hours. When it has risen, beat the dough and from then on keep in a cool place until ready to roll out. Cut the salmon into small pieces and fry lightly in butter, just to stiffen them. Remove and allow to cool.

Cook the rice in water (or stock). Fry the mushrooms and onion lightly in butter, add parsley, Madeira, salt, pepper, nutmeg, and chives, then add salmon and simmer for a few minutes. Remove from heat.

Using two-thirds of the dough, roll out the bottom sheet, which has to be thicker than the top covering. Put on a lightly greased baking sheet. Spread the filling, avoiding the edges, in layers : first half the rice. Then arrange the salmon, scatter mushrooms and their juices over it, follow with a layer of hard-boiled eggs, and finally another layer of rice. Dot with tiny pieces of butter. Roll out the rest of the dough, cover the filling carefully with it. Moisten the edges slightly to make the dough stick together and draw up the edges of the lower sheet of pastry, so that they cover the edge of the upper sheet. Cut a slit in the top to enable steam to escape, brush the top with melted butter, sprinkle with breadcrumbs, and bake in a moderately hot oven, 204°C (400°F or Gas Mark 5) for one hour. Remove from oven, pour three to four tablespoons melted butter into the 'chimney hole' in the centre, and serve.

Fish dishes

Truites aux amandes

4 Servings

4 brook trout
1 dl (1 gill or $\frac{1}{2}$ cup) milk
flour
salt and pepper
90g (3oz or 6 tablespoons) butter
120g (4oz or $\frac{3}{4}$ cup) blanched almonds
squeeze lemon juice

Clean the trout, wash, dry on a cloth, dip in milk, and roll in flour seasoned with salt and pepper. Fry in two tablespoons butter until golden on both sides, remove, put on a heated serving dish, and keep hot.

Slice the almonds longwise into slivers. Add the rest of the butter to the frying pan in which the fish was cooked, heat, put in almonds, and brown them and the butter. Spoon a portion of the almonds over each trout. Add a dash of lemon to the browned butter and serve with the fish. Delicious with new boiled potatoes, tossed in butter, and sprinkled with chopped chervil.

Fillets of sole with cod roe quenelles

4 Servings

8 sole fillets
60g (2oz or $\frac{5}{8}$ cup) fresh, sliced mushrooms
0·5 litre (1 pint or 2 cups) good fish stock
240g (8oz or 1 cup) cod's roe
1 slice stale bread
salt and pepper
1 tablespoon chopped parsley
3 eggs
3 tablespoons oil
2 medium-sized, sliced onions
breadcrumbs
100ml (4fl oz or $\frac{1}{2}$ cup) dry white wine
$\frac{1}{2}$ teaspoon grated lemon rind
1 teaspoon cornflour

Fish dishes

strained juice of 2 lemons
pinch cayenne pepper

Wash and dry the fillets of sole. Put a few slices of mushroom on each fillet, roll it up, and secure with a cocktail stick. Make a good strong fish stock (page 259) and strain.

Dip the roe in water, leave for a few minutes to remove excess salt, then squeeze out.

Soak bread in water, squeeze, and add to roe. Season with salt and pepper, add parsley, and pound in a mortar or put through a blender. Work in one tablespoon oil and add one lightly beaten egg. If the mixture is too liquid, sprinkle in a tablespoon breadcrumbs. Mix well.

Heat remaining oil in a casserole and lightly fry onions. Put in rolled fillets, season, add wine and enough stock just to cover the fish. Bring to the boil, cover, reduce heat, and simmer for seven to eight minutes. Taking a little of the cod's roe mixture at a time, shape into little quenelles, add to sole fillets, continue to simmer for fifteen minutes.

Take the fillets out of the casserole, arrange on a heated serving dish, surround with quenelles, and keep hot. Strain the liquor in which the fish was cooked, add to it remaining stock, and bring to the boil. Add lemon rind.

Dilute cornflour with two tablespoons lemon juice, blend into stock, simmer, stirring for two to three minutes, until the sauce thickens, keep hot without allowing to boil.

Beat remaining eggs with the rest of the lemon juice until frothy. Dilute with two ladlesful of hot, but not boiling, stock, adding it a little at a time. Remove stock from heat. Pour the egg liaison into the stock, stir, ladle some of the sauce over the fish, sprinkle with cayenne, and serve. Serve the rest of the sauce separately.

Don't let the sauce boil after adding the egg liaison, or it will curdle.

Fish dishes

Fillets of sole in aspic

6 Servings

12 small sole fillets
2 tablespoons butter
seasoning
fish fumet (page 259)
1 long cucumber or 12 small tomatoes
2·5dl ($\frac{1}{2}$ pint or 1 cup) fish aspic (page 258)
cod roe pâté (page 6)

Flatten sole fillets, spread with a little butter, season to taste, roll up each one into a little horn, secure with a cocktail stick, and cook slowly in good, concentrated fish *fumet*. While the fish is cooking, make 'stands' for the little fillet horns – either small scooped-out tomatoes, or cucumber, peeled, cut into chunks, and hollowed out to make suitable 'pedestals'. Dip both the 'pedestals' and the cooled, drained fillets in cold fish aspic jelly and fix the rolled fillets to the 'pedestals'. Carefully extract the cocktail sticks – when the aspic sets. Arrange on a dish, put a spoonful of cod roe pâté into each horn, and serve.

Fillets of sole with tehina

Either sole, lemon sole, or plaice fillets can be used for this dish. If it is intended as an *hors-d'oeuvre*, the ingredients indicated will suffice. If you wish to serve it as a main course – and it makes an attractive summer meal – double the quantities.

4 Servings

4 fillets of sole
salt and pepper
2–3 tablespoons cod roe pâté (page 6)
1 chopped, hard-boiled egg
1 tablespoon lemon juice
tehina (page 10)
1 tablespoon chopped parsley
black olives for garnish

Wash, dry, and skin the fillets. Cut them across into strips about 5cm (2 inches) wide, season with salt and pepper.

Fish dishes

Preheat oven to 190°C (375°F or Gas Mark 4). Mix cod roe pâté with chopped, hard-boiled egg.

Spread pieces of fish with roe and egg mixture, roll up, and secure with cocktail sticks. Put in an ovenproof dish, add lemon juice, cover, and bake for twenty minutes. Remove, allow to cool. Coat with tehina, sprinkle with parsley, garnish with black olives, and serve cold.

Lithuanian pike with mushrooms

This recipe can be used with equal success for any other kind of fish fillets, cod, haddock, hake, halibut, etc.

6 Servings

1kg (2lb) pike fillets
salt and pepper
4 tablespoons butter or margarine
1 large, chopped onion
240g (8oz or 2½ cups) sliced, fresh mushrooms
1 tablespoon chopped dill
1 teaspoon grated lemon rind
140ml (6fl oz or ¾ cup) fish stock (page 259) or water
140ml (6fl oz or ¾ cup) cream
1 teaspoon cornflour
1 tablespoon cold water
2 raw yolks

Cut the fish into pieces, season with salt and pepper. Heat butter, fry onion until transparent, add mushrooms, and simmer until they soften. Add parsley and lemon rind, stir, and put in fish. Little by little add stock, blend in cream, cover, and simmer on very low heat for twenty minutes. Transfer fish and mushrooms with a perforated spoon to a fairly deep, heated serving dish and keep warm while you finish off the sauce.

Blend cornflour with cold water, add to the pan juices, and simmer gently, stirring until the sauce thickens.

Remove from heat. Dilute yolks with a couple of tablespoons of hot but not boiling sauce, mix, then stir the diluted yolks into the sauce. Reheat if necessary, without allowing the sauce to come to the boil, pour over fish, and serve.

Fish dishes

Dag filé (fried fillets of fish)

Fried fillets of fish are as popular in Israel as fish and chips in England. If you go to a modest restaurant, which may have only two or three main courses on the menu, you can bet your bottom lira that one of them will be *dag filé* (pronounced 'filay').

The fillets are usually dipped in seasoned egg, then matzo crumbs or cornmeal, and fried in hot olive oil. The seasoning can include a dash of cayenne, paprika, mace, turmeric or other spices.

4 Servings

720g (1½lb) fish fillets (plaice, sole, halibut, cod, haddock, hake, etc.).
1 egg
1 tablespoon milk
salt and pepper
pinch mace
matzo meal or breadcrumbs
oil

Wash and dry the fillets carefully. Mix egg with milk, season with salt, pepper, and mace. Dip fillets in egg, then in matzo meal. Pat down to coat all over, then shake lightly to shed surplus crumbs. Use enough oil to submerge the fillets. Heat oil until a blueish haze begins to rise. Put the fillets in a few at a time, to prevent sudden cooling of the oil temperature, as this would make the fillets soggy. Fry until brown all over, drain on paper, garnish with fried parsley (page 53), and serve piping hot.

East European baked stuffed bream

Bream cooked this way is particularly good, but the recipe can be applied to other kinds of fish: haddock, gurnet, carp:

6 Servings

1·5kg (3lb) bream, clean and ready for cooking
salt
180g (6oz or ¾ cup) butter or margarine
1 chopped onion
3 chopped stalks celery
1 chopped apple

Fish dishes

180g (6oz or 2 cups) soft breadcrumbs
pinch thyme
1 tablespoon chopped parsley
salt and pepper
1–2 eggs
pinch paprika
1 tablespoon flour
lemon cut in wedges

Slit the bream along the stomach and carefully remove the backbone. Wash, dry on soft cloth, and sprinkle with salt on the inside. Heat half the butter and fry onion and celery until soft. Add apple and breadcrumbs, cook together for two to three minutes, stirring. Remove from heat, add thyme and parsley, season to taste with salt and pepper, bind with egg, and mix the stuffing well. Preheat oven to 190°C (375°F or Gas Mark 4). Stuff the bream, stitch up with thread, put in a well buttered baking dish, and season. Melt remaining butter and baste the fish with it. Mix flour with paprika and dust the fish with it. Bake for fifty to sixty minutes.

Lift the bream out on to a heated serving dish. Remove stitches, spoon the pan juices over the fish, garnish with lemon wedges, and serve.

Hake in orange sauce, Israeli recipe

4 Servings

480g (1lb) hake
flour
salt and pepper
oil for frying
2·5dl (½ pint or 1 cup) fresh orange juice
1 teaspoon cornflour, diluted in 2 tablespoons cold water

Cut fish into portions. Mix flour with salt and pepper and coat fish pieces with it, then fry them in oil. Drain fish, put in a deep dish, cool.

Bring orange juice to the boil, stir in cornflour, simmer until the sauce thickens, pour over fish, allow to cool. Chill and serve with orange salad with poppy seeds (pages 164–5).

Seventeenth century silver wine cup
in the Jewish Museum, London

Meat dishes

Meat dishes

Moroccan etalya (beef, avocado, and olive salad)

4 Servings

16 black, stoned olives
50ml (2fl oz or ¼ cup) red wine
1 slice white bread
120g (4oz or ⅔ cup) blanched almonds
120g (4oz or ¾ cup) pine kernels
4–5 cloves garlic
120ml (¼ pint or ½ cup) olive oil
salt and white pepper
1 tablespoon tarragon vinegar
1½ tablespoons lemon juice
360g (12oz or 1½ cups) cold, cooked, sliced beef
360g (12oz or 1¼ cups) cooked potatoes
3 tablespoons salad dressing*
1 tablespoon chopped chives
240g (8oz or 1¼ cups) sliced cucumber
1 red sweet pepper, seeded and shredded
2 avocado pears

Put the stoned olives in a small bowl, pour the wine over them, and leave to stand for at least one hour. Soak the slice of bread in a little water.

Pound the almonds, pine kernels, and garlic, or pass through a blender to make a smooth paste and transfer to a bowl. Squeeze out the bread and add to the paste. Start adding oil little by little, stirring as for mayonnaise, until all the oil is used up. Season to taste with salt and pepper, add vinegar and one tablespoon lemon juice. Blend well and chill the sauce until ready to serve.

Arrange the beef slices, overlapping them slightly in the middle of a serving dish. Dice the potatoes, toss in salad dressing, sprinkle with chives, and spoon around the beef slices. Garnish with cucumber and red pepper.

Cut the avocado pears in half, remove stone, and sprinkle the cut halves with half a tablespoon of lemon juice. Drain the olives and fill the avocado pears with them. Add to strategic points of the salad dish and serve with the pine kernel sauce.

* To make salad dressing, mix three parts oil with one part vinegar or lemon juice, and salt and pepper to taste.

Meat dishes

Klops with hard-boiled eggs

Klops is an East European improved version of a meat loaf. Both this recipe and the one which follows look attractive when cut; one with whole hard-boiled eggs in the middle, the other stuffed with mushrooms and an omelette and rolled like a Swiss roll. Both can be served with a mushroom or tomato sauce, or cold for a Sabbath lunch. If you intend to serve klops cold, leave it in the tin until it cools down completely, then turn out and slice.

6 Servings

60g (2oz or 1 cup) fresh breadcrumbs
stock
1kg (2lb) beef
1 large, finely grated onion
1 tablespoon chopped parsley
1 finely grated carrot
salt and pepper
pinch nutmeg
2 beaten eggs
margarine
6 hard-boiled eggs

Soak the breadcrumbs in a little stock. Put the beef through a mincer with breadcrumbs. Add onion, parsley, and carrot.

Season to taste with salt and pepper, add nutmeg and beaten eggs, and mix well.

Grease a loaf tin generously with margarine. Shell the eggs. Preheat the oven to 235°C (450°C or Gas Mark 7). Put half the meat mixture into the loaf tin, pressing down firmly. Put whole hard-boiled eggs in a line down the middle, cover with the rest of the meat. Scatter a few pieces of margarine over the top and bake for ten minutes. Reduce heat to 190°C (375°F or Gas Mark 4) and continue to bake for forty-five to fifty minutes.

Meat dishes

Klops with mushrooms and omelette

6 Servings

120g (4oz) white, crustless bread
100ml (4fl oz or $\frac{1}{2}$ cup) stock
1kg (2lb) minced beef or veal
1 tablespoon chopped parsley
1 finely grated carrot and large onion
salt and pepper
pinch nutmeg
2 beaten eggs and 3 eggs for omelette
30g (1oz or $\frac{1}{2}$ cup) grated breadcrumbs
60g (2oz or $\frac{3}{4}$ cup) sliced mushrooms
margarine

Soak the bread in stock, flake with a fork, add to minced meat. If the
mixture does not look smooth enough, put through a mincer. Add onion,
parsley, carrot, salt, pepper, nutmeg, and two beaten eggs. Mix
thoroughly. Preheat oven to 235°C (450°F or Gas Mark 7). Grease a
baking tin with margarine. Sprinkle a board with grated breadcrumbs,
put the beef on it, and roll out, or spread with your fingers, into a flat
pancake, smoothing it out to a thickness of about 1·5 cm ($\frac{3}{4}$ inch).

Fry mushrooms lightly in two tablespoons margarine. Arrange the
mushrooms in an even flat layer over the meat. Lightly grease an omelette
pan, which should be slightly smaller in diameter than the circle of meat.
Beat the eggs and fry a pancake omelette; cook it on one side only.

When the underside of the omelette is done, turn it out carefully, cooked
side up, on to the circle of meat. Roll up like a Swiss roll, to enclose the
omelette completely. Patch up any splits, sprinkle with breadcrumbs,
put in a baking tin, dab with small pieces of margarine, and bake for
fifteen minutes. Reduce heat to 190°C (375°F or Gas Mark 4) and bake for
thirty-five to forty minutes.

Shashlyk

This is considered to be a Georgian dish by the Russians but, under the
name of kebab, it is popular throughout the Middle East, the Balkans, and
all stations to Pakistan and India.

Meat dishes

The Greeks undoubtedly had a word for it – *souvlakia* after *souvla*, the Greek word for skewer. It is said that the origins of the dish go back to the tribal horsemen of the Caucasus and the Asiastic steppes, who only had camp fires for cooking.

It is interesting to note the different methods of marinating the meat, which all shashlyk or kebab cooks consider essential. Local produce and religious taboos decree the marinating ingredients. The Georgians, who go in for vineyards, marinate it in red wine; the Moslems to whom wine is forbidden, use oil; the Indians use yoghurt. The Israelis, who cultivate both olives and lemons in abundance, marinate their meat for shashlyk in a seasoned mixture of olive oil and lemon juice.

Shashlyk is best grilled over charcoal and should be served as soon as it is done. Make your guests wait for it, as they would for a *soufflé*. Otherwise, if you allow cooked shashlyk to stand, it will turn tough and leathery.

6 Servings

1kg (2lb) steak
100ml (4fl oz or ½ cup) olive oil
2 cloves minced garlic
1½ tablespoons chopped parsley
1 teaspoon salt
½ teaspoon pepper
2 tablespoons lemon juice
120g (4oz) button mushrooms
3 onions
360g (12oz) tomatoes
1–2 green peppers

Cut the meat into 2·5-cm (1-inch) cubes. Mix oil, garlic, parsley, salt, pepper, and lemon juice. Put the meat into this mixture and leave in a cool place for one to two hours, turning from time to time.

Wash and dry mushrooms. Slice onions and tomatoes. Seed peppers and cut into square pieces to match the meat cubes. Thread the meat on greased skewers, alternating with onions, tomatoes, mushrooms, and pepper. Cook over charcoal barbecue or very hot grill, turning to ensure even cooking. The outside should be well browned but the inside tender and pink.

Meat dishes

Pickled beef (corned beef)

Pickled beef, corned beef, or salt beef, is delicious hot or cold. The liquid in which it is ultimately cooked makes a very good broth. The procedure is simple though time consuming. It is advisable to pickle more than you may require for a meal and the number of servings, therefore, is not indicated.

You can serve it hot, with boiled vegetables and dumplings, then cold with a salad, and finally no one would consider it a hardship to eat a snack or a sandwich of salt beef on rye bread, with a home-pickled cucumber as a garnish. So don't be afraid to have too much – it can't be wasted.

Pickling
2–3kg (4–6lb) brisket of beef
4 litres (4 quarts) water
480g (1lb or 2 cups) coarse salt
30g (1oz) saltpetre
2–3 crushed cloves garlic (optional)
2–3 bay leaves
2–3 tablespoons sugar

Cooking
warm water
5–6 smallish onions
3–4 quartered carrots
3 sliced stalks celery
1 parsnip, cut in chunks
2 young turnips, cut in chunks
2–3 cloves
pinch brown sugar
peppercorns to taste
onion dumplings (page 264)

To pickle the brisket, wash and dry it. Bring water with pickling ingredients to the boil, simmer for seven to eight minutes, skimming until the surface is clear. Strain into a pickling crock and allow to cool completely. Then put the brisket in, cover with a plate heavy enough to press it down, and keep it submerged in the brine. Cover the top with a piece of butter muslin and leave for eight to ten days in a refrigerator or a very cool larder, turning the meat every two or three days.

Meat dishes

To cook, take the brisket out of the brine, rinse, and dry. Put in a saucepan, add enough warm (not cold) water to cover the meat and bring to the boil. Skim, cover, and simmer for two hours. Add the rest of the ingredients, except the dumplings, simmer for one hour. Add dumplings, simmer for thirty-five to forty minutes.

Put the beef on a heated serving dish, surround with its vegetables and dumplings, ladle some of its broth over it, and serve. Use the rest of the broth for making soup.

Beef Stroganoff

6 Servings

720g ($1\frac{1}{2}$lb) fillet of beef
1 teaspoon salt
$\frac{1}{2}$ teaspoon pepper
2 medium-sized onions
120g ($\frac{1}{4}$lb or $\frac{1}{2}$ cup) vegetable margarine
120g ($\frac{1}{4}$lb or $1\frac{3}{4}$ cup) sliced mushrooms
1 tablespoon flour
1 tablespoon tomato purée
1 teaspoon made mustard (English)
2·5dl ($\frac{1}{2}$ pint or 1 cup) stock
1–2 tablespoons lemon juice
1 tablespoon chopped parsley

Wash the meat, trim away gristle, and two hours before it is needed cut into 'straws' – i.e. strips about 2·5cm (1 inch) long and not more than 5mm ($\frac{1}{4}$ inch) thick – sprinkle with salt and pepper, and leave to stand. Slice the onions and fry in margarine, add mushrooms, and fry together for two to three minutes. Add the meat, and fry together for five to six minutes, stirring with a wooden fork. Sprinkle in flour, and fry for another two to three minutes. Put in tomato purée and mustard, dilute with stock, and bring to the boil. Add lemon juice, cover with a lid, and simmer gently for fifteen minutes. Bring to the boil, sprinkle with chopped parsley, and serve with new potatoes.

For an extra touch, you can *flambé* this dish, i.e. sprinkle it with a tablespoon of brandy, set it alight, then extinguish with lemon juice and finish off as described.

Meat dishes

Beef strudel

This is a grand and very luxurious dish, a sort of Jewish answer to
boeuf en croûte. Most of the preparation can be done well in advance.
The actual baking will only take about half an hour:

6–8 Servings

1·5kg (3lb) fillet of beef
margarine
strudel dough (page 188) or puff pastry (page 189)
salt and pepper
oil
chopped chicken liver (page 16)

Heat the oven until very hot 245°C (475°F or Gas Mark 8). Brush the
fillet with melted margarine and brown quickly in the oven to sear it. As
soon as it browns, remove and allow to cool completely. Make the strudel
dough, or puff pastry, as described, using oil or margarine instead of
butter. Cut the fillet into 'pages', i.e. without slicing right through, so
that the bottom part remains whole. Season to taste, spread a layer of
chopped liver between each 'page', and gently sandwich together. Put the
fillet on a rolled out piece of dough, spread remaining chopped liver over
it, smooth down, and wrap in pastry to enclose the meat completely.
Make slanting cuts on the top to mark the meat slices, to make it easier to
cut for serving. Put on a baking sheet.

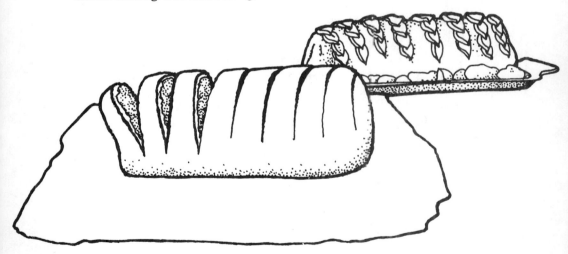

Meat dishes

At this stage the strudel can be put in the refrigerator and kept until you are ready to bake it.

Preheat oven to 205°C (400°F or Gas Mark 5). Brush strudel with oil or melted margarine and bake for fifteen minutes. Reduce heat to 175°C (350°F or Gas Mark 3) and continue to bake for fifteen to twenty minutes or until the strudel is golden.

Liver strudel

This is a complete contrast to the extravagant beef strudel, which uses a choice cut of meat and chopped chicken liver, and is intended for specially festive occasions. This more modest strudel illustrates the genius of the Jewish cooks from Eastern Europe, where poverty taught them to make cheaper cuts and leftovers of meat into palatable and attractive dishes. Ox liver, spleen (milt), lung, intestines, are all used in a great variety of dishes.

8 Servings

720g (1½lb) ox liver
4 tablespoons flour
salt and pepper
60g (2oz or 4 tablespoons) chicken fat
2 finely chopped onions
240g (8oz or 1 cup) minced, cooked meat (optional)
strudel dough (page 188) using melted margarine or oil instead of butter

Slice the liver. Season flour with salt and pepper. Roll liver in seasoned flour. Heat chicken fat and light fry onions. Add liver and brown. If you have any roast or boiled meat, add to liver. Put the mixture through a mincer, check seasoning. Roll out dough, spread liver mixture over it, roll up, brush with a little melted margarine or oil, and bake as described in recipe for beef strudel.

Meat dishes

Grilled spare ribs

These are not the thick shoulder pieces, but the end bones of ribs, 10 to 12cm (4 to 5 inches) long with only a little meat on them.

Spare ribs is one of many dishes which originated in the Orient and became happily naturalized in many countries.

The composition of the marinade or basting mixture varies greatly. The original oriental recipe relies on fresh ginger and soya sauce; in the Pacific pineapple juice is used; and in America every barbecue owner boasts of having a formula of his own, though, in my opinion, they tend to use too much tabasco.

The recipe which follows was sent from Canada. Spare ribs must be well done and require slow grilling over low heat:

4 Servings

12–16 spare ribs
100ml (4fl oz or ½ cup) salad oil
1–2 cloves crushed garlic
1 teaspoon ground ginger
1 teaspoon salt
½ teaspoon pepper
50ml (2fl oz or ¼ cup) lemon juice
2 tablespoons finely chopped green pepper
1 tablespoon soya sauce
2 tablespoons brown sugar, or
4 tablespoons honey
½ teaspoon dry mustard
2–3 tablespoons white wine vinegar

Wash ribs in cold water and dry on a cloth. Combine the rest of the ingredients and heat to boiling point, to make sauce. Put ribs on grill and cook slowly over low heat. If you are using a charcoal grill, keep the ribs about 10cm (4 inches) above the coals. Baste with hot sauce. Cook for at least one hour, turning and basting frequently.

Arrange ribs on a heated serving dish, spoon remainder of hot sauce over them, and serve.

Meat dishes

Baked spare ribs

Prepare ribs and basting sauce as described in recipe for grilled spare ribs. Lightly oil a shallow roasting dish big enough to take all the ribs in one layer. Preheat oven to 175°C (350°F or Gas Mark 3).

Spread ribs with basting sauce, put in the oven and bake for twenty minutes. Turn, baste, and bake for thirty minutes. Repeat turning and basting, cook for another twenty minutes, and serve.

Many cooks advocate baking the ribs for an hour, then finishing off for twenty to thirty minutes on a charcoal grill, turning and basting with the sauce.

Beef casserole with dumplings

6 Servings

720g (1½lb) stewing steak
3–4 tablespoons dripping
480g (1lb or 4 cups) sliced onions
salt and pepper
1 teaspoon paprika
2·5dl (½ pint or 1 cup) water
juice of ½ lemon
small pinch caraway seeds
small pinch marjoram
1 tablespoon flour
2·5dl (½ pint or 1 cup) stock
180g (6oz or 1 cup) peeled, quartered tomatoes
dumplings (page 264)

Cut the steak into bite-size pieces. Heat dripping and *sauté* onions until soft and transparent, add meat, and brown evenly on all sides. Season with salt, pepper, and paprika, add water, lemon juice, caraway seeds, and marjoram, cover, and simmer for one and a half hours. Blend in flour, dilute gradually with stock, add tomatoes, cover, and continue to simmer for another hour. Prepare dumplings and serve with the casserole.

Meat dishes

Roast beef and Yorkshire pudding

There is very little that can match up to a prime joint of roast beef and
Yorkshire pudding. No wonder the dish has entered into the repertoire of
English Jewish cookery. The recipe is strictly Yorkshire. The only
adaptation to make it accord with the Jewish Dietary Laws is the
substitution of water for milk in the pudding batter. Cooked in the
traditional Yorkshire way, it is excellent.

In less affluent days, Yorkshire mothers had to find economical means of
filling the empty stomachs of their families, a job which Jewish mothers
have brought to a fine art. Yorkshire pudding used to be served on its own,
before the joint, thus making the meat go further.

beef joint: sirloin, rib or topside
120g (4oz or 1 cup) plain flour
salt
1 egg
2·5dl ($\frac{1}{2}$ pint or 1 cup) water

Heat the oven until very hot 235°C (450°F or Gas Mark 7 or 8). Put the
top shelf of the oven in the mid-way position and roast the joint in a baking
tin or straight on the grid, if you use a gas oven, with a pan placed on the
shelf below to catch the dripping. For a traditionally made roast beef and
Yorkshire pudding, a gas oven is much better, because the pudding is then
cooked underneath the joint and catches all its lovely juices. Roast joint
in a hot oven for twenty minutes, then reduce to 190°C (375°F or Gas
Mark 4). Allow fifteen minutes per 0·5 kilo (pound) and fifteen minutes over.

As soon as you put the meat in, start preparing the batter for the Yorkshire
pudding. Sift the flour with a good pinch of salt into a mixing bowl,
make a well in the middle, drop in the egg, and pour a little water over it.
Beat with a whisk, drawing the flour in little by little and gradually
adding more water until the batter acquires a creamy consistency, free of
lumps. Cover, and leave to stand in a cool place.

Half an hour before the beef is ready, start cooking the pudding. Pour off
surplus fat from the pan in which the dripping has collected under the
joint, but retain the meat juices which have run into it. (If an electric oven
is used, take a couple of tablespoons of dripping from the roasting dish
and heat it in a baking pan, before adding batter.) Pour the Yorkshire
pudding batter into the dripping pan and replace it under the joint so

Meat dishes

that, during its baking, it will become impregnated with the beef juices flowing into it. Bake for twenty minutes, then put the pudding on a shelf above the joint to give the top a lovely golden colour. Serve with roast potatoes and horseradish (pages 260–1).

Boeuf bourguignon

The original French recipe includes diced bacon rashers which have been omitted and beef dripping is used throughout instead of butter.

6 Servings

1kg (2lb) lean beef
2·5dl (½ pint or 1 cup) red wine
4 sprigs parsley
sprig thyme
1 bay leaf
90g (3oz or 6 tablespoons) dripping
1 sliced onion
1 tablespoon flour
1dl (¼ pint or ½ cup) meat stock
120g (4oz or 1½ cups) button mushrooms
12 button onions
salt and pepper

Marinate – that is, let the beef stand – in red wine, seasoned with the parsley, thyme, and bay leaf, for three hours. Remove the beef and strain. Melt dripping in a pan, fry onion till golden, add beef, brown it. Remove, stir in flour, add stock – slowly stirring as you do so – then add the wine in which the beef has marinated. Replace the beef in this sauce and simmer, covered for three hours. Slice the mushrooms and fry them in 30g (1 oz) dripping with button onions until golden.

Season to taste. Place the beef on a hot dish, surround it with mushrooms and onions, and serve the sauce in which the beef has cooked in a sauce-boat.

Meat dishes

Fondue bourguignonne

This French invention really is not fondue at all, because there is no 'melting' involved, but it is a nice way of making your guests cook their own meal.

Prepare it for as many people as would sit comfortably around your table, all of whom must be able to reach the cooking pan, standing (over a spirit lamp, a candle, or a charcoal burner) in the middle of the table. Each participant should be given a plate containing a portion of meat cut in cubes, a small saucer for the sauces of his choosing, and a fork with the longest possible handle. Each guest impales a cube of meat on his fork, plunges it into the pan of sizzling fat, and cooks it to his or her taste, then dunks it into one of the sauces, which both flavour and cool the meat.

8 Servings

1kg (2lb) good steak
0·5 litre (1 pint or 2 cups) oil
mayonnaise sauce (page 250)
tomato sauce (see below)
horseradish (page 260)

Make your sauces and arrange them and horseradish in bowls on the table around the central cooking pan. Cut meat into bite-size cubes, and keep cool until ready to distribute it.

Heat oil in the pan, put it on the table burner, and your work is done! Serve with crisp French bread.

Sweet and sour meat balls in tomato sauce

This is a universal favourite among all Jewish communities from Russia to Canada. Different communities tend to use different flavourings for their minced meat preparations.

Syrian Jews add chopped mint to the mixture, the Balkan communities use cumin, in Israel sesame sauce is popular in the shape of tehina (page 10). This is a Russian variation.

Served with mashed potatoes, or better still, boiled rice, it makes a very good main course:

Meat dishes

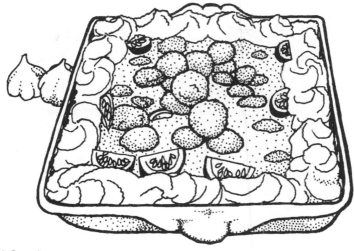

6–8 Servings

1kg (2lb) minced beef
1–2 pounded clove garlic
1 finely chopped and 2 thinly sliced onions
5 tablespoons oil for frying
salt and pepper
2 beaten eggs
1 tablespoon flour
2 tablespoons tomato purée
2·5dl ($\frac{1}{2}$ pint or 1 cup) stock
1 small bay leaf
1–1$\frac{1}{2}$ teaspoons sugar
juice of $\frac{1}{2}$ lemon
1 tablespoon chopped dill or parsley

Fry garlic and chopped onion in tablespoon oil, mix with minced beef,
season to taste with salt and pepper. Add eggs and blend well. Form
into walnut-sized balls and fry in hot oil until uniformly brown.
Transfer meat balls to a casserole. In the oil left from cooking the meat
balls, fry sliced onions until soft, stir in flour, and cook together for two to
three minutes. Add tomato purée and cook stirring for one minute, little
by little blend in stock. Check seasoning, add bay leaf, sugar, and lemon
juice. Bring to the boil, then pour the sauce over the meat balls and put in a
slow oven – 150°C (300°F or Gas Mark 2) for thirty-five to forty minutes.

Meat dishes

Moussaka

This recipe is a good example of the international nature of ORT and the way the dish is adapted to make it acceptable in orthodox homes. The dish is of Greek origin, but is popular throughout the Middle East, and was contributed by Madame D. Aboulker, ORT member in France.

The 'naturalization' consists of using vegetable margarine instead of butter, white sauce instead of béchamel, and sprinkling the top with grated breadcrumbs instead of cheese for the gratin surface, none of which in any way spoils the quality of the moussaka. The recipe provides a most satisfactory way of using up a small amount of meat.

5–6 Servings

5–6 medium-sized aubergines
salt and pepper
olive oil
60g (2oz or ¼ cup) vegetable margarine
1 finely chopped onion
720g (1½lb) minced beef or veal
120g (4oz or 1¼ cups) ripe, peeled, sliced tomatoes
1 tablespoon chopped parsley
1dl (1 gill or ½ cup) red wine
60g (2oz or ½ cup) grated breadcrumbs
0·5 litre (1 pint or 2 cups) white sauce for meat dishes (page 248)
½ teaspoon grated nutmeg

Remove stalks from aubergines, slice them, and sprinkle generously with rock salt. Leave to stand for an hour, to draw away bitterness. Rinse, drain, dry on a cloth, and fry in oil to brown on both sides. Remove, drain, and keep warm.

Heat half the margarine and fry the onion until it becomes soft, add meat, and brown quickly. Add tomatoes, parsley, seasoning to taste, moisten with wine, and simmer gently for fifteen to twenty minutes. Remove from heat, add two to three tablespoons white sauce, and mix well. Grease an ovenproof dish, line it with aubergine slices, purple side downwards. Proceed to fill the dish with alternate layers of mince and slices of fried aubergine, sprinkling each layer with breadcrumbs and a few tiny pieces of margarine, and bake in a moderately hot oven 205°C (400°F or Gas aubergine skins, purple side up. Flavour white sauce with nutmeg, pour

Meat dishes

it over the dish, sprinkle the top with breadcrumbs, dot with small pieces of margarine, and bake in a moderately hot oven 205°C (400°F or Gas Mark 5) for forty to forty-five minutes.

Let the dish stand for a few minutes, turn out on to a serving dish, and serve. Or serve the moussaka in the same dish, as it comes out of the oven.

When aubergines are unavailable, moussaka, made as above, but using zucchini (baby marrows) is good. There is also a splendid moussaka, using layers of minced lamb and artichoke hearts, and omitting tomatoes.

Puchero

This is a super stew of Argentinian origin which provides three dishes in one. The stock makes excellent soup, the meat is served with mustard and the vegetables, in as great a variety as the season or pocket permits, make the third dish:

6 Servings

1·5kg (3lb) beef shank
2 onions
2 carrots
2 leeks
2 stalks celery
several sprigs parsley
1 bay leaf
1 small white cabbage
3 corn cobs
6 potatoes
salt and pepper

Cut the meat into portions and put in a big saucepan with 3 litres (3 quarts) salted, boiling water. Skim until the surface is clear. Peel and quarter onions and carrots, trim leeks, and cut in half lengthwise, cut celery into chunks. Add all these vegetables and parsley to the meat, allow to come to the boil again, then reduce heat, and simmer on very low heat for one and a half hours. Cut cabbage into six wedges, corn cobs into 5-cm (2-inch) chunks. Peel and quarter potatoes.

Add this second lot of vegetables to the stew. Season to taste, simmer until all vegetables are tender.

Meat dishes

Sauerbraten

8–10 Servings

Marinade
0·5 litre (1 pint or 2 cups) vinegar
0·5 litre (1 pint or 2 cups) water
salt and pepper
1 dozen peppercorns
1 bay leaf
1 sliced carrot
1 sliced onion
2–3 stalks shredded celery
2 cloves
2kg (4lb) rump or sirloin
3 tablespoons dripping
2 medium-sized, chopped onions
2 large, peeled, chopped tomatoes
2·5dl ($\frac{1}{2}$ pint or 1 cup) stock (or water with bouillon cube)
1 tablespoon sugar
juice of 1 lemon
2·5dl ($\frac{1}{2}$ pint or 1 cup) red wine
120g (4oz or $\frac{3}{4}$ cup) seedless raisins
potato dumplings (page 265)

Bring vinegar and water to the boil with one tablespoon salt, peppercorns, bay leaf, sliced carrot, onion, celery, and the cloves, simmer for fifteen minutes, and allow the marinade to cool.

Wipe the meat with a damp cloth, put in an earthenware crock, pour marinade over it, cover, and leave to marinate for three to four hours, turning the meat periodically. Drain the meat and strain the marinade.

Heat dripping in a large casserole, brown the meat all over, add chopped onions, tomatoes, stock, sugar, and lemon juice. Moisten with the wine, and equal amounts of marinade, cover with a well-fitting lid, and simmer gently for three hours, adding more marinade if the liquid evaporates too much.

Meat dishes

Soak raisins in enough warm water to cover for half an hour, strain. Remove meat from casserole, slice, arrange on a heated serving dish, and keep hot. Boil down pan juices, dilute with strained marinade if the sauce is too thick, season to taste, and strain into a clean saucepan. Add raisins, reheat, pour over the meat, and serve garnished with potato dumplings.

Dried fruit tzimmes

6–8 Servings

90g (3oz or $\frac{1}{2}$ cup) dried apricots
90g (3oz or $\frac{1}{2}$ cup) dried prunes
0·5 litre (1 pint or 2 cups) cold water
1·25 kilo (2$\frac{1}{2}$lb) brisket of beef
1 large, chopped onion
salt and pepper
1 tablespoon shredded parsley
$\frac{1}{2}$ teaspoon ground ginger
pinch cinnamon
6 cloves
boiling water
1kg (2lb) potatoes cut in large dice (or dumplings, page 265)
60g (2oz or 4 tablespoons) chicken fat or beef dripping
3 tablespoons flour
60g (2oz or 4 tablespoons) sugar
1–2 glasses red wine

Snip apricots and prunes into bite-sized pieces, put in a small pan with water, simmer on low heat for thirty-five to forty minutes.

Put meat in a large saucepan, add onions, cover with boiling water, bring to the boil, and skim until the surface is clear. Add salt, pepper, parsley, ginger, cinnamon, and cloves. Cover and simmer for half an hour. Add potatoes or dumplings. Strain apricots and prunes, reserve the liquid. Add fruit to casserole. Simmer until tender. Heat chicken fat or dripping, fry flour until it browns slightly, stir in liquid in which the dried fruit was soaked and the wine. Add sugar, cook the sauce for two to three minutes, pour over the contents of the casserole, and finish cooking in the oven as described in recipe for carrot and chicken tzimmes.

Meat dishes

Meat coulibiac

6–8 Servings

puff pastry (page 189)
500–720g (1–1½lb) steak
vegetable margarine
1 bunch, chopped spring onions
240g (½lb or 3½ cups) sliced mushrooms
30g (1oz or ¾ cup) chopped parsley
salt and pepper
stock
sieved breadcrumbs

Prepare the puff pastry as described, using vegetable margarine.

Cut the steak into strips, fry in three tablespoons margarine. When brown on all sides, add spring onions, mushrooms, and parsley. Mix, and cook together for five minutes. Season with salt and pepper, and moisten with two or three tablespoons stock. Allow to cool.

Using two-thirds of the pastry, roll out the bottom sheet, which has to be thicker than the top covering. Put on a lightly greased baking sheet. Spread the filling, avoiding the edges. Dot with tiny pieces of margarine. Roll out the rest of the pastry, cover the filling carefully with it. Moisten the edges slightly to make the pastry stick together and draw up the edges of the lower sheet of pastry, so that they cover the edge of the upper sheet. Cut a slit in the top to enable steam to escape, brush the top with melted margarine, sprinkle with breadcrumbs, and put in a refrigerator for half an hour. Bake in a hot oven 230°C (450°F or Gas Mark 7) until golden.

Carbonnade à la flammande

4 Servings

1kg (2lb) lean stewing steak
1 sliced onion
60g (2oz or 4 tablespoons) margarine
1 lump sugar

Meat dishes

1 teaspoon French mustard
sprig thyme
½ bay leaf
salt and black pepper
1 tablespoon flour
2·5dl (½ pint or 1 cup) pale ale

Cut the beef into 2·5-cm (1-inch) cubes. Fry onion in margarine, add meat, and brown. Add sugar, French mustard, thyme, and bay leaf, season, sprinkle with flour, and cover with pale ale. Bring to the boil, and stir. Cover and simmer for two hours.

Hungarian goulash

4–6 Servings

500g (1lb) lean beef
240g (½lb) lean veal
60g (2oz or ¼ cup) dripping
2 medium-sized, chopped onions
1 clove chopped garlic
240g (½lb or 2 cups) peeled, sliced tomatoes
1 seeded, sliced green pepper
5dl (1 pint or 2 cups) stock (or water with bouillon cube)
480g (1lb or 2 cups) potatoes, cut in large dice
1 teaspoon salt
¼ teaspoon black pepper
1 dessertspoon paprika
small pinch caraway seeds

Cut the beef and veal into 2·5-cm (1-inch) cubes. Heat the dripping, quickly brown the meat, add onions and garlic, and continue to brown. Transfer to a thick-bottomed saucepan, add tomatoes and green pepper, moisten with stock, cover, and simmer for one hour or more, till the meat begins to be tender. Add potatoes, season with salt and pepper to taste, heighten with paprika, add caraway seeds, cover, and continue to simmer until the potatoes are done.

Meat dishes

Beef with quinces

Traditional dish among Rumanian Jews:

6 Servings

480g (1lb) beef
2 tablespoons dripping
water
480g (1lb) quinces
1 sliced onion
salt, pepper
1 tablespoon chopped dill (or parsley)

Cut meat into pieces, allowing three to four per person. Melt dripping in a
pan, put the meat in, and brown lightly. Add enough water to cover the
meat and simmer very gently for one hour. Slice the quince, peel, and core,
and add to the pan. Fry the onion lightly, and add to meat. Season with
salt and pepper to taste, and simmer until tender. Turn out into a heated
dish, sprinkle with chopped dill, and serve.

Keema (Indian minced meat and lettuce curry)

4 Servings

0·5kg (1lb) lean minced beef or veal
2 tablespoons oil
2 medium-sized, chopped onions
2 chopped cloves garlic
240g ($\frac{1}{2}$lb or 2 cups) peeled, sliced tomatoes
1 tablespoon ground coriander
1 teaspoon each of: ground turmeric, ginger, cumin, and chilli
2 heads coarsely shredded lettuce
salt

Heat the oil and brown the onion and garlic lightly. Add tomatoes and all
the ground spices, cook together for ten minutes, stirring all the time.
Add lettuce, mix, simmer for five minutes, then add meat, season with
salt to taste, and cook, stirring from time to time until the meat is done,
serve.

Meat dishes

Moroccan beef and olive casserole

6 Servings

0·5kg (1lb) beef
50ml (2fl oz or 4 tablespoons) oil
2 crushed cloves garlic
6 shredded stalks celery
1 teaspoon chilli pepper
salt
300ml (12fl oz or 1½ cups) water
240g (8oz or 1¼ cups) pitted olives
1–2 tablespoons lemon juice

Cut the meat into uniform cubes. Heat oil and fry garlic for two minutes. Add beef and brown all over. Reduce heat, add celery, season with chilli pepper and salt to taste, moisten with water, cover, and simmer for one hour. Add olives, simmer for twenty minutes. Add lemon juice, cook for a further five minutes, and serve with rice.

Guzeli (Persian tongue and pineapple mould)

6 Servings

3 tablespoons olive oil
1 tablespoon tarragon vinegar
½ tablespoon fresh, chopped mint
salt and pepper
1 medium-sized pineapple
1 tablespoon chervil*
0·5 kilo (1lb or 2 cups) cooked, diced tongue
60g (2oz or 6 tablespoons) stuffed olives

Combine oil, vinegar, mint, salt, and pepper, mix well, and leave the dressing until required. Peel and dice the pineapple, adding juice to dressing. Chop chervil.

Put tongue, pineapple, and chervil through a mincer. Strain dressing over the mixture, stir well. Press into a lightly oiled mould. Turn out onto a serving dish, smooth the surface, stud with olives, and serve.

* If fresh chervil is not available, parsley may be substituted.

Meat dishes

Chilli con carne

This is the most popular Mexican dish, and the only concession to
non-Mexican palates I have made is to reduce the amount of chilli powder,
which can be very fierce. For those who like it hot, this can be increased.
I have also omitted the cream:

4 Servings

120g (4oz or $\frac{1}{2}$ cup) red kidney beans
500g (1lb) steak
1–2 tablespoons oil
2 finely chopped onions
1 clove crushed garlic
240g ($\frac{1}{2}$lb or 1 cup) peeled, chopped tomatoes
1$\frac{1}{2}$ tablespoons chilli powder or 1 teaspoon tabasco sauce
4 tablespoons water
1 green pepper, seeded and sliced
1 tablespoon flour
pinch pounded caraway seeds
salt

Soak the beans in water overnight. Mince the steak. Heat the oil, and fry
the onion and garlic on low heat until the onion softens and becomes
transparent. Add meat, and brown, stirring with a fork and breaking up
any 'lumps'. Drain, and add the beans, stir, add tomatoes, tabasco, water,
and green pepper. Cover and simmer for one hour, shaking the pan and
stirring carefully from time to time. Mix flour and caraway seeds, and
blend into the mixture in the pan.

Chilli con carne is normally served with tortillas, which are eaten as bread
in Europe. They are made of corn (maize) soaked in water and slaked lime,
allowing 30g (1 ounce) of slaked lime to $\frac{1}{2}$ kilo (1 pound) of corn. The corn
is simmered gently in the same water until soft, drained, pounded into a
smooth paste, rolled out very thinly, and baked on an ungreased griddle.

Meat dishes

Ox tongue with almonds and raisins

Common to all Middle East countries:

6–8 Servings

1 ox tongue
3 litres (6 pints or 3 quarts) water
salt
1 sliced onion
1 sliced carrot
a few celery leaves (optional)
1 sprig parsley
1 bay leaf
10 peppercorns
180g (6oz or 2 cups) blanched, coarsely chopped almonds
120g (4oz or $\frac{3}{4}$ cup) washed raisins
1 teaspoon grated lemon rind
2dl ($\frac{1}{2}$ pint or 1 cup) red wine
3 tablespoons sugar
3 tablespoons water
2 tablespoons dripping
2 tablespoons flour
4 tablespoons vinegar

Soak and wash the tongue, put in a stockpot with water and one tablespoon salt, bring to the boil, skim, add onion, carrot, celery, parsley, bay leaf, and peppercorns, simmer for three hours, then remove and drain, but keep the liquor. Rinse tongue with fresh water, and peel off the outside skin completely. Before it is required, reheat the tongue in its own cooking liquor while you are making the sauce.

Put almonds and raisins into a small saucepan with wine, bring to the boil, reduce heat, simmer for five minutes, add lemon rind, remove from heat, and leave covered. Boil up sugar with water to make a thick syrup, blend in dripping and flour, dilute with 0·25 litre ($\frac{1}{2}$ pint) of the strained liquor in which the tongue was cooked, stir, add vinegar, check seasoning, simmer for five minutes stirring constantly. Add wine with almonds and raisins, heat until boiling is established, stir, simmer for five minutes.

Slice the tongue, arrange on a serving dish, pour the sauce over it, and serve.

Meat dishes

Shami kebab (fried kebab)

This recipe comes to us with the compliments of ORT in India, where it is as popular as falafel in Israel. Roadside cooks in India serve it with unleavened bread. The only adjustment I had to make was to omit yoghurt as a binding agent and use egg instead:

4 Servings

0·75kg (1¼lb) lean lamb
2 onions
1–2 chillies
2·5cm (1 inch) piece fresh ginger*
1 clove garlic
¾ teaspoon coriander
salt
pepper
0·5 litre (1 pint or 2 cups) water
1 beaten egg
dripping or vegetable fat

Wash the meat, cut off all fat. Chop onions, chillies, ginger, and garlic. Mince the lamb with onions, chillies, ginger, and garlic. Mix well, add coriander, and season with salt and pepper to taste. Put in a saucepan, add water, stir, and simmer until there is no more sign of water. Mince the cooked mixture once more or pass through a blender to reduce to a smooth paste. Bind with egg, shape into small cubes, and fry in fat until uniformly brown.

* If fresh ginger is not available, powdered ginger may be used.

Spring navarin of lamb (or mutton)

This is a superb French stew, and although you can use large carrots and turnips, cutting them down to look like small ones, the great charm of this dish depends on all the ingredients being 'spring', i.e. young:

6 Servings

1kg (2lb) shoulder of lamb
salt and pepper
pinch sugar

Meat dishes

2 tablespoons dripping
2 tablespoons flour
stock or water
2 medium-sized tomatoes, peeled and chopped
1 clove crushed garlic
bouquet garni
12 small onions, peeled
12 baby carrots
12 baby turnips
12 small new potatoes
240g ($\frac{1}{2}$lb) fresh, shelled peas
120g ($\frac{1}{4}$lb) French (string) beans

Cut the meat into 60-g (2-ounce) pieces, season with salt and pepper, and sprinkle with sugar (sugar is essential, it will add a delicious caramel flavour to the gravy).

Heat the dripping in a deep oven casserole, brown the meat, sprinkle with flour, stir, and let it colour lightly. Dilute with enough stock or water to cover, blending the *roux* in thoroughly. Add tomatoes, garlic, and bouquet garni, bring to the boil, cover, and simmer in the oven set at 190°C (375°F Gas Mark 4) for one hour.

With a perforated spoon, take out the pieces of lamb, strain the sauce into a bowl, and rinse out the casserole, to make sure it has no bone splinters left in it. Put meat back in the casserole, pour in sauce, bring to the boil, add onions, carrots, turnips, and potatoes. Put back in the oven, reduce heat to 175°C (350°F or Gas Mark 3) and continue to simmer for twenty minutes. Lower oven temperature to 150°C (300°F for Gas Mark 2). Add peas and beans, taste for seasoning, cook for twenty minutes, and serve.

Meat dishes

Boulfaf (lamb's liver on skewers, Moroccan style)

4 Servings

480g (1lb) lamb's liver
2 tablespoons oil or melted margarine
salt and pepper
cumin

Wash and dry the liver.

Heat the grill and sear the liver quickly on all sides, then cut into pieces about 2·5cm (1 inch) square. Brush with oil, season the squares of liver with salt and pepper to taste, sprinkle lightly with cumin, thread on skewers, allowing six or eight squares per skewer.

Grill for six to seven minutes until nicely browned all over.

Minced lamb in spinach leaves, Persian style

4 Servings

500g (1lb) lean lamb
1 medium-sized onion
1–2 cloves garlic
salt and pepper
pinch cayenne
500g (1lb) leaf spinach
3 tablespoons oil
juice of ½ lemon
1·5dl (1½ gills or ¾ cup) tomato juice
boiled rice

Pass the lamb through a mincer with onion and garlic a couple of times to ensure smoothness of mixture. Season to taste with salt, pepper, and cayenne. Taking a teaspoon of minced lamb at a time, shape into small balls. Dip spinach leaves into boiling water to soften them.

Using two spinach leaves as a wrapping, envelope the little balls in them. Heat oil in a *sauté* pan, pack the spinach rolls into it, sprinkle with lemon juice, moisten with tomato juice, cover with an upturned plate to prevent the rolls floating out in all directions, simmer for one and a half hours, and serve with hot fluffy rice.

Meat dishes

Lemon lamb

There are many traditional recipes for lamb among all Jewish communities. Roast shoulder of lamb with dried apricots and raisins, for example, is traditional *Rosh Hashana* dish among Jews of Alsace; oriental Jews have a dish of the same cut cooked covered with mint leaves. This recipe is common to several Middle East countries:

4 Servings

720g (1½lb) stewing lamb
3 tablespoons oil
1 thinly sliced lemon
salt and pepper
½ teaspoon cinnamon
small pinch saffron
2dl (½ pint or 1 cup) hot stock

Cut the lamb into uniform pieces, and brown in oil. Cover with lemon slices, sprinkle with cinnamon, and season to taste with salt and freshly ground pepper. Dilute saffron in hot stock, add to pan, stir well, cover, and simmer gently for one hour, or until the lamb is tender.

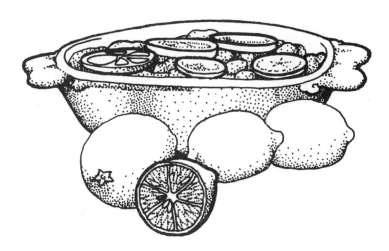

Meat dishes

Canadian minted lamb chops

4 Servings

4 thickly cut lamb chops
100ml (4fl oz or ½ cup) oil
4 tablespoons lemon juice
120g (4oz) mint jelly (page 286)
salt and pepper

Have the butcher cut the chops about 5cm (2 inches) thick. Put in a dish, sprinkle with oil and lemon juice, and leave to macerate for one to two hours.

Heat the grill. Take chops out of marinade and grill over medium heat, turning after twelve to thirteen minutes to brown the other side. Don't overcook.

Melt mint jelly over simmering water and use for basting chops during grilling. Just before serving, season to taste.

Crown of lamb

This is a great English dish. It looks elegant and tastes delicious. Serve with glazed chestnuts (page 153), new potatoes, and mint sauce (page 252) or redcurrant jelly (page 286):

2·5kg (5lb) crown of lamb
water
salt
cooked garden peas

Trim the bones, join the ends to form a circle or 'crown'. Cover tips of bones with oiled paper. Start roasting in a hot oven 220°C (450°F or Gas Mark 7) for fifteen minutes. Reduce heat to 175°C (350°F or Gas Mark 3) add two tablespoons hot water to the pan. Season meat with salt, and roast for one hour, basting frequently.

Put 'crown' on a dish, fill the middle with green peas. Replace oiled paper with paper frills on bone tips.

Meat dishes

Alsace lamb with chestnuts

4 Servings

3 tablespoons dripping
1kg (2lb) neck of lamb
1 large, chopped onion
2 large, thinly sliced carrots
2 tablespoons chopped parsley
1dl (1 gill or ½ cup) dry white wine
500g (1lb) chestnuts
salt and pepper

Heat the dripping in a pan large enough eventually to take all ingredients. Brown the piece of lamb evenly all around. Add onions and carrots, *sauté* until the vegetables are coated with a film of fat and begin to look glazed. Season, sprinkle with parsley, moisten with wine, cover, and simmer gently for two hours.

Slit the chestnuts on the pointed side, put them in a tin with a little water, roast in the oven for fifteen minutes, and peel while hot. Add to the casserole, cook for a further half hour, and serve.

Oriental spiced lamb

6 Servings

720g (1½ lb) lean lamb
3 tablespoons dripping
juice of 2 oranges and shredded peel of 1 orange
4–5 tablespoons chopped walnuts
3 tablespoons seedless raisins
salt and pepper
boiled rice
2 teaspoons allspice

Pass the lamb through a mincer twice, brown in dripping, pressing with a wooden fork to break down any lumps. Add orange juice, simmer for twelve minutes. Add orange peel, walnuts, and raisins. Season with salt and pepper to taste, cover, and simmer gently for twenty minutes. Arrange the hot cooked rice as a border, fill the middle with the cooked lamb, sprinkle with allspice, and serve.

Meat dishes

Vienna schnitzel

The name of this dish proclaims its origin but it is a familiar one in its slightly modified form on Jewish menus all over the world:

5–6 Servings

1kg(2lb) fillet of veal
flour
salt and pepper
2 beaten eggs
breadcrumbs
120g (4oz or $\frac{1}{2}$ cup) chicken fat or oil
3 hard-boiled eggs
5–6 anchovy fillets
5–6 stoned olives
1 peeled, sliced lemon

Cut veal into *escalopes*, flatten to make them very thin. Put a little flour in a paper bag, season with salt and pepper, and shake to mix well. Dip *escalopes* in seasoned flour, then in beaten egg, and finally in breadcrumbs, pressing well to make them adhere.

Heat fat and fry *escalopes* until golden on both sides. Shell eggs and chop the white and the yolks separately.

Arrange schnitzels on a heated serving dish, top each with an olive wrapped in anchovy fillet. Garnish with egg whites and yolks in separate group. Put the lemon slices around the dish and serve.

Veal in aspic

This is an excellent way of presenting veal for a cold buffet:

8 Servings

aspic jelly (pages 257–8)
1·5kg (3lb) cold roast fillet of veal
3 hard-boiled eggs
salt and pepper
3 tablespoons sliced, stuffed olives
1–2 sliced pickled cucumbers
3 tablespoons diced, cooked carrots

Meat dishes

3 tablespoons cooked peas
1 tablespoon chopped parsley
lemon wedges
horseradish (pages 260–1)

Pour a thin layer of aspic jelly into a mould, tilt it to line bottom and sides, and put in a refrigerator. As soon as jelly lining the mould sets, decorate bottom and sides with slices of hard-boiled egg, olives, and cucumber.

Spoon a little jelly to secure these decorations and chill until they set.

Put veal in the middle of the mould, season, garnish with carrots and peas, sprinkle with parsley, spoon over some aspic jelly to seal down these ingredients, and chill to set them. Add the rest of the aspic jelly. Chill until set hard, preferably overnight.

To serve, dip mould for a moment into warm water, wipe, and turn out on to a chilled dish. If you have any aspic left over, pour it into a shallow mould and leave until firm, then cut the jelly into triangles or 'wolf's teeth' croûtons. Serve with lemon wedges and grated horseradish. See chrain (page 260).

Veal with aubergines, Sephardic traditional dish

4 Servings

1kg (2lb) diced veal
olive oil
1 chopped onion
pinch marjoram
2 peeled, sliced tomatoes
pinch cinnamon
salt and pepper
1dl (1 gill or ½ cup) sherry
4 sliced aubergines
flour

Fry veal in oil, add onion, cook until it softens, sprinkle in marjoram, add tomatoes, cinnamon, salt, pepper, and sherry, and simmer gently. Dredge aubergines with flour, fry in oil until golden on both sides. Garnish the veal with aubergines, and serve with plain boiled rice.

Meat dishes

Veal with dumplings

6 Servings

120g (4oz or $\frac{1}{2}$ cup) margarine
1 small, chopped onion
1 diced carrot
1 stick shredded celery
$\frac{1}{2}$ chopped parsnip
1kg (2lb) veal, cut in cubes
salt and pepper
2 tablespoons flour
2·5dl ($\frac{1}{2}$ pint or 1 cup) stock (or water with bouillon cube)
1 teaspoon grated lemon rind
$\frac{1}{2}$ teaspoon nutmeg
1 tablespoon chopped parsley
240g (8oz or 2 cups) grated breadcrumbs
2 raw egg yolks

Melt 60g (2 ounces or $\frac{1}{4}$ cup) margarine and lightly fry the onion, carrot, celery, and parsnip. Add veal, brown quickly, then reduce heat, season to taste, and simmer until tender. Stir in flour, dilute with stock, add lemon rind, nutmeg, and parsley, and leave on lowest possible heat. Soak breadcrumbs in stock. Blend 60g (2oz or $\frac{1}{4}$ cup) margarine with egg yolks, season with a pinch of salt, add slightly squeezed out breadcrumbs, mix well, shape into dumplings with a dessertspoon, and poach the dumplings in slightly salted boiling water, until they float up to the surface (about ten minutes). Drain carefully, add to veal, and serve.

Veal with brains

4–5 Servings

180g (6oz) calf's brain
vinegar
margarine
1 finely chopped onion
360g (12oz or $1\frac{1}{2}$ cups) minced veal
$\frac{1}{2}$ tablespoon flour
2·5dl ($\frac{1}{2}$ pint or 1 cup) stock or water
salt and pepper

Meat dishes

juice of $\frac{1}{2}$ lemon and $\frac{1}{2}$ teaspoon grated lemon rind
120g (4oz or $1\frac{1}{2}$ cups) chopped mushrooms
3 eggs
1 tablespoon breadcrumbs

Soak the brains in cold water for one hour, remove skin and any traces of blood, bring to the boil in enough water to cover, with a dash of vinegar, for ten minutes, drain, plunge into cold water, allow to cool.
Heat 60g (2oz) margarine, fry the onion until it becomes soft, add veal, and cook gently until tender. Sprinkle with flour, stir it in well, dilute with stock, and season. Leave simmering gently for five minutes.

Meanwhile, drain and dry the brains, slice, fry lightly in one tablespoon margarine, and add to veal with lemon juice and rind. Toss the mushrooms in the margarine left from frying the brains and add to the mixture. One by one, blend in eggs. Grease four to five ramekin dishes, divide the mixture between them, sprinkle with breadcrumbs, dot with tiny pieces of margarine, put in a preheated oven 218°C (425°F or Gas Mark 6), bake for ten minutes, and serve.

Minced veal in almond sauce

4 Servings

240g ($\frac{1}{2}$lb or $1\frac{1}{4}$ cups) cooked, minced veal or lamb
salt and pepper
1 egg
60g (2oz or $\frac{2}{3}$ cup) ground almonds
1 tablespoon chopped parsley
2·5dl ($\frac{1}{2}$ pint or 1 cup) water
2 tablespoons olive oil
juice of $\frac{1}{2}$ lemon

Put the meat into mixing bowl, season well, bind with egg, blend thoroughly, and shape into small balls. Put almonds in a pan, add parsley and water, bring to the boil, season, incorporate oil, and as soon as boiling is re-established, drop in the meat balls. Make sure they are covered with the liquid, reduce heat, and simmer under a lid for one and a half hours. Taste for seasoning, heighten with a dash of lemon juice, and serve very hot with rice or mashed potatoes.

Meat dishes

Ossibuchi

The name of this Italian dish means 'hollow bones', which is precisely
what is meant to be left on your plate by the time justice is done. The
traditional ossi buchi alla Milanese is usually served with a risotto dressed
with melted butter and grated Parmesan cheese. We have dispensed with
this, and the sauce provides ample dressing.

6 Servings

1·25–1·5kg (2½–3lb) shin-bone veal
salt and pepper
flour
6 tablespoons oil
1 chopped onion
2 small, diced carrots
½ bay leaf
1–2 stalks diced celery
1dl (¼ pint or ½ cup) veal stock
1dl (¼ pint or ½ cup) dry white wine
1kg (2lb or 6 cups) ripe, peeled, diced tomatoes
2 tablespoons chopped parsley
1 clove chopped garlic
1 tablespoon grated lemon peel

Have the veal sawn into 5-cm (2-inch) pieces, wipe with a damp cloth.
Season flour with salt and pepper and roll the chunks of shin in it, then
brown in oil for ten minutes. Remove from frying pan, and fit the bones in
a *sauté* pan in an upright position (not flat), to prevent the bone marrow
flowing out. In the fat left from browning the bones, fry the onion, carrots,
bay leaf, and celery, for a few minutes, to soften the vegetables and to give
them a film coating of oil. Moisten with wine, cook to reduce the wine by
half, and add the mixture to the bones. Add stock and tomatoes, cover, and
simmer for two hours. (Do not allow the sauce to dry out. Add more stock
and wine, if necessary.) Carefully remove the veal on to a serving dish and
keep warm. Strain the sauce, put back in a pan, reheat, and pour over the
veal. Mix parsley, garlic, and lemon peel, sprinkle over ossibuchi, and
serve with plain rice.

Meat dishes

Liver, Venetian style

4 Servings

olive oil
4 large onions
500g (1lb) calf's liver
flour
salt and pepper

Heat a little oil, enough to cover the bottom of a heavy pan. Slice the onions very thinly and sweat them very slowly, keeping the heat very low, for half an hour, by which time they should turn a beautiful, translucent yellow. Cut the liver into thinnest possible slices – really wafer thin – lightly dredge with flour, and fry quickly to brown both sides – this should take no more than two minutes. Season to taste. Using the onions as a luxurious foundation, arrange the liver on top and serve at once.

Calf's liver with artichokes

4 Servings

500g (1lb) calf's liver
flour
3 tablespoons olive oil
1 chopped onion
4 tender artichokes
juice of $\frac{1}{2}$ lemon
salt and pepper
1 tablespoon chopped parsley

Cut the liver into slices 5mm ($\frac{1}{4}$ inch) thick and dredge lightly with flour. Heat olive oil and fry the onion until it becomes soft and transparent. Cut down the stalks of the artichokes (only the very tender variety is suitable for this treatment, either green or violet coloured), pick off only the outside layer of leaves, cut off the tips of the leaves with a sharp knife, cut each artichoke into quarters, and at once plunge into a bowl of cold water with lemon juice added, to prevent discoloration. When all the artichokes have been quartered, drain them, dry on a cloth, and add to onion. Simmer gently for fifteen to twenty minutes. Add liver, brown quickly on both sides, season with salt and pepper, sprinkle with parsley and lemon juice, simmer with the seasoning for a couple of minutes, and serve.

Meat dishes

Lashon im zeitim (calf's tongue with olives), Israeli recipe

4 Servings

1 calf's tongue
water
salt
1 medium-sized onion
1 medium-sized carrot
30g (1oz or 2 tablespoons) dripping
25·dl ($\frac{1}{2}$ pint or 1 cup) veal stock
8 large, chopped olives

Put the tongue in a pan, cover with cold water, bring to the boil, skim, add a
little salt, simmer, for one and a half hours, drain, allow to cool, and skin
(see ox tongue, page 97). Dice the onion and carrot, and fry in dripping.
Add tongue, brown on all sides, add stock and olives, cover, simmer on
very low heat for one hour, and serve.

Sweetbread vol-au-vent

2 Servings

2 vol-au-vent cases (page 130)
240g ($\frac{1}{2}$lb) sweetbreads
1 teaspoon lemon juice
2 tablespoons margarine
60g (2oz or $\frac{3}{4}$ cup) sliced mushrooms
salt and pepper
1 tablespoon Madeira or sherry
1dl (1 gill or $\frac{1}{2}$ cup) white sauce for meat dishes (page 248)

Soak the sweetbreads in cold water for one hour, changing the water from
time to time. Put in a pan with enough cold water to cover, with lemon
juice added to it, bring to the boil, reduce heat, simmer for five minutes,
drain, rinse with cold water. Remove membranes and any discoloured
parts, and dice the sweetbreads. Fry them lightly in margarine with the
mushrooms, season to taste. Blend Madeira into the sauce, add
sweetbreads, mix well, check seasoning. Proceed to fit vol-au-vent cases
as described.

Meat dishes

Fried sweetbreads

4 Servings

2 pairs calf's sweetbreads
1 beaten egg
breadcrumbs
margarine
slivers of truffle (optional)
cooked asparagus tips

Soak sweetbreads in water for one hour. Put in a saucepan, cover with cold salted water, bring to the boil, simmer for five minutes. Cool under running water, drain, and trim. Cut the sweetbreads into slices, dip in beaten egg and breadcrumbs, fry in margarine. Garnish with slivers of truffle and cooked asparagus tips. Sprinkle with juices left in the pan.

Poultry dishes

Figure based on an eighteenth century Derby Ware Jewish Pedlar
in the Jewish Museum, London

Chicken stuffed with almonds, semolina, and raisins

4 Servings

1 plump chicken
70g (2¼oz or ¾ cup) blanched almonds
105g (3½oz or ½ cup) couscous semolina, or rice
150g (5oz or 1 cup) seedless raisins
105g (3½oz or 7 tablespoons) margarine
small pinch ground nutmeg
1 medium-sized, chopped onion
pinch ground ginger
pinch saffron

Have the chicken ready for stuffing. Chop the almonds roughly.

Steam the semolina as for couscous. If using rice instead of semolina,
drop it into boiling water for one minute, then rinse with cold water.
(Or steam it in a couscous marmite and cool, to separate the grains.) Pound
the raisins in a mortar or chop finely.

In a large bowl assemble almonds, semolina or rice, and raisins. Add two
tablespoons margarine, nutmeg, and salt to taste. Mix well. Stuff the
chicken, sew up, and truss.

Heat a braising dish with one tablespoon margarine. Cook the onion until
it softens. Add ginger and cook for two to three minutes. Pound the saffron
with a pinch of salt, add to onion, and place the stuffed chicken on top.

Add enough water so that it half covers the chicken. Bring to the boil.
Little by little, add the remaining margarine. Cook on a brisk heat for
about two hours until the flesh comes away easily from the bones. By this
time the water should have evaporated and the chicken browned. Serve on
a preheated dish.

The director of the ORT school in Morocco, who kindly supplied this and
other Moroccan recipes, goes on to give this lyrical advice on how to eat
this dish: 'Rub the chicken with a piece of bread, then dip it in the sauce
accumulated in the bottom of the dish and taste this perfumed croûton.
Delicately, with epicurean fingertips, detach the scalding flesh, snap the
breast bone to release the sweet blond forcemeat – and you are in for a
surprise which will dazzle your palate.'

Poultry dishes

Spiced chicken with orange juice and olives

4 Servings

2 large frying chickens, jointed
60g (2oz or 4 tablespoons) chicken fat or vegetable oil
salt and pepper
1 teaspoon paprika
2 medium-sized onions, sliced into rings
200ml (8fl oz or 1 cup) orange juice
90g (3oz or $\frac{1}{4}$ cup) honey
2 tablespoons lemon juice
pinch powdered ginger and nutmeg
2–3 cloves
120–180g (4–6oz or $\frac{1}{2}$–$\frac{3}{4}$ cups) stoned, ripe olives

In an orthodox household the chicken must first be koshered. To do
this, the chicken is put into a bowl, reserved entirely for this operation,
covered completely with cold water, and left to soak for half an hour.
Every particle of blood must be carefully washed away before the
chicken is taken out of the water. It is then placed on a perforated wooden
board, sprinkled with salt, and left to drain for an hour. After this, it is
rinsed throughly and used as directed in the recipe.

Brown the chicken lightly in chicken fat or oil, season to taste with salt,
pepper, and paprika. When nicely and uniformly brown, transfer to an
ovenproof dish. In the fat left over from browning the chicken, fry the
onions lightly and sprinkle over chicken.

Mix orange juice with honey, lemon juice, ginger, nutmeg, and cloves.
Bring to the boil, stirring all the time, and add to chicken. Blend in, add
olives, cover with a well-fitting lid, and bake in the oven preheated to
190°C (375°F or Gas Mark 4) until tender. Start testing for readiness after
forty-five minutes.

Spring chickens with grapefruit

4–6 Servings

2–3 spring chickens, split in half
flour

Poultry dishes

90g (3oz or 6 tablespoons) chicken fat or vegetable oil
1½ tablespoons brandy
1·5dl (1½ gills or ⅔ cup) chicken stock
3–4 tablespoons sherry
juice of ½ grapefruit
1 grapefruit, divided into segments
salt and pepper

Cut each halved spring chicken into quarters, dredge with flour, and brown quickly in fat on all sides. Season. Pour brandy over the chickens and ignite. Continue to cook until done.

Put chickens on serving dish and keep hot. Dilute the pan juices with stock, sherry, and grapefruit juice. Stir well, cook down to reduce the liquid by half. Season to taste. Remove all pith and membranes from the grapefruit segments and garnish the chickens. Pour the sauce over them and serve.

Chicken in aspic

4–6 Servings

1·5 litres (3 pints or 6 cups) liquid aspic jelly (pages 257–8)
1·5kg (3lb) chicken
tarragon leaves

Prepare stock for aspic jelly as described and poach the chicken in it until tender. Make sure there is enough stock to immerse the chicken completely. Remove the chicken and leave to cool.

Clarify and strain the aspic and leave until it begins to look syrupy, without allowing it to set.

Divide the chicken into portions, skin them, and lay out on a grid placed over a dish. Space the pieces so they don't touch. Coat each portion with several layers of aspic, spooning it over them and letting each layer set before applying the next. Transfer chicken portions to a serving dish, decorate with tarragon leaves, spoon over them the remaining aspic jelly and any that has collected in the dish, and chill.

Serve with avocado and grapefruit salad (page 165).

Poultry dishes

Chicken with almonds, Peruvian style

4–6 Servings

1 roasting chicken
3–4 tablespoons olive oil
1 large, chopped onion
stock (or water with a bouillon cube)
1dl (1 gill or ½ cup) dry white wine
8–10 black peppercorns
60g (2oz or ⅓ cup) blanched, peeled almonds
1–2 crushed cloves garlic
1 tablespoon margarine
1 sprig parsley
2 hard-boiled yolks
3 tablespoons sherry

Joint the chicken, fry in oil until golden. Remove and put chicken in a saucepan. In the same fat fry the onion. Add to chicken with all residue. Add enough stock just to cover the chicken. Bring to the boil, cover, and simmer for thirty minutes. Add wine and whole peppercorns. Fry almonds and garlic in margarine, then pound in a mortar with yolks and margarine into a smooth paste, or blend in a blender. Add sherry, stir well, and pour the mixture into the pan with the chicken. Simmer for twenty minutes and serve.

Chicken a la Kiev

4 Servings

2 small frying chickens
180g (6oz or ¾ cup) vegetable margarine
salt and pepper
2 beaten eggs
breadcrumbs
oil for deep frying

Remove the four fillets, taking off breast and wing for each portion. (The rest of the chickens can be used for another dish.) Skin and carefully bone the fillets in such a way as to keep each in one piece and to leave a small bone attached to each fillet.
Beat fillets to flatten and season.

Poultry dishes

Cut margarine into uniform 'fingers', season, roll slightly to give them cigar shapes, and chill thoroughly.

Put a piece of frozen seasoned margarine on each fillet, fold the flesh over it, and roll up the fillet neatly into a cigar shape with the bone sticking out at one end. It is essential to enclose the margarine completely. Dip in beaten egg, roll in breakcrumbs. Do this twice to make the coating adhere and to seal the margarine inside it. Keep in a refrigerator until ready to fry.

Heat the oil and deep fry the chicken for four to five minutes, until uniformly golden. Before serving put a paper frill on each bone. Garnish with lemon wedges and watercress and serve on a croûton of fried bread, or on a baked foundation of puff pastry. The classical accompaniment is straw potatoes and garden peas.

Chicken vindaloo
Vindaloos are specialities of southern India and are usually fiery. The amount of chillies for the vindaloo paste can be increased or decreased, dependent on how you like your curry. Duck, goose, and chicken lend themselves particularly well to vindaloo recipes. If fresh lime juice is not available, use lemon juice or vinegar.

4 Servings

1 chicken
2–3 cloves garlic
2 medium-sized onions
4 tablespoons chicken fat
2 tablespoons vindaloo paste (see over)
2 tablespoons lime juice
salt

Joint the chicken. Chop garlic and onions. Heat the chicken fat and fry the garlic and onions until soft. Add vindaloo paste and lime juice, simmer for five minutes very gently, taking care not to burn the mixture. Add chicken to pan, stir, moisten with 1 dl (1 gill or $\frac{1}{2}$ cup) water, cover, and simmer until tender. Do not allow the juices to dry out, add more liquid if necessary, though it should not be needed if the heat is kept really low. Taste for seasoning and serve with rice.

Poultry dishes

Vindaloo paste

5–6 seeded, fresh red chillies
1cm ($\frac{1}{2}$ inch) slice fresh, green ginger
1$\frac{1}{2}$ teaspoons coriander
1 teaspoon cumin
1–2 cloves garlic
$\frac{1}{4}$ teaspoon powdered turmeric

Combine all the ingredients and pound in a mortar or blend in a liquidizer to make a smooth paste. Use as directed.

Elachi murghi (cardamom spring chicken)

Elachi means cardamom. This famous dish spread from the Mogul courts to many countries. Its spicy stuffing is the secret of its popularity. Ghee, or clarified butters (page 260) would normally be used for this dish in India, but here chicken fat is used as a substitute. Ideally it should be roasted on a spit. If you have to use the oven, make sure the bird is on a trivet in the roasting pan, above the pan juices. Only young tender chicken is suitable for Elachi Murghi.

4 Servings

2 spring chickens
salt
2 medium-sized onions
1 teaspoon ground cardamom and black peppercorns
120g (4oz or $\frac{1}{2}$ cup) chicken fat
120g (4oz or $\frac{1}{2}$ cup) chicken livers
45g (1$\frac{1}{2}$oz or 1 cup) fresh breadcrumbs

Wipe the chickens and rub with salt on the inside. Chop the onions, heat three tablespoons chicken fat, and fry the onions until they begin to soften. Add cardamom and peppercorns, reduce heat, and continue to cook, stirring for six to seven minutes. Chop the chicken livers and add to onions. Cook until they change colour. Season with salt to taste. Simmer for seven to eight minutes. Remove from heat, add breadcrumbs, mix well, check seasoning, divide the mixture in half, and stuff each chicken. Brush with chicken fat and roast for thirty-five to forty minutes, basting with chicken fat or pan juices from time to time. Serve with a salad.

Poultry dishes

Tzimmes

The Yiddish word derives from the German *zum* and *essen* and roughly means 'to eat with'. Traditionally, it is a side dish of sweetened vegetables, particularly carrots, and fruit. Tzimmes can also be served as a dessert. More often it is 'eaten with' and even cooked with a joint of brisket or a fat chicken, in a spicy casserole. Because of the great variety of ingredients, which had to be peeled, scrubbed, sliced, simmered, and spiced, the word has become synonymous with a complicated chore. 'She makes a tzimmes of it' means 'she blows it up into a full scale production, makes an exaggerated fuss'. Also, perhaps because some samples of tzimmes were not entirely successful, another humorous expression has evolved: 'a proper tzimmes' – i.e. a real hash or mess, a right stew.

Carrot and chicken tzimmes

6 Servings

1 jointed, boiling fowl
2 quartered onions
salt
0·5kg (1lb) carrots, in thick slices
1kg (2lb) potatoes, cut in large cubes
60g (2oz or 4 tablespoons) chicken fat
3 tablespoons flour
60g (2oz or 4 tablespoons) sugar
pepper
2–3 tablespoons lemon juice

Put the chicken and onions in a pan, cover with boiling water, bring to the boil, skim, cover, season with salt, and simmer for one and a quarter hours. Add carrots and onions and simmer on low heat until tender. Transfer chicken and vegetables to an oven proof casserole with a perforated spoon. Strain the liquid and reserve.

Heat chicken fat, brown the flour in it, little by little stir in 0·5 litre (1 pint or 2 cups) of the liquid in which the chicken and vegetables were cooked. Add sugar, dissolve thoroughly, continue to simmer for a few minutes to concentrate. Season with salt and pepper to taste, add lemon juice, pour over the contents of the casserole, and finish cooking in the oven, preheated to 190° (375°F or Gas Mark 4) for twenty-five to thirty minutes.

Poultry dishes

Roast turkey

This is a traditional English recipe. Sausage meat or veal forcemeat is used for stuffing the crop and chestnut stuffing for the body. The time honoured accompaniments are roast potatoes, brussels sprouts, gravy, bread sauce, and cranberry sauce. There are endless variations of the stuffing. You can use mushroom, liver and mushroom, or sage and onion stuffing. In the Balkans sauerkraut stuffing is popular, in Persia turkey is cooked with tangerines and the crop is stuffed with a mixture of chopped almonds and sultanas. There are some splendid Jewish stuffings for turkey: noodle and poppy seed; matzos, moistened with stock, mixed with glazed onions and broken walnuts, flavoured with thyme, and bound with egg; liver, rice, and mushroom; farfel cooked in chicken fat, then simmered in chicken soup with onion, carrot, and celery.

A slightly sweetened stuffing, either rice, noodle or farfel, mixed with chopped apple, prunes or raisins, is used for *Rosh Hashana*.

10–15 Servings

4–5kg (8–10lb) turkey, dressed, ready for cooking
salt
veal forcemeat (page 261)
chestnut stuffing (page 261)
melted margarine
large sheet aluminium foil
bread sauce (pages 248–9) and cranberry sauce (page 250)

Preheat oven to 235°C (450°F or Gas Mark 7).

Wipe turkey inside and out with clean, damp cloth. Rub with salt and brush with margarine, inside and outside. Stuff the crop with veal forcemeat and secure the flap with a small skewer or stitch it up. Fill the body with chestnut stuffing and secure. If you are stitching the cavities, remember to remove the thread before serving. Give the bird another brushing with melted margarine, wrap it in foil, place on a rack in a roasting tin, and put in the hot oven. Cook for fifteen minutes. Reduce heat to 190°C (375°F or Gas Mark 4). Allow fifteen minutes per 0·5kg (1lb) roasting time.

Half an hour before the end of cooking, unwrap the bird, continue roasting, basting frequently to make the skin brown and crisp. Transfer the turkey to a heated serving dish and keep hot. Make the gravy (page 247) and serve.

Poultry dishes

Roast goose, Jaffa style

8–10 Servings

one 2–2·5kg (4–5lb) goose, ready for cooking
1kg (2lb or 4½ cups) seasoned mashed potato, mixed with
2 tablespoons freshly grated orange peel
flour
apple sauce (page 249) or gooseberry sauce (page 249)
Goose yields a great deal of fat during cooking, therefore, if roasting in
the oven, don't let it lie in the basting fat, but roast it on a trivet set in the
pan. Better still, roast it on a spit. Allow eighteen minutes per 0·5 kilo
(per pound) cooking time.

Prepare the goose for roasting, stuff with the potato and orange peel
mixture, and truss. Prick the breast with a fork to let the fat run out and
roast in a hot oven, 204°C (400°F or Gas Mark 6) for the first thirty
minutes breast down. Cook for two to two and a half hours, until tender.
Pour off fat as it accumulates. When nearly done, dust breast with flour,
baste with fat in the roasting pan, and put back in the oven to 'froth it'.

Remove trussing string, put the goose on a heated dish. Serve with apple
or gooseberry sauce and giblet gravy.

Detail from a Megillah in the Jewish Museum, London

Poultry dishes

Stuffed necks

Whenever a chicken, goose, duck or turkey is roasted, the neck is usually destined to provide stock for the gravy. Some people still like necks of fowl boiled in soup, but I find that skin is totally out of favour.

Thrifty Jewish mothers have invented a way of not wasting the skin of birds' necks, but turning them into savoury sausages.

The stuffing varies from community to community. Central European and East European Jews use the heart and liver of the appropriate poultry, minced and mixed with a veal forcemeat, breadcrumbs, matzo meal or semolina, soaked in a little stock, and chopped onion and parsley; Mediterranean Jews add chopped almonds or walnuts; and the further East we go the more exotic the spices used for flavouring.

The stuffed neck can be gently simmered in stock, then browned in goose or chicken fat, but they are best of all roasted with the bird. Put it in the pan at the same time as the bird and roast, until crisp and nicely brown.

1 skin of goose neck
heart and liver of goose
120g (4oz or $\frac{1}{2}$ cup) breadcrumbs or matzo meal moistened with a few tablespoons stock
3–4 tablespoons goose fat
2 tablespoons finely grated onion
1 tablespoon chopped parsley
salt and pepper
grated rind and juice of $\frac{1}{2}$ lemon
1 beaten egg

Wash the skin, tie up one end tightly.

Chop goose heart and liver, mix with the rest of the ingredients, and stuff the neck with the mixture loosely, to allow for expansion during cooking. Sew up opening, prick the neck with a fork, and roast with the goose, basting with the pan juices periodically.

To serve: slice, put on a plate, and spoon a little of the pan juices over the neck.

Poultry dishes

Duck with olive stuffing

4 Servings

1 duck, ready for cooking
240g (8oz or 1¼ cups) stoned, green olives
120g (4oz or 1 cup) breadcrumbs
salt and pepper
1 egg, slightly beaten
90g (3oz or 6 tablespoons) dripping
1–2 tablespoons brandy
1dl (1 gill or ½ cup) stock

Chop half the olives and the duck's liver. Soak the breadcrumbs in water and squeeze out. Add to chopped olives and liver. Season with salt and pepper, bind with egg, and mix well.

Stuff the duck with this mixture, sew up opening, truss, and brown the duck in hot dripping on both sides. Add brandy and stock, season, and cook for forty to sixty minutes. Add the rest of the olives and continue to cook for ten to fifteen minutes, until the duck is tender.

Duck with walnut and pomegranate sauce

4 Servings

360g (12oz or 1½ cups) sliced, cooked duck
120g (4oz or 1 cup) peeled, blanched walnuts
2·5dl (2 gills or 1 cup) pomegranate juice
2·5dl (2 gills or 1 cup) chicken stock
½ teaspoon sugar
salt and pepper

Pound the walnuts in a mortar and put in a saucepan with pomegranate juice and the stock. Add sugar, mix well, and cook stirring constantly until the sauce acquires an oily appearance. Season to taste with salt and pepper, add duck, heat through, and serve with boiled rice.

Pasta, rice, and cereal dishes

Pasta, rice, and cereal dishes

Noodle paste

240g (8oz or 2 cups) flour
7·5g (¼oz or 1½ teaspoonful) salt
2 whole eggs, lightly beaten
2 yolks
cold water

Sift the flour and salt, add eggs and yolks and enough cold water to make a firm paste. Roll out, fold twice, leave for an hour before using.

Samosas

Indian samosas can be triangular, round or crescent shaped. Savoury samosas with a lightly curried filling make excellent snacks and cocktail accompaniments.

4–6 Servings

180g (6oz or 1½ cups) flour (plain)
salt
4 tablespoons ghee (or clarified butter page 260)
100ml (4fl oz or ½ cup) curds or yoghourt
1 medium-sized onion
1½ teaspoons fresh ginger
1 tablespoon coriander
1 teaspoon chilli powder
0·5kg (1lb or 2¼ cups) mashed potato
1½ teaspoons salt
1–1½ teaspoons garam-masala (see page 262)
1½ tablespoons sieved mango (or 1 tablespoon lemon juice)
2 teaspoons dried pomegranate seeds (optional)
1–2 tablespoons milk
fat or oil for deep frying

Sift flour and a pinch of salt into a bowl, stir in three tablespoons ghee and the curds, knead gently into a dough, roll into a ball, cover with a bowl, and leave to stand for twenty-five to thirty minutes while you prepare the stuffing for the samosas. Chop the onion and ginger. Pound coriander.

Pasta, rice, and cereal dishes

Heat the remaining ghee and lightly fry the onion, just to soften it. Add coriander, ginger, and chilli. Stir and simmer for two to three minutes. Add potato purée, season to taste with salt, blend in garam-masala and mango pulp. Pound pomegranate seeds and add to potato mixture. Simmer on low heat to evaporate moisture – the stuffing should be on the dry side. Remove from heat and allow to cool.

Roll out the dough very thin and cut into 6- to 7-cm (2½- to 3-inch) squares, put a generous teaspoon of the stuffing in each square, leaving the edges clear. Brush the edges with a little milk or water, fold corner to corner to make a triangle, and press well to seal the edges.

Heat fat and deep fry a few samosas at a time until golden brown on both sides. Drain on kitchen paper and keep hot while you fry the rest. Serve with mint chutney (page 264).

Mediterranean rice soufflé with chicken livers and Marsala

6 Servings

240g (8oz or 1 cup) rice
1 litre (2 pints or 4 cups) chicken broth or water with stock cube
120g (4oz or ½ cup) margarine
2 tablespoons flour
salt and pepper
240g (8oz or 1 cup) chicken livers, cut in thin strips
2 tablespoons Marsala or sherry
4 beaten yolks of egg and 4 whites of egg, beaten stiff

Cook the rice in chicken broth for eighteen to twenty minutes. At the end of cooking, stir in half the margarine. Remove from heat. Season the flour with salt and pepper, dredge the liver with it, brown in margarine, then add Marsala and simmer for five minutes. Add to rice and mix well. Leave until lukewarm.

Grease a large *soufflé* dish and preheat oven to 190°C (375°F or Gas Mark 4). Stir yolks into the rice and chicken liver mixture, blend well, check seasoning. Fold in whites of egg, put the mixture into the prepared *soufflé* dish, and bake for fifteen to seventeen minutes. Serve at once.

Pasta, rice, and cereal dishes

Oriental rice with salted peanuts

6–8 Servings

480g (1lb or 2 cups) rice
60g (2oz or 4 tablespoons) margarine
$\frac{1}{2}$ teaspoon salt
1 litre (1 quart) chicken stock
1 tablespoon chopped parsley
1 clove chopped garlic
small pinch celery seed
90g (3oz or $\frac{1}{2}$ cup) salted peanuts

Cook the rice in melted margarine in a heavy pan on low heat, stirring, until pale golden. Season with salt, add stock and the rest of the ingredients, except peanuts.

Stir, cover with a well fitting lid, and simmer on low heat for twenty-five minutes. Chop the peanuts roughly, stir into rice, and serve.

Mushroom pilaf

3–4 Servings

0·5 litre (1 pint or 2 cups) stock
salt
60g (2oz or 4 tablespoons) margarine
240g (8oz or 1 cup) rice
360g ($\frac{3}{4}$lb or 4 cups) fresh button mushrooms
1–2 tablespoons strong meat gravy (optional)
freshly grated pepper
3–4 peeled, sliced tomatoes
parsley

Season stock, add one tablespoon margarine, and bring to the boil.

Wash and drain the rice thoroughly, add to stock, stir once, cover, boil fast for five minutes. Lower heat and simmer gently for twelve minutes. Remove from heat. Leave to stand for half an hour. Stir gently with a wooden spoon.

Pasta, rice, and cereal dishes

Heat the remaining margarine and cook the mushrooms on low heat for eight to ten minutes. Flavour with good meat gravy, heat through without boiling, check seasoning.

Arrange the rice in a ring, fill the centre of the dish with mushrooms and their sauce, surround with a border of tomato slices, decorate with parsley, and serve at once.

Kreplach

These are triangular or square, ravioli-like, pasta pockets with various fillings. They can be boiled in water, drained, and served on their own or in soup; they can be savoury or sweet. Kreplach are traditionally served on *Purim* (see page 224), *Rosh Hoshanah*, the festival commemorating the birthday of the world, the day before *Yom Kippur* – the Day of Atonement. There is a particularly delicious type of kreplach, eaten on the festival of *Shavuot* – the Pentecost, with a filling of sweetened cottage cheese and raisins, served smothered with sour cream and sprinkled with sugar.

To serve with soup, cook the kreplach in boiling salted water for twelve to fifteen minutes, or until they float to the surface, drain, and add to soup.

Pasta, rice, and cereal dishes

Savoury kreplach

noodle paste (page 126)
0·5kg (1lb or 2 cups) minced, cooked meat
1 tablespoon finely grated onion
1 tablespoon chopped parsley
salt and pepper to taste
pinch powdered ginger
1–2 eggs, dependent on size

Prepare noodle paste as described.

Combine meat (beef, veal, beef sausage meat, chicken), onion, parsley, salt, pepper, and ginger. Mix well, stir in eggs to bind the mixture. Put the noodle paste on a lightly floured board, roll out thinly, cut into squares not bigger than 5cm (2 inches).

Put a teaspoon of the filling in the middle of each square, fold into a triangle, press to enclose the filling, then bring the two corners together and press hard to seal the edges. Leave on a floured board for an hour or so, to dry.

Cook in boiling salted water, drain by removing them carefully with a perforated spoon, and use as required.

Vol-au-vent and bouchées

Vol-au-vent and bouchées provide an excellent way of using up otherwise insufficient quantities of meat or fish to make a delicious and substantial dish.

Roll out puff pastry made with vegetable margarine to a thickness of 2cm ($\frac{3}{4}$ inch). To make a perfect round shape, put a dish on top of the pastry, and trace out the shape with the point of a knife. Cut out, leaving the edges clean, without dragging the pastry. Place on a wet baking sheet, mark the inner ring, and cut down to about half the thickness of the pastry. Brush the marked top with beaten egg. Mark slanting cuts outwards from the inner ring, to facilitate lifting the baked 'lid', put in a very hot oven 245°C to 260°C (450°F to 500°F or Gas Mark 8 to 9) for ten minutes, then reduce heat to 205°C (400°F or Gas Mark 5). When baked, remove inner ring, carefully scoop out the soft inside, return to oven for a moment to seal the scooped-out surface and your case is ready to be filled when required.

Pasta, rice, and cereal dishes

Vol-au-vent is also a splendid standby for buffet meals, and has the advantage of being good served hot or cold. The important rules to remember are: for cold vol-au-vent, both the pastry-case and the filling must be cold before the filling is put in. If they are to be served hot, heat them separately and fill just before serving. Instead of making one large vol-au-vent, you can make small bouchées, prepared in exactly the same way but much smaller in size. Cut out circles of required size, put on a damp baking sheet, mark out top with a smaller pastry cutter, and proceed as above.

Bourekas

These are puff pastry pasties traditionally served among Syrian Jewry during *Shavuot*. The filling is usually made of goat cheese, or a mixture of grated cheese and cream cheese.

Similar pasties with savoury fillings are popular both in Greece and Turkey and are known as *bourekakia*.

puff pastry, made with vegetable margarine (page 189)
240g (8oz or 1 cup) cooked, mashed potato
240g (8oz or 2 cups) grated goat or Cheddar cheese
1 tablespoon margarine
salt and pepper
2 eggs
120g (4oz or ¾ cup) sesame seeds

Prepare pastry, give it three turns of rolling out and leave in refrigerator. Combine potato, cheese, and margarine, season, and mix well. Preheat oven to 190°C (375°F or Gas Mark 3).

Roll out pastry very thinly, cut into 7-cm (3-inch) squares. Put a spoonful of filling on each square, fold into triangles, and pinch to seal edges. Beat eggs, brush the patties, sprinkle generously with sesame seeds, and bake for thirty minutes or until golden.

Pasta, rice, and cereal dishes

Kasha (baked buckwheat)

500g (1lb or 2⅔ cups) buckwheat
1 teaspoon salt
60g (2oz or 4 tablespoons) chicken fat or margarine water

Sort the buckwheat and pick out any black grains. Roast it in an ungreased frying pan, stirring and taking care not to burn, until pale golden. Put in an ovenproof dish, season with salt, stir in chicken fat, and pour in enough boiling water to cover. Bake in a slow oven, 135°C (275°F or Gas Mark 2) for two and a half to three hours.

Kasha (buckwheat) and mushroom pie

6–8 Servings

quick puff pastry (page 189)
0·5kg (1lb or 2⅔ cups) buckwheat
4 tablespoons chicken fat or margarine
1 finely chopped onion
240g (½lb or 3 cups) finely sliced mushrooms
juice of ½ lemon
salt and pepper
beaten egg

Cook the buckwheat as described (see kasha above). Fry the onion in two tablespoons chicken fat until soft. Add mushrooms, toss together for three to four minutes, add to buckwheat, sprinkle with lemon juice, season with salt and freshly grated pepper, and blend in remaining chicken fat.

Roll out three-quarters of the pastry, leaving the rest to make the top. Line a pie dish and fill it with buckwheat and mushroom mixture. Roll out the remaining pastry, cover the pie, crimp the edges, make a slit in the centre to allow steam to escape during baking, and put the pie in a refrigerator for twenty-five to thirty minutes. Preheat the oven to 218°C (425°F or Gas Mark 6). Brush the pie with egg, bake for twenty-five to thirty minutes.

Pasta, rice, and cereal dishes

Potato and kasha pirozhki

Pirozhki are patties, with various fillings, which make excellent accompaniments to borsch and other soups. They are served on the side, instead of bread. Among the popular fillings are: fish, liver, meat, mushroom, carrot, cabbage and hard-boiled egg, or spring onions and hard-boiled egg, and of course buckwheat – or kasha. The filling can be enclosed in puff pastry, yeast dough or potato pastry, as in the recipe which follows:

6–8 Servings

kasha (page 132, using half quantity)
3–4 tablespoons oil
2 large, chopped onions
salt and pepper
1kg (2lb or 4 cups) hot, mashed potato
1 tablespoon margarine
2 eggs
self-raising flour
1 beaten egg

Prepare the kasha as described. Heat oil and fry the onion until soft, but do not brown. Add to kasha, season to taste with salt and pepper, and stir well.

Mash the hot potato with margarine, add eggs, season, and adding flour as required, make a pliable dough. Roll out on a lightly floured board to a thickness of 5mm ($\frac{1}{4}$ inch) and cut into circles with a round pastry cutter.

Put a spoonful of kasha filling on each circle, fold over into crescent shapes, and pinch the edges securely. Add a pinch of salt to the beaten egg and brush the pirozhki with it to give them an attractive gloss.

Preheat oven to 190°C (375°F or Gas Mark 4). Bake for twenty to twenty-five minutes.

Pasta, rice, and cereal dishes

Sambousek

These are similar to the Syrian bourekas, but yeast dough is used instead of puff pastry and the filling is a mixture of spinach and grated cheese. The sambousek are traditional among Lebanese Jews:

Dough
30g (1oz or 2 cakes) fresh yeast
1 teaspoon sugar
200ml (8fl oz or 1 cup) lukewarm milk
salt
240g (8oz or 1 cup) melted margarine or
120g (4oz or ½ cup) oil
1 egg
480g (1lb or 4 cups) flour

Filling
480g (1lb) fresh spinach
90g (3oz or ¾ cup) grated cheese (Cheddar, Gruyère or Parmesan)
2–3 tablespoons finely chopped onion
black pepper
2 beaten eggs

To complete
1 yolk
1 teaspoon water
90g (3oz or 9 tablespoons) sesame seeds

Blend yeast with sugar and dilute with milk. Mix well and leave to stand for fifteen to twenty minutes. Put flour in a bowl, make well in the centre, pour in yeast, add margarine, egg, and one teaspoon salt, and mix well. Knead until the dough is smooth and stops being sticky. Shape into a ball, cover with a cloth, and leave to rise until it doubles in bulk.

Pick over and wash spinach thoroughly, put in a bowl, scald with boiling water, and leave for five minutes. Drain well, chop roughly, mix with cheese and onion, season with salt and pepper, stir in beaten eggs.

Taking pieces of dough the size of a hen's egg, roll out into circles to a thickness of 5mm (¼ inch). Put a spoonful of filling in the middle of each circle, pinch the edges to seal into plump semi-circles. Leave to stand for thirty minutes. Preheat oven to 205°C (400°F or Gas Mark 5). Put sambouseks on a lightly greased baking sheet. Mix yolk with a pinch of

Pasta, rice, and cereal dishes

salt and a teaspoon water and brush sambouseks to give them a nice gloss. Sprinkle with sesame seeds and bake for twenty-five to thirty minutes, or until they are golden.

Carving of Manna pot at Capernaum

Vegetable dishes

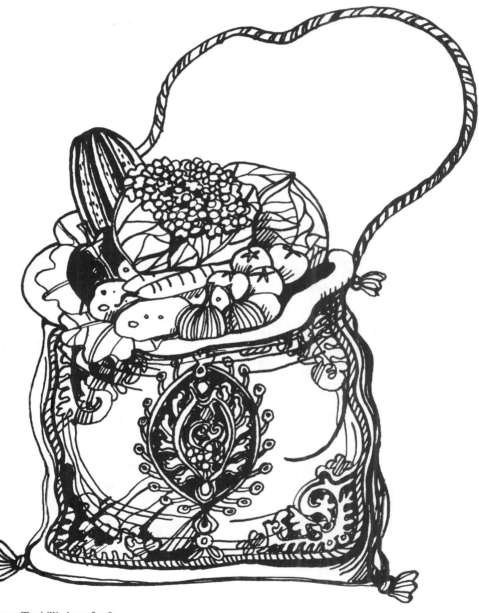

Derived from a Tephillin bag of 1789
in the Jewish Museum, London

Artichokes, Jewish style

This is one of the best ways of eating artichokes, but only young tender ones should be used. Keep the stalk long – up to 7 to 10cm (3 to 4 inches). The artichokes when served look like exotic golden blooms, each petal crisp and curly. This is achieved by deep frying the artichokes first, then dipping them into hot fat once more, just before serving.

4 Servings

8 artichokes
juice of 1–2 lemons
salt and pepper
1 litre (1 quart or 4 cups) oil

Peel the stalks, removing all woody substance. Trim off artichoke tips, discard outer coarse leaves. Holding the artichoke by the stem, press down gently, to open it up. Extract the choke with a knife, taking care not to damage the artichoke. Drop each artichoke as it is ready into a bowl of water acidulated with lemon juice, to prevent their going black.

Put oil to heat. Drain artichokes, dry carefully on a soft cloth, sprinkle with salt and pepper between the leaves. Deep fry artichokes, a few at a time, for seven to eight minutes, turning occasionally to ensure even cooking. Drain on absorbent kitchen paper and leave for two to three hours, or until required.

Reheat oil, taking each artichoke by the end of the stalk, quickly dip into boiling oil. As soon as they turn dark golden and curl up, remove, drain on paper, season with fine dry salt, and serve at once.

Vegetable dishes

Jerusalem artichokes with rice

4 Servings

2·5dl ($\frac{1}{2}$ pint or 1 cup) olive oil
3–4 chopped shallots
240g (8oz or 1$\frac{1}{2}$ cups) peeled, quartered tomatoes
1kg (2lb) Jerusalem artichokes
0·75 litre (1$\frac{1}{2}$ pints or 3 cups) water
salt and pepper
juice and grated rind of 1 lemon
2 tablespoons chopped dill

Heat the oil, add shallots, and fry until just transparent. Add tomatoes and simmer together for seven to eight minutes. Peel and slice artichokes, add to shallot and tomato mixture, moisten with 50ml ($\frac{1}{2}$ cup or 8 tablespoons) water, cover, and simmer for fifteen minutes. Do not stir, but shake the pan from time to time. Season, add remaining water, and simmer gently until artichokes are tender. (The cooking time varies, dependent on how young they are.)

Cook the rice separately, for twelve minutes, drain and add to artichokes. Sprinkle in lemon juice and rind, check seasoning, simmer uncovered for five to six minutes, decant into a serving dish, and chill. Serve cold, sprinkled with dill.

Asparagus quiche

4 Servings

Pastry
300g (10oz or 2$\frac{1}{2}$ cups) flour
1 egg
6 tablespoons oil
$\frac{1}{2}$ teaspoon salt
cold water

Filling
1kg (2lb) asparagus
0·5 litre (1 pint or 2 cups) double cream
4 eggs
salt and pepper

Vegetable dishes

Heap the flour on a pastry board. Make a well in the centre and in it put egg, oil, and salt and work mixture with fingertips, adding a little cold water when necessary, until you have a smooth ball. Allow to rest several hours before rolling out. Meanwhile, prepare asparagus : snap off tough lower ends, scrape, wash in running water, tie in bundles, cook in salted water until just tender, and drain carefully.

Roll out pastry and line a flan tin with it. Prick it with a fork on bottom and sides. Bake in a 218°C (425°F or Gas Mark 6) oven for ten minutes.

Beat the cream and eggs together until thoroughly blended. Season with salt and pepper. Pour the mixture into the partially cooked pastry shell. Bake ten minutes longer.

Cut off the top 50mm (2 inches) of the asparagus. Remove the quiche from the oven and stick the asparagus tips into the filling, tip sides up. Put back into the oven for five minutes or until the custard has set. Serve hot.

Aubergines (egg-plants) sandwiched with tomato, Bessarabian recipe

4–6 Servings

2–3 aubergines
2 tablespoons olive oil
1 carrot
1 parsnip
1 onion
2–3 tomatoes
1 teaspoon salt
¼ teaspoon pepper
tomato fondue (page 260)

Wash the aubergines, cut in thin slices longways, fry each slice in oil, and remove. Clean the carrot, parsnip, and onion, cut in very thin slices and *sauté* in the oil in which the aubergines were fried. Add peeled and chopped tomatoes, season with salt and pepper. Sandwich a little of this mixture between each slice of aubergine, place them in an ovenproof dish, and press together to make the aubergines appear whole. Cover with fondue and bake in the oven for fifteeen to twenty minutes at 218°C (425°F or Gas Mark 6).

Vegetable dishes

Aubergines (egg-plants) with almond sauce, Sephardic style

4 Servings

8 aubergines
1½ teaspoons salt
120g (4oz or 1 cup) flour
olive oil
1 chopped onion
1 peeled, chopped tomato
2·5dl (½ pint or 1 cup) water
60g (2oz or ⅔ cup) roasted, pounded almonds
1 teaspoon sugar

Peel the aubergines and cut lengthwise into slices 1cm (½ inch) thick.
Season with salt and leave in a colander for about an hour. Dip in flour
and fry in hot olive oil. Heat some olive oil in a saucepan and fry the
onion. When it is golden, add tomato and fry together. Pour in sufficient
water for the sauce. Add almonds and sugar, check seasoning, adding salt
if necessary. Cook for a few moments, add aubergines, cover the pan, and
simmer gently for half an hour.

Fried aubergines (egg-plants) with yoghourt, Yemeni recipe

4 Servings

2–3 aubergines
salt
olive oil
0·25 litre (½ pint or 1 cup) yoghourt
1–2 cloves pounded garlic (optional)

Wash the aubergines, but do not peel them. Slice, sprinkle with salt, and
leave for half an hour. Rinse off salt, dry the aubergine slices on a cloth,
then sprinkle with fine dry salt and fry in very hot olive oil. There should
be quite a lot of oil, at least 5mm (¼ inch) in the pan. As soon as one side is
golden, turn and fry the other side. Drain off surplus oil on kitchen paper
and arrange the aubergines on a serving dish. Serve cold.

Stir garlic into yoghourt and either dress the aubergines with it or serve it
separately.

Vegetable dishes

Holishkes (stuffed cabbage leaves)

6 Servings

12 cabbage leaves
1 small, chopped onion
3 tablespoons oil
0·5kg (1lb 2 cups) minced, raw beef
4–5 tablespoons cooked rice
salt and pepper
2·5dl ($\frac{1}{2}$ pint or 1 cup) stock
1 sliced onion
120g (4oz or $1\frac{3}{4}$ cups) sliced, fresh mushrooms
1 tablespoon flour
2 tablespoons tomato paste
$1\frac{1}{2}$ teaspoons sugar
60g (2oz or 6 tablespoons) sultanas (optional)
juice of $\frac{1}{2}$ lemon
1 tablespoon chopped dill (or parsley)

Choose a good white cabbage, pick off the largest leaves, slice off the central stem to make the leaves flatter and more pliable. Put cabbage leaves in a bowl, cover with boiling water, leave to stand for three minutes. This should be enough to soften them. Drain, dry carefully on a soft cloth.

Fry chopped onion in one tablespoon oil until soft. Add meat, brown lightly, add rice, season to taste, and stir in two to three tablespoons stock. Remove from heat. Put a generous portion of meat stuffing on each cabbage leaf, fold in the sides, and roll up into neat parcels.

Heat remaining oil and fry the cabbage rolls to brown lightly on all sides. If you fry them flap side first they will not unroll. Transfer to an ovenproof casserole.

In the oil left from frying the cabbage rolls, fry sliced onion until soft. Add mushrooms and fry for two to three minutes. Sprinkle in flour, fry to make a *roux*, add tomato paste, then gradually stir in remaining stock. Bring to the boil, add sugar, sultanas, and lemon juice, season to taste, and pour the sauce over the cabbage. Put in the oven preheated to 175°C (350°F or Gas Mark 3) and cook uncovered for twenty-five to thirty minutes. Sprinkle with dill and serve in the casserole.

Vegetable dishes

Machshee batzal (stuffed onions)

This is a Sephardic speciality and can be served as a first course or a light lunch or supper dish:

6 Servings

6 large onions
boiling water
180g (6oz or $\frac{3}{4}$ cup) minced lamb
3 tablespoons oil
2 tablespoons ground almonds
1 teaspoon chopped parsley
pinch allspice
salt and pepper
3–4 tablespoons stock or water
1 tablespoon lemon juice
tomato fondue (page 260)
2–3 tablespoons breadcrumbs

Peel onions, drop whole into boiling salted water, and simmer until tender. Drain, leave to cool.

Heat two tablespoons oil, fry lamb until brown, add almonds, parsley, allspice, salt and pepper, stock, and lemon juice. Simmer on low heat for ten minutes. Cut onions into halves and separate layers. Fill these onion shells with stuffing and put into a lightly greased wide ovenproof casserole. Continue in layers of stuffed onions until all is used up.

Spoon tomato fondue over the top. Heat remaining tablespoon oil and fry breadcrumbs in it. Scatter fried breadcrumbs over the contents of the casserole. Bake uncovered in a preheated oven 175°C (350°F or Gas Mark 3) for twenty-five to thirty minutes.

Swiss onion flan (pie)

6 Servings

unsweetened short pastry (see flan cases page 225)
1kg (2lb or 8 cups) sliced onions
3–4 tablespoons butter

Vegetable dishes

3 eggs
1dl (1 gill or ½ cup) single cream
salt and pepper

Prepare the pastry and line a large flan tin but do not bake. Fry the onions in butter over gentle heat until soft and pale golden. Fill the flan case with onions. Whisk the eggs with cream, salt, and pepper and pour into the flan.

Bake for five minutes in the oven preheated to 220°C (425°F or Gas Mark 6), then reduce heat to 175°C (350°F or Gas Mark 3) and bake until flan case is cooked and the filling brown on top and just firm to the touch.

Bambali (cheese mushroom soufflé)

6 Servings

120g (4oz or 1½ cups) button mushrooms
2 tablespoons lemon juice
0·5 kilo (1lb or 2 cups) cottage cheese
0·5 litre (1 pint or 2 cups) sour cream
1–2 teaspoons grated lemon rind
celery or onion salt
paprika
4 egg whites
2 tablespoons butter
60g (2oz or ½ cup) toasted breadcrumbs
60g (2oz or ⅓ cup) slivered almonds

Preheat the oven to moderate temperature 190°C (375°F or Gas Mark 4).

Wipe the mushrooms, slice, and sprinkle with lemon juice. Mash the cottage cheese, mix with half the sour cream. Add mushrooms and lemon rind, season to taste with salt and paprika, and mix well. Beat the whites of egg until very stiff and fold into the cheese and mushroom mixture.

Using half the butter, well grease a soufflé dish, pour mixture into it, sprinkle with breadcrumbs, dot with remaining butter, scattering it over the top in tiny pieces, and bake in the oven for forty-five to fifty minutes.

Whisk the remaining sour cream. Spread over the top of the cheese and mushroom soufflé, spike with slivered almonds, sprinkle with a little paprika to add colour, put back in the oven for ten to twelve minutes, and serve at once.

Vegetable dishes

Leek omelette

Leeks have been a much loved vegetable since the biblical times. *Numbers* 11.5 says '. . . we remember the leeks and the onions . . .'

Here is a recipe which makes a good starting or a light main course:

4–6 Servings

0·5kg (1lb) leeks
6 eggs
salt and pepper
oil

Trim leeks, leaving only white part. Wash carefully. Cook in salted boiling water until just tender. Drain, cut into slices, leave to cool.

Beat eggs, season with salt and pepper, add leeks, and whisk to mix. Grease a straight-sided frying pan lightly with oil, heat thoroughly, pour the omelette mixture in, and fry, lifting the sides carefully to let liquid egg flow underneath. When the omelette is set and the underside is browned, turn out on to a heated plate, take to the table at once, cut into wedges like a cake, and serve.

Honeyed sprouts

This is one of the tzimmes type dishes of sweetened vegetables. Traditionally, it is served at *Rosh Hashanah* – the beginning of the year, or the New Year, and celebrates the creation of the world. Jewish calendar is governed by the 354/355-day lunar year. To bring the dates in line with astronomical periods, a thirteenth month is introduced as required. This ensures that the Passover and other holidays are kept always at their proper time. The year 1973 corresponds to the year 5733 of the Jewish calendar.

4 Servings

720g (1½lb) brussels sprouts
salt
180g (6oz or ½ cup) honey
pinch grated nutmeg
2 teaspoons lemon juice

Vegetable dishes

Tear off any coarse outer leaves, cut through the stem at the bottom, and wash sprouts. Leave them in cold salted water for fifteen to twenty minutes. Drain and put in a pan without adding any liquid. The water they have absorbed during soaking should be enough to cook them, but if your heat is too high and they begin to show signs of drying out, add a couple of tablespoons of water. In this way you preserve the flavour, the colour, and the vitamins of the sprouts.

Cook for six to seven minutes only. Add honey, sprinkle in nutmeg and lemon juice. Simmer for two to three minutes to heat through again and serve.

Honeyed sprouts are excellent with roast turkey or chicken.

Red cabbage

6–8 Servings

1 red cabbage
olive oil
1–2 finely sliced onions
pinch salt
freshly ground black pepper
45ml (1½fl oz or 3 tablespoons) water
45ml (1½fl oz or 3 tablespoons) vinegar
4 cooking apples
lemon juice
1–2 tablespoons castor sugar

Wash the cabbage, trim off outside coarse leaves, and shred it. Lightly oil an ovenproof dish and put in cabbage and onion in layers. Season with salt and pepper, sprinkle with water and vinegar. Bake in the oven set at 177°C (350°F or Gas Mark 3) for one hour.

Peel and slice apples finely and sprinkle with lemon juice to prevent discoloration. When they are all sliced, add to cabbage, sprinkle with sugar, and bake gently for another hour. Stir in a tablespoon of olive oil and serve. Excellent with goose or duck.

Vegetable dishes

Belgian cabbage and chestnut purée

6–8 Servings

1kg (2lb) chestnuts
1 head white cabbage
0·5 litre (1 pint or 2 cups) stock
salt and pepper
2 tablespoons margarine

Slit the chestnuts, bring to the boil in cold water, simmer to loosen skin, then drain, shell, and skin. Put chestnuts into a pan, cover with boiling water, and simmer until tender.

Cut cabbage into pieces, cook in stock until tender. Drain and chop. Rub both chestnuts and cabbage through a sieve or purée in a blender. Reheat, season to taste, blend in margarine, and serve.

Sarmi or dolma (stuffed vine leaves)

Under various names this famous dish has been popular for many centuries in many Asian, Middle Eastern, Balkan, and North African countries. In oriental Jewish communities sarmi is traditionally served during *Succoth* – harvest festival.

The composition of the stuffing can vary according to the imagination of the individual cooks. Generally speaking, sarmi made with meat stuffing are served hot. If sarmi are intended as an *hors-d'oeuvre* in oil (page 15), no meat is used in the stuffing. One recipe for each variety of sarmi is given.

Fresh vine leaves are available wherever there are vineyards. They should be dipped in salted boiling water for a moment, to blanch them before stuffing. In less generous climates, vine leaves can be bought in tins and jars, packed in brine. They need no blanching, only draining and rinsing to wash off brine.

Vegetable dishes

Sarmi (vine leaves stuffed with lamb)

6 Servings

0·5kg (1lb) or 2 cups) minced, lean lamb
1 large, minced onion
3 tablespoons oil
6 tablespoons uncooked rice
juice of 3 lemons
1 teaspoon cinnamon
salt and pepper
500g (1 pint) jar vine leaves
lamb bones
300g (10oz or 2 cups) fresh, peeled, quartered tomatoes
1dl ($\frac{1}{4}$ pint or $\frac{1}{2}$ cup) dry white wine
fresh mint
egg and lemon sauce (page 251).

Heat oil and fry onion. Add meat and fry to brown lightly. Remove from heat, add rice, pine kernels, juice of one lemon, cinnamon, and salt and pepper to taste. Mix well and allow the stuffing to cool. Place a vine leaf rough side up, put a generous teaspoonful of stuffing on it, fold in the stem, then the sides, and roll up tightly into a finger-like cylinder about 7cm (3 inches) long. Continue until all are made.

Put the lamb bones on the bottom of a large *sauté* pan and cover with any left over vine leaves. This is to make a foundation for the sarmi. Pack the stuffed vine leaves on this foundation in layers. Add tomatoes and wine. Put a plate upside down over the sarmi, to press down and prevent their breaking up during cooking.

Simmer for one and a quarter to one and a half hours. Remove plate. Sprinkle in remaining lemon juice. Leave to rest for twelve to fifteen minutes. Carefully transfer to a heated serving dish, garnish with fresh mint leaves, and serve with egg and lemon sauce. Any liquid left in the *sauté* pan should be strained and used for the sauce. While the sauce is being made, the stuffed vine leaves should be kept hot.

Vegetable dishes

Potato latkes

Latkes are a versatile kind of potato pancakes. They used to be served as a traditional *Chanukah* speciality. Nowadays latkes are served at any time, perhaps because with their delicious crispness they are as tempting as the best and blondest of chips.

6 Servings

6 medium-size potatoes
pinch bicarbonate of soda
30g (1oz or ¼ cup) flour
2 beaten eggs
salt and pepper
fat for frying

Peel potatoes, put in a bowl, cover with cold water, and leave to soak for thirty minutes. Drain, grate on a fine grater, and pour off the liquid which comes out of the potatoes. Put potatoes in a mixing bowl, add bicarbonate of soda, eggs, and seasoning. Mix well. Heat a little fat in a frying pan and drop in the mixture in spoonfuls. Brown on one side, turn to brown the other side, remove from pan, drain on kitchen paper, and keep hot. Latkes can be served as accompaniment to other dishes, or in their own right, with grated cheese, sour cream or apple sauce (page 249). As a variation they can be flavoured with finely grated onion, which should be added to potatoes during mixing. As a dessert, latkes can be served with sugar and cinnamon.

Potato and walnut latkes

4 Servings

120g (4oz or 1 cup) halved walnuts
0·5kg (1lb or 2¼ cups) mashed potatoes
2 eggs
salt and pepper
fat for frying

Reserve four tablespoons walnuts for garnish, chop the rest. Mix mashed potatoes with chopped nuts, beat in eggs, season to taste, and mix well. Heat a little fat and fry as described in recipe for potato latkes.
Serve hot garnished with walnut halves.

Vegetable dishes

Beans in tomato sauce, Rumanian recipe

4 Servings

480g (1lb) string beans
water
1 large, thinly sliced onion
480g (1lb) peeled, sliced tomatoes
4 tablespoons olive oil
salt and pepper

Top and tail the beans, remove any strings, wash. Cook in two to three tablespoons of water for seven to eight minutes. Add the rest of ingredients, season to taste, cover, simmer for twenty minutes, and serve.

Cauliflower, Polish style

4–6 Servings

1 large cauliflower
120g (4oz or ½ cup) butter or margarine
salt
pepper
3 hard-boiled egg yolks
2 tablespoons chopped parsley
3 tablespoons white breadcrumbs

Boil the cauliflower as described, and drain. Heat half the butter in a pan which should be large enough to take all the flowerets in one layer. As soon as butter begins to sizzle and to take on a light brown colour, put the flowerets in one by one, season with salt and freshly ground pepper, and fry on a lively fire, turning them with a fork, to brown lightly on all sides.

Arrange in a serving dish. Chop yolks, or rub through a sieve, mix with parsley, and scatter the mixture over the cauliflower.

Add the rest of the butter to the pan, fry the breadcrumbs until golden, and pour breadcrumbs and butter over the cauliflower.

Vegetable dishes

Hungarian cauliflower loaf

6 Servings

1 large cauliflower
0·25 litre ($\frac{1}{2}$ pint or 1 cup) white sauce (page 248)
salt and pepper
3 eggs
2 tablespoons tomato paste
45g (1$\frac{1}{2}$oz or 3 tablespoons) butter or margarine
1kg (2lb) peeled tomatoes
2 tablespoons chopped parsley
paprika

Wash and trim the cauliflower. Cook in boiling salted water for fifteen to twenty minutes or until tender. Drain thoroughly and pass through a sieve or blender. Mix the cauliflower with the sauce, season with salt and pepper.

Beat two eggs and one egg yolk until well blended. Add the eggs and the tomato paste to the cauliflower. Mix well. Beat the remaining egg white until stiff and fold into the cauliflower. Pour into a greased mould and place in a pan of hot water. Bake forty-five minutes at 177°C (350°F or Gas Mark 3).

At the same time, heat the butter or margarine in a shallow pan over moderate heat. Add the tomatoes cut in pieces, sprinkle with salt, pepper, and chopped parsley. Cook uncovered for forty-five minutes.
Unmould the cauliflower on to a heated dish. Strain the sauce over the loaf. Serve very hot. Sprinkle with paprika.

Carrot and dumpling tzimmes

Proceed as for carrot and chicken tzimmes (page 119), omitting the chicken, onions, and potatoes.

Cook the carrots in chicken or beef stock for fifteen minutes. Place dumpling (pages 168–9 and 264) among the carrots, make sure you have enough stock to cover carrots completely. Cover with a lid and simmer until tender. Then make the sauce and finish off as described in recipe for carrot and chicken tzimmes. The dumpling mixture can either be shaped into one loaf or into smaller, individual dumplings.

Vegetable dishes

Carrots in yoghourt

This recipe is common to all Middle East countries.

4 Servings

480g (1lb) carrots
water
salt
beaten egg
60g (2oz or 8 tablespoons) breadcrumbs
3–4 tablespoons olive oil
1 clove pounded garlic
0·25 litre (½ pint or 1 cup) yoghourt

Peel carrots, quarter, cook in enough salted water to cover for fifteen minutes, and drain. Dip in beaten egg then in breadcrumbs. Fry in oil until golden, drain, arrange on a dish, and leave until cold.

Whisk yoghourt with garlic, pour over carrots, chill, and serve.

Carrots with caraway seeds

4 Servings

0·5kg (1lb) carrots
0·25 litre (½ pint or 1 cup) water
salt
45g (1½oz or 3 tablespoons) butter or margarine
1 tablespoon flour
pinch caraway seeds
1 tablespoon finely chopped parsley

Choose young carrots, scrape, and dice. Bring water to the boil, season with salt, put in carrots, cook for ten minutes, and strain, reserving the cooking liquid. Keep the carrots warm, while you prepare the sauce.

Melt butter, blend in flour, cook until the mixture browns lightly, dilute with water left from cooking carrots, adding it little by little and stirring constantly. Add caraway seeds and carrots, check seasoning, stir gently. Sprinkle with parsley and serve.

Vegetable dishes

Carrot pie

60g (2oz or 4 tablespoons) butter or margarine
30g (1oz or 4 tablespoons) flour
3 egg yolks and egg whites
salt and pepper
480g (1lb or 2 cups) cooked, mashed carrots
1½ tablespoons grated onion

Melt butter, blend in flour, and cook a pale brown *roux*. Remove from heat, cool slightly. Beat yolks lightly, season, and stir into *roux*. Add mashed carrots and onion and mix well. Beat whites with a small pinch of salt until stiff and fold into the carrot mixture.

Pour into a buttered *soufflé* dish, lined with oiled greaseproof paper, set in a pan of hot water, and bake in the oven 190°C (375°F or Gas Mark 4) for thirty minutes. Remove from oven, leave to 'rest' for five minutes, turn out on to a warm dish, take off paper band, and slice to serve.

Stuffed peppers, Sephardic style

6 Servings

6 large sweet peppers
olive oil for deep frying
1 crushed clove garlic
1 minced onion
360g (12oz or 1½ cups) minced beef
1 grated carrot
6 tablespoons cooked rice
salt and pepper
1 egg
1 raw yolk
1–2 tablespoons flour
2 sliced onions
1 tablespoon tomato purée
100ml (4fl oz or ½ cup) white wine
lemon juice

Cut a disk out of the stem end of the peppers and keep for 'lids'.
Carefully scoop out seeds, wash peppers, and put upside down to drain.

Vegetable dishes

In two tablespoons oil fry garlic for two minutes. Add minced onion and carrot. Fry gently until soft.

Combine beef with garlic, onion, carrot, and rice. Season well with salt and pepper, bind with egg, and mix the stuffing well. Put oil to heat. Fill the peppers with the stuffing, brush with yolk, seal the 'lids' on, and dust with flour. Deep fry the peppers in smoking hot oil, drain, arrange on a serving dish, and keep hot.

Fry sliced onions until soft in one to two tablespoons oil. Stir in one tablespoon flour. Add tomato purée, season to taste, and blend in wine. Simmer for a few minutes to cook the flour. Just before serving, add a dash of lemon juice.

Glazed chestnuts

4 Servings

1½ tablespoons margarine
1 tablespoon sugar
240g (8oz or 2 cups) shelled and skinned chestnuts (page 284)
100ml (4fl oz or ½ cup) meat stock
salt and pepper

Melt margarine gently, add sugar, and as soon as it dissolves, put in chestnuts. Cook until the chestnuts go pale brown. Add stock, season to taste, cover, and simmer until the chestnuts are tender and acquire a glaze.

Egg and cheese dishes

Decorative motif from a German Chanuka lamp of 1770
in the Jewish Museum, London

French herbed eggs

6 Servings

6 hard-boiled eggs
180g (6oz or 1½ cups) cooked, chopped mushrooms
butter
salt
cayenne pepper
0·5 litre (1 pint or 2 cups) Mornay sauce (page 251)
1 tablespoon finely chopped parsley
1 tablespoon finely chopped chives
1 small bunch watercress
French dressing (pages 253–5)

Halve the eggs lengthwise. Rub the yolks through a sieve and mix them with mushrooms, one and a half tablespoons butter, half a teaspoon salt, and a little cayenne. Using a pastry bag with a fluted nozzle, force the mixture into the egg whites, heaping it high. Mix Mornay sauce with parsley and chives and spread a layer of the sauce in individual baking dishes, arrange the eggs on this foundation and bake in the oven 177°C (350°F or Gas Mark 3) just to heat through. Garnish with watercress tossed in French dressing.

Eggs milanese

4 Servings

180g (6oz or 1½ cups) spaghetti
salt and pepper
4 hard-boiled eggs
30g (1oz or 2 tablespoons) butter or margarine
1 tablespoon finely chopped onion

Boil the spaghetti in plenty of salted water for ten minutes, drain, and season. Keep hot. Cut the eggs into halves, remove yolks, mash with half the butter and onion, season with salt and pepper. Pound to a paste and fill the egg whites with it. Arrange stuffed eggs in an ovenproof dish, surrounded with spaghetti, dot with remainder of butter in small pieces, put in a hot oven 218°C (425°F or Gas Mark 6) or under a grill to brown the tops of eggs, and serve.

Egg and cheese dishes

Canadian eggburgers

4 Servings

4 large, round rolls
4 slices of cheese
1 tablespoon butter
4 eggs
salt and pepper
1 small onion, cut into rings

Split the rolls, put split side up on a baking sheet, cover half of the splits
with cheese slices cut to match (the other halves will be used as 'caps').
Put both cheese-covered and plain halves of halves of rolls in the oven,
or under a grill to melt the cheese, and toast the rolls. Fry the eggs in
butter, turn once, season to taste, and arrange on the cheese-covered
halves, top with onion rings, cover with 'caps', and serve with any
piquant sauce, pickles or mustard.

Jewish spring onion omelette

2 Servings

3 eggs
1 tablespoon chopped spring onions
salt and pepper
1 tablespoon water
1 tablespoon margarine

Break the eggs into a bowl, season with salt and pepper, add spring onions
and water, whisk, and fry on a fairly high flame, shaking the pan from time
to time to ensure even cooking. When the omelette begins to thicken,
fold the sides with a palette knife, put on a heated plate or dish, folded side
down, top with a dab of margarine, and serve at once.

French jellied tarragon eggs

Arrange soft boiled or poached eggs in moulds coated with
tarragon-flavoured aspic jelly (page 257) and decorated with blanched
tarragon leaves. Fill the moulds with jelly and chill to set. Turn the eggs
out at the last moment, arrange in a circle, fill the centre with chopped jelly.

Egg and cheese dishes

Sardine meringue, Sephardic style

4 Servings

1 large tin sardines
2·5dl ($\frac{1}{2}$ pint or 1 cup) white sauce (page 248)
seasoning
butter
3 yolks
3 whites of egg
onions cut in rings
stuffed olives

Drain the sardines, remove tails and bones, mash, and mix with white sauce. Season to taste, allow to cool, add yolks, stir well, and pour into a lightly buttered *soufflé* dish. Beat the whites with a small pinch of salt until stiff, pile over the sardine mixture, smooth the top lightly, and decorate by carefully arranging a layer of thin onion rings in whatever pattern pleases you. Put an olive, stuffing upwards, in the centre of each onion ring, put in the oven 177°C (350°F or Gas Mark 4), bake for twenty-five to thirty minutes, and serve.

Jaffa carrot soufflé

4 Servings

4 egg yolks
1 tablespoon grated onion
360g (12oz or 1 cup) raw, grated carrot
shredded flesh of 1 orange
grated rind of 1 orange
2·5dl ($\frac{1}{2}$ pint or 1 cup) white sauce (page 248)
salt
pepper
4 egg whites, beaten stiff
butter for greasing dish

Combine yolks with onion, carrots, orange flesh, and rind. Gradually stir sauce into this mixture, check seasoning. Fold in egg whites, pour into a prepared *soufflé* dish, stand in a pan of hot water, and bake in the oven 190°C (375°F or Gas Mark 4) for fifty minutes. Serve in the same dish.

Egg and cheese dishes

Swiss egg and cheese casserole

6 Servings

6 slices bread with crusts cut off
60g (2oz or 4 tablespoons) garlic butter (page 259)
6 eggs well beaten
salt and pepper
$\frac{1}{4}$ teaspoon dry mustard
paprika
1dl (1 gill or $\frac{1}{2}$ cup) cream
240g ($\frac{1}{2}$lb or 2 cups) grated cheese
300ml (12fl oz or 1$\frac{1}{2}$ cups) dry white wine

Spread bread slices with garlic butter and put in a well-greased
casserole, buttered side down. Season eggs to taste with salt, pepper,
mustard, and paprika, beat in cream, add grated cheese and wine. Mix well,
pour over bread, and bake in a moderate oven 177°C (350°F or Gas Mark
5) for twenty to twenty-five minutes. Serve at once.

Fondue

This must be the best known Swiss speciality. It is very easy to make and
provides an attractive informal meal. This recipe comes from
Neuchâtel. Gruyère cheese is best for it. Neuchâtel is specified but you
can use any reasonably dry white wine for fondue:

4 Servings

1 clove cut garlic
0·5 litre (1 pint or 2 cups) Neuchâtel white wine
0·5kg (1lb or 4 cups) mixed, grated Gruyère and Emmenthal cheese
1 clove pounded garlic
pinch ground nutmeg
pepper to taste
1 teaspoon flour
1 tablespoon kirsch

Rub around the inside of the fondue dish with a cut clove of garlic. Warm
the wine in the dish over low heat, then mix in the grated cheese. Cook
gently, stirring all the time, until cheese blends with the wine. Add
remaining garlic, nutmeg, and pepper, and bring to boil. Dilute cornflour

Egg and cheese dishes

with kirsch and stir into mixture, cook for two to three minutes, until the fondue thickens.

Send to the table, keep hot over a spirit lamp, to keep constantly simmering. Serve with French bread, which the guests spike on forks and dip into the fondue.

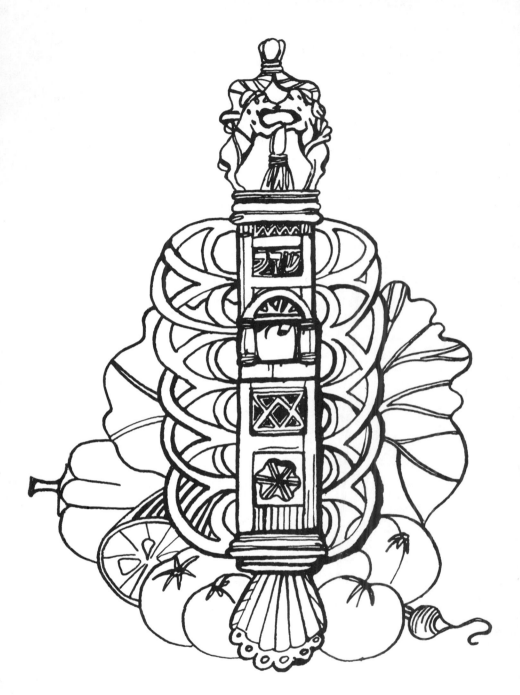

Salads

Italian fifteenth century ivory case Megillah
in the Jewish Museum, London

Israelis are great salad eaters. Salads of every description appear on their tables for every meal, including breakfast.

Whatever vegetable or fruit is in season and all the herbs, which the Jews have used since biblical times, go into salads.

The old Eastern European favourites of radishes in sour cream, cucumber and tomato salads, various cabbage salads are all popular. There are substantial *kibbutznik* salads, with up to a dozen vegetables, hard-boiled eggs, olives, and lashings of sour cream or yoghourt among the ingredients. From a vast number of recipes, I have chosen several which are both typical and unusual.

Sephardic orange, onion, and olive salad

4 Servings

4 oranges
1 large Spanish onion
1 dozen black olives
lemon and oil dressing (page 255)

Peel the oranges, remove all pith, and slice thinly. Peel and cut onion into thin rings. Arrange orange slices and onion rings in a salad dish. Garnish with olives, sprinkle with salad dressing, and serve cold.

Leek apple and tomato salad

2 Servings

2 leeks
1 large cooking apple
lemon juice
2–3 tomatoes
pinch sugar
2 tablespoons mayonnaise (page 250)

Using only white part of leeks, wash thoroughly, dry, and slice. Peel and core the apple, cut into thin slices, and dip these in lemon juice. Peel tomatoes and slice. Put leeks, apple, and tomatoes into a salad dish, sprinkle with sugar, season with salt and pepper to taste, dress with mayonnaise.

Salads

Iraqi minted salad

4 Servings

2 tomatoes
1 cucumber
small bunch radishes
6 spring onions
1 red pepper
1 green pepper
salt and pepper
5–6 tablespoons oil and lemon juice salad dressing (page 255)
15g ($\frac{1}{2}$oz 3 tablespoons) fresh mint leaves
1 tablespoon chopped parsley

Peel and dice tomatoes, cucumber, and radishes. Shred spring onions and peppers. Mix all vegetables, season, dress with salad dressing, arrange in a dish, in layers, alternating with a layer of mint leaves, sprinkle with parsley, garnish with a few mint leaves, and serve very cold.

Persian cucumber salad, with mint and yoghourt dressing

4 Servings

360g (12oz or 3 cups) peeled, sliced cucumber
salt
1 tablespoon tarragon vinegar
$\frac{1}{2}$ teaspoon castor sugar
3 tablespoons fresh, chopped mint
4 radishes
100ml (4fl oz or $\frac{1}{2}$ cup) yoghourt

Sprinkle cucumber with salt and put into a colander or dish which allows drainage. Put a saucer on top and leave for thirty to forty minutes. Press out surplus liquid and put cucumber into a mixing bowl.

Mix vinegar with sugar and mint, stir well, and leave until the sugar dissolves. Cut the radishes into roses. Mix vinegar with yoghourt, spoon dressing over cucumber, stir carefully, put into individual salad bowls, decorate with a radish rose, and serve.

Salads

Salat karpas ve mandarinot (celery and tangerine salad)

4 Servings

3 tablespoons olive oil
½ teaspoon garlic juice
1 tablespoon tarragon vinegar
salt and pepper
½ tablespoon fresh mint
1 head celery
4 seedless tangerines
2–3 tomatoes
2–3 shelled, hard-boiled eggs

Add garlic juice to olive oil. Mix vinegar with salt and pepper. Chop mint finely. Combine vinegar, mint, and olive oil in a small bottle and shake well. Leave until needed.

Trim off upper branches of the celery, remove outer stems, and cut off root. Wash celery very carefully; keep it under a running tap to wash away all earth. Dry well, remove fibres, and cut stems into bite-sized pieces.

Peel tangerines, pick off pith fibres, and divide the fruit into segments. Peel and slice tomatoes. Chop hard-boiled eggs. Arrange celery and tangerines in layers in a salad bowl. Sprinkle with chopped egg.

Shake the mint and garlic flavoured dressing to blend well, pour it over the salad, and mix. Garnish with tomato slices.

Ukrainian sauerkraut and carrot salad

4 Servings

480g (1lb or 2 cups) sauerkraut
240g (8oz) carrots
pepper
2 tablespoons salad oil

Wash and drain sauerkraut and put in a salad dish. Grate carrots, add to sauerkraut. Season, sprinkle with oil, mix, and serve cold.

Salads

Salat melon im gvina levana (cream cheese and melon salad)

4 Servings

360g ($\frac{3}{4}$lb or $1\frac{1}{2}$ cups) cream cheese
0·5dl ($\frac{1}{2}$ gill or $\frac{1}{4}$ cup) mayonnaise (page 250)
1 melon
30g (1oz or 3 tablespoons) salted almonds
salt
lettuce cups
salad dressing (pages 253–5)

Put the cheese and mayonnaise into a mixing bowl. Cut melon in half, de-seed and dice the flesh, add to cheese; reserving a small amount of melon for garnish. Add almonds to the cheese mixture, season to taste with salt. Spoon cheese and melon mixture into crisp lettuce cups, garnish with reserved melon. Sprinkle with salad dressing and serve.

Cream cheese salad with olives and cranberry jelly

6 Servings

180g (6oz or 2 packages) cream cheese
1dl (1 gill or $\frac{1}{2}$ cup) mayonnaise (page 250)
2·5dl (2 gills or 1 cup) whipped cream
240g (8oz or 1 cup) cranberry jelly
180g (6 oz or 1 cup) shredded pineapple (fresh or tinned)
60g (2oz or $\frac{1}{2}$ cup) chopped olives
4–5 tablespoons finely chopped celery

Mix cream cheese with mayonnaise, blend in cream. Cut cranberry jelly into dice and add to cheese together with the pineapple, olives, and celery. Press into a mould and chill until set.

Orange salad with poppy seed, Israeli recipe

4 Servings

4 oranges, peeled
1 tablespoon sugar
small pinch salt

Salads

¼ teaspoon dry mustard
3 tablespoons olive oil
1 tablespoon vinegar
¼ teaspoon finely grated onion (optional)
½ teaspoon poppy seeds

Cut oranges into very thin slices, remove seeds, arrange slices on a serving dish. Combine the rest of ingredients, except poppy seeds, in a jar and shake well. Pour over orange slices, chill. Just before serving, sprinkle with poppy seeds.

Avocado, grapefruit, and orange salad

4 Servings

1 grapefruit
1 orange
1–2 avocados, dependent on size
lemon juice
1 red sweet pepper
salad dressing (page 253–5)
2 tablespoons pomegranate seeds (optional)

Peel grapefruit and orange, remove pith, and divide into segments. Halve avocado, discard stone, cut into slices lengthwise, and dip at once in lemon juice to prevent discoloration. Shred red pepper. Arrange slices of avocado and segments of grapefruit and orange on a dish, slightly overlapping them. Garnish with red pepper, sprinkle with salad dressing, and scatter pomegranate seed on top. You need the seeds of one fresh pomegranate for the above.

Sabbath dishes

Based on a silver spice tower
in the Jewish Museum, London

Sabbath, in spite of coming every week, remains a special day.

Exodus 20:10 commands that on the Sabbath the Jews shall not work, 'nor thy son, nor thy daughter, thy manservant, nor thy maidservant, nor thy cattle, nor the stranger that is within thy gate . . . .'

The word *shabat* means 'rest' and on the Sabbath rest is decreed by the scriptures for man and beast.

In the hectic existence of our time I find the idea of having one day of complete rest every single week, without doing anything and feeling virtuous about it, very attractive.

The Sabbath family meal is a festive occasion. Lesson 11 of my first Hebrew reader, entitled 'What does a Jew need for a Sabbath?' teaches that among the musts on the Sabbath table is wine, candles and cholla (page 186). It says: 'There is no Sabbath if there are no candles on the table' and about wine: 'Without wine there is no rejoicing, without rejoicing there is no Sabbath'.

Among the dishes of the Sabbath feast are such favourites as chopped liver or herring, olives, gefilte fish with horseradish, chicken soup with noodles, or perhaps a dumpling soup, chicken, and a dessert.

All of these can be prepared a day in advance. In an orthodox household, however, the proper dish to offer after Synagogue service on the Sabbath, is cholent (page 168). It is an overnight stew of ancient Sephardic origin. See also Sabbath eggs (page 169).

There are innumerable variations of cholent, different cuts of beef or a boiling fowl can provide the main ingredient; the Iraqi community favours chick peas, burghul, and pumpkin; the European community prefers haricot or butter beans and potatoes or, best of all, dumplings.

Sabbath dishes

Cholent

6 Servings

240g (8oz or 1¼ cups) haricot or butter beans
4 tablespoons oil
1 chopped onion
180g (6oz or ⅞ cup) rice
6 peeled, quartered tomatoes
6 peeled potatoes
salt and pepper
pinch cinnamon and cumin
1kg (2lb) fat brisket
dumplings (page 169)
1 tablespoon sugar
boiling water

Choose a large ovenproof dish with handles and a very well-fitting lid. A tight lid is important because the cholent must be securely sealed to prevent it drying out during the long cooking process.

Soak the beans for five hours and drain. Turn on the oven set at 205°C (400°F or Gas Mark 5). Heat oil, fry onion until soft and transparent, add rice, and fry together until the rice acquires a pale golden colour. Do not allow to brown. Add tomatoes, cook stirring for five minutes, and remove from heat.

Put half the beans, fried rice, and potatoes on the bottom of the casserole. Season with half the salt, pepper, cinnamon, and cumin. Put the brisket and dumplings in the middle. Pack in the rest of the ingredients, add remaining seasoning and spices, sprinkle with sugar, and pour in enough boiling water to cover.

Put greaseproof paper over the top, cover tightly with a lid, put in the middle of the oven. As soon as boiling is established, reduce oven heat to 120°C (250°F or Gas Mark ½) and leave until you are ready to serve lunch the following day.

Sabbath dishes

Dumplings for cholent

120g (4oz or 1 cup) self-raising flour
30g (1oz or ⅓ cup) semolina
45g (1½oz or 3 tablespoons) finely chopped suet or raw chicken fat
1 tablespoon finely grated onion
2 teaspoons finely chopped parsley
salt and pepper
pinch nutmeg
1 beaten egg

Combine all ingredients (use suet for beef cholent and chicken fat for a fowl), season, bind with egg, and mix well. Divide and shape into the required number of dumplings. Cook as described (cholent, page 168).

Sabbath eggs

This is the traditional way of preparing eggs which, with cholent (page 168) are served in orthodox households on the Sabbath. Both dishes are cooked slowly, in a cool oven, overnight. Thus they can be put in the oven on Friday and the family can have a hot meal for Sabbath lunch without having to do any cooking on the day of rest. The recipe is literally thousands of years old.

Allow two eggs per person, put them in an ovenproof dish with two to three tablespoons oil, a pinch of pepper, two *unpeeled* medium-sized onions and enough water to cover. Cover with a double layer of greaseproof paper, then with a well-fitting lid and bake in the oven set at 121°C (250°F or Gas Mark ½) for at least twelve hours. These eggs are equally good hot or cold. The onion peel gives them a lovely brown colour.

Sabbath dishes

Cold fish in egg sauce

This is one of the traditional dishes for the Sabbath meal.

The advantage of such cold dishes is that they can be made well in advance:

6 Servings

1½kg (3lb) any good quality fish
court bouillon (page 257)
salt and pepper
2 raw yolks
2 tablespoons butter or margarine
1 tablespoon lemon juice
½ teaspoon mace
1–2 tablespoons chopped parsley
cooked asparagus tips for garnish (optional)

Cut the fish into portions.

If you have a fish kettle, put the portions on the strainer. If not, wrap them in butter muslin and gently lower into a pan of simmering court bouillon. This prevents the pieces of fish breaking up. Simmer gently for twenty-five to thirty minutes. Do not allow the liquid to boil fast.

Remove the fish to a serving dish, unwrapping it of course if you used muslin, season to taste. Continue to cook the liquid in which the fish was done. Boil down to reduce by half, remove from heat, and strain.

Using a double saucepan, dilute yolks with a ladle of the fish liquor. Add the rest of the liquor and lemon juice and cook, stirring over simmering water until the sauce thickens.

Check seasoning, add mace, stir, and pour the sauce over the fish, sprinkle with parsley, cool, and chill. Serve garnished with cooked asparagus tips dressed with vinaigrette.

Sabbath dishes

Hake and sour cream mould

Any good white fish can be substituted for hake. This dish makes an excellent first or main course for a summer Sabbath meal:

6 Servings

720g (1½lb) hake and fish head and extra bones for fish stock
fish stock (page 257)
30g (1oz or 2 tablespoons) unflavoured gelatine
1 tablespoon lemon juice
2 sliced, hard-boiled eggs
2 tablespoons cucumber slices
100ml (4fl oz or ¼ cup) sour cream
100ml (4fl oz or ¼ cup) mayonnaise (page 250)
1 teaspoon freshly grated horseradish

Prepare fish stock and simmer fish as described in recipe for cold fish in egg sauce (page 170). Remove fish, cool, and flake. Boil down fish liquor to concentrate, (see *fumet* page 259) and strain.

Soften gelatine with lemon juice and a tablespoon of cold water, then dilute with 100ml (4fl oz or ¼ cup) hot fumet. Stir until gelatine dissolves completely.

Line a fish mould with a thin veneer of liquid gelatine, tilt it to coat evenly, and put in refrigerator to set this lining. Decorate the mould with slices of hard-boiled egg and cucumber and seal with a few drops of liquid gelatine. Chill the mould again. These operations should not take long,

but nevertheless make sure your liquid gelatine does not set into a jelly. It needs to be just syrupy in consistency.

Combine sour cream, mayonnaise, flaked fish, horseradish, and half-set gelatine. Whisk, pour into mould, and chill. Unmould and serve with a plain green salad.

Sabbath dishes

Jellied fish steaks

This is another cold fish dish which is suitable for the Sabbath meal. It is of Middle Eastern origin. To make sure that the sauce turns into lovely jelly, use good fish stock using the head and some extra bones, skin and the bits and pieces trimmed off the fish. (See fish fumet page 259). When the steaks are cut for you, ask the fishmonger to let you have some extra fish bones for stock. (See also fish aspic page 258).

6 Servings

6 cod steaks
4 tablespoons olive oil
1–2 cloves crushed garlic
0·5 litre (1 pint or 2 cups) good fish stock (page 257)
juice of 2 lemons
salt and pepper
3 tablespoons chopped parsley
1 thinly sliced lemon

Wash the cod steaks and dry on a cloth. Heat oil and fry garlic for two to three minutes, without browning.

It is best to cook the fish steaks in the fish kettle, on a strainer. If you haven't got a fish kettle, cook fish wrapped in muslin, which should be discarded after cooking. See recipe for cold fish in egg sauce (page 170).

Transfer oil and garlic to fish kettle, add fish stock, lemon juice, salt and pepper to taste, and bring to a gentle boil. Put in fish and simmer on low heat until done. Do not overcook.

Lift the cod steaks with a perforated spoon and arrange on a serving dish deep enough to take both the fish and the liquid. Taste the liquid for seasoning, correct and add more lemon juice if necessary, and strain over the fish. Cool, garnish with lemon slices, and chill.

Sabbath dishes

Sabbath cake

This is a traditional, delicate sponge cake. It is important to bake it in a very moderate oven. If the oven is too hot, the cake will fail to rise properly and will lack lightness; or it will rise too quickly and not have the strength to stand up as proudly as it should to greet the Sabbath. If the oven is not hot enough, you may have a heavy wodge forming on the bottom. Among other vital rules is the sifting of the flour three or four times and really thorough beating with a whisk at all stages of mixing the batter. This cake is sometimes split, filled, and covered with a cream icing, but personally I prefer the Sabbath cake in its natural state, lightly dusted with icing sugar.

120g (4oz or 1 cup and 2 tablespoons) sifted cake flour
small pinch salt
6 raw yolks
grated rind and juice of 1 lemon
180g (6oz or ¾ cup) castor sugar
6–7 whites of egg
½ teaspoon cream of tartar
1 tablespoon icing sugar, or
chocolate butter icing (page 266)

Preheat oven to 175°C (350°F or Gas Mark 3).

Sift the flour with salt at least three times and leave it in a sifter. Beat yolks until thick, gradually beat in lemon rind and juice. Add half the sugar and continue to beat thoroughly until egg and sugar are completely amalgamated and the mixture is light and fluffy. Fold in flour, sifting it in little by little.

Whisk egg whites with cream of tartar and, as they begin to stiffen, little by little incorporate the remaining sugar, beating all the time. Fold the whites into the yolk mixture very gently, delicately lifting it.

Pour the batter into an ungreased pan, a tube pan if you have one for preference. Bake for fifty to sixty minutes. Invert the pan over a wire cake rack and leave to cool completely before removing the pan.

Arrange on a dish and dust the top with icing sugar. Or, if you prefer it with a filling, split, spread with icing, sandwich, and smooth the remaining icing on top.

Passover dishes

Italian Faience Pottery Passover Plate c. 1850
in the Jewish Museum, London

Passover dishes

The Passover – *Pesach* – commemorates Israel's deliverance from slavery in Egypt as told in the *Book of Exodus*. This Festival of Freedom is celebrated by a *Seder*, a combination of a religious service and a family dinner.

During Passover week yeast or leaven of any kind may not be used and it is usual in orthodox families to reserve special table and kitchen utensils for this festival. Matzo, unleavened bread, is used throughout the week as a symbol of the bread of affliction which the Israelites, fleeing from Egypt, baked in haste without waiting for the dough to rise.

Matzo meal replaces ordinary flour in the kitchen; it can be used for thickening soups and sauces, for coating foods instead of breadcrumbs, for making noodles, dumplings, pie crusts, cakes, and biscuits, etc.

In addition to matzo, tradition decrees other symbolic foods for the *Seder* table: bitter herbs (usually horseradish) to recall the bitterness of slavery; a roasted egg symbolizing the sacrificial offerings at the Temple; roasted shank bone, representing the Paschal lamb; charoseth – (see recipe on page 178) a mixture of chopped nuts and fruit, representing the clay from which the Jews made bricks while slaving for the pharaohs; parsley, celery or lettuce, representing spring crops; a bowl of salt water for dipping foods requiring salting, as a reminder of the tears shed during slavery.

Each place setting has a wine glass and wine is served to all. A spare glass of wine, known as Elijah's Cup, is left on the table. The *Haggadah* of Passover is also at every place setting. It is customary to invite to a *Seder* friends, neighbours, and particularly some lonely person, such as a traveller away from home.

Many delicious dishes are served at a family *Seder* and it is a festive occasion. The following are among the most popular Passover dishes: chicken soup with almond dumplings, charoseth, coconut pyramids, cremslach, matzo and red wine pudding, cinnamon balls, etc. Recipes for all these dishes are given in the book.

Passover dishes

Cremslach

These fritters are a traditional Passover dessert. They are excellent served hot, with rum sauce or red wine sauce (page 250–1):

8 Servings

2 matzos
360g (12oz or 3 cups) fine matzo meal
90g (3oz or 1 cup) ground almonds
½ teaspoon cinnamon
120g (4oz or ¾ cup) dried fruit
90g (3oz or 6 tablespoons) castor sugar
3 eggs
fat for frying

Break matzos, soak in cold water until soft. Squeeze out surplus liquid, put matzo in a mixing bowl, break up with a fork, add matzo meal, almonds, cinnamon, fruit, and 60g (2oz or ¼ cup) sugar.

Separate yolks and whites. Add yolks to matzo mixture and blend well. Whisk egg whites until stiff, fold into mixture.

Heat fat and drop the mixture into it a spoonful at a time. Fry the cremslach, turning once, until golden brown on both sides. Drain on kitchen paper and keep hot. Sprinkle with remaining sugar and serve.

Filled cremslach

These are more elaborate cremslach than the previous recipe. Any good preserve can be used in the filling and the cremslach can be served hot or cold:

10 Servings

300ml (12fl oz or 1½ cups) water
140ml (6fl oz or ¾ cup) oil
480g (1lb or 4 cups) fine matzo meal
180g (6oz or 1½ cups) sugar
pinch salt
pinch powdered cinnamon
4 eggs
480g (1lb or 1⅓ cups) full fruit jam

Passover dishes

90g (3oz or ¾ cup) roughly chopped almonds or walnuts
fat for frying
few tablespoons castor sugar

Heat water and oil and bring to the boil together.

Mix matzo meal with sugar, dilute with hot water and oil mixture.
Stir well and leave to stand for twenty to twenty-five minutes. Add salt and
cinnamon, beat eggs in one by one. Taking a little mixture at a time, shape
into flat patties.

Mix jam with chopped almonds, add a little matzo meal to absorb surplus
liquid. Put a little of this filling on each patty, fold, seal edges, and flatten
into shape as before.

Heat fat, fry cremslach as described in previous recipe. Drain on kitchen
paper, sprinkle with castor sugar, and serve.

Beolas

These are traditional Tunisian Passover fritters for which matzo meal is
used instead of flour. They make an interesting dessert, reminiscent of
baba, impregnated with jasmine or orange-blossom flavoured syrup or
honey. They are very easy to make and the preparation takes surprisingly
little time:

120g (4oz or ½ cup) sugar
100ml (4fl oz or ½ cup) water
1 teaspoon grated lemon rind
3 eggs
2 tablespoons fine matzo meal
2 tablespoons ground almonds
oil for deep frying
few drops jasmine essence or orange-blossom water

Heat sugar and water to dissolve, add lemon rind, and boil for four to five
minutes. Strain.

Beat eggs, add matzo meal and almonds, and mix well. Heat oil, drop
mixture in spoonfuls, fry until lightly browned on all sides. Drain on
absorbent kitchen paper, put in a glass dish. Add jasmine essence or
orange-blossom water to syrup, pour over fritters, cool, chill, and serve.

Passover dishes

Charoseth

Different Jewish communities have different versions of charoseth, dependent on what ingredients are available locally.

The Yemenis used chopped dates and dried figs, flavoured with coriander, and heightened with chilli pepper. In Israel the chopped or grated mixture may include pine kernels, peanuts, bananas, apples, dates, and sesame seeds, mixed with a little matzo meal, and bound with red wine.

The recipe which follows comes from Eastern Europe:

240g (8oz or 2 medium-sized) apples, peeled and cored
90g (3oz or 9 tablespoons) seedless raisins
90g (3oz or ½ cup) blanched almonds
1 tablespoon candied peel
cinnamon

Finely chop or mince all the ingredients, add cinnamon to taste, then shape the mixture into little balls.

Matzo pudding

4 Servings

4–5 matzos
175ml (7fl oz or ⅞ cup) sweet red wine
60g (2oz or ¼ cup) margarine
pinch mixed spice
120g (4oz or ¾ cup) mixed, dried fruit

Passover dishes

90g (3oz or 1 cup) roughly chopped walnuts
90g (3oz or 6 tablespoons) brown sugar
2–3 eggs
2 tablespoons castor sugar

Put the matzos in a dish, cover with red wine, and leave to soak just until they soften. Turn on oven to moderate heat, 190°C (375°F or Gas Mark 5). Gently melt margarine. Lightly grease a baking dish. Mix spice, dried fruit, chopped nuts, and brown sugar. Separate yolks from whites. Stir yolks into fruit and nut mixture. Beat whites until very stiff. Put a layer of wine-flavoured matzo in the greased ovenproof dish, sprinkle with melted margarine, follow with a layer of fruit and nut mixture, and top with a coating of egg white.

Continue in this manner until all ingredients are used up, finishing off with a layer of egg white. If there is any wine left over from soaking the matzos, spoon it over the pudding. Bake for forty minutes. Sprinkle with castor sugar and return to the oven for six to seven minutes.

Serve with rum sauce (page 251) or red wine sauce (page 250).

Matzo brie

This is recommended as a breakfast dish at Passover time:

4 Servings

4 matzos
hot water
4 eggs
salt
margarine or maize oil for frying
sugar

Soak the matzos in hot water and break them into small pieces. Break the eggs over the matzos, season to taste. Heat margarine or oil and fry the egg and matzo mixture.

Serve with a sprinkling of salt or sugar, whichever is preferred.

Passover dishes

Matzo meal pancakes

4 Servings

4 eggs
4 tablespoons matzo meal
margarine or maize oil for frying
1 lemon, cut in wedges and sugar or
jam

Beat the eggs briskly with matzo meal to make pancake batter. Heat margarine or oil and fry pancakes, brown on both sides. Serve hot with lemon and sugar or jam.

Passover sponge cake I

The difference between Passover sponge cake and any other sponge cake is that no ordinary flour is used, because it may contain some form of leaven. Matzo, being free of yeast, is eaten instead of bread, to recall the unleavened bread baked by the Jews during the flight from Egypt when the need for haste ruled out the use of leaven. Fine matzo meal is used for coating food for frying, for stuffings, for thickening soups and sauces, and for making cakes and biscuits during Passover.

90g (3oz or $\frac{1}{2}$ cup) fine matzo meal
90g (3oz or 9 tablespoons) potato flour
180g (6oz or $\frac{3}{4}$ cup) unsalted butter or margarine
4 eggs
180g (6oz or $\frac{3}{4}$ cup) castor sugar
grated rind of 1 lemon

Grease a 20-cm (8-inch) cake tin. Cut a circle of waxed paper to fit the bottom of the tin, put it in, and brush lightly with butter. Preheat oven to 190°C (375°F or Gas Mark 4).

Sift matzo meal and potato flour into a mixing bowl. Gently melt butter or margarine over lowest possible heat. Separate eggs and cream yolks with sugar until the mixture is light. Stir in butter, add matzo meal and potato flour. Sprinkle in lemon rind and mix well. Whisk egg whites until stiff, fold into the cake mixture, pour into prepared tin, and bake for seventy to seventy-five minutes.

Passover dishes

Remove from oven, put upside down on a wire cake rack, and leave to cool before removing tin. This cake can also be flavoured with orange rind or vanilla.

If you want to make it into a layer cake, slice the cake into layers, spread with your favourite jam, and sandwich together.

Passover sponge cake II

This really is the true sponge cake, nearly as light as air. The recipe requires neither butter, or any other shortening, nor milk. Its spongy lightness is achieved by air which is beaten into the eggs. The cake will float or sink, dependent on your deftness with the whisk:

1 tablespoon butter or margarine for greasing cake tin
180g (6oz or $\frac{1}{4}$ cup) castor sugar
1 teaspoon potato flour
4 eggs
90g (3oz or $\frac{1}{2}$ cup) fine matzo meal

Lightly grease a 20-cm (8-inch) cake tin. (A spring-form pan or round tin with removable bottom is best.) Preheat oven to 175°C (350°F or Gas Mark 3).

Separate the eggs. Beat the yolks with half the sugar, until the sugar is thoroughly absorbed and the mixture is light and fluffy. This complete amalgamation of sugar is vital.

Beat the whites with clean, dry beaters, gradually incorporating remaining sugar, until you have a stiff meringue. Sift matzo meal, then little by little fold it into the yolks and sugar mixture, just to blend it in. Avoid hard stirring.

With a whisk or spatula gradually and gently fold the yolk and matzo meal mixture into the stiffly beaten whites. Again do not stir, just fold in gently to blend the two mixtures.

Pour into prepared tin and bake for one to one and a quarter hours. Remove from oven, invert on wire rack, and leave until cold before removing baking tin.

Passover dishes

Cinnamon balls

These are eaten at Passover time:

4 Servings

2 egg whites
120g (4oz or $\frac{1}{2}$ cup) castor sugar
240g (8oz or $2\frac{2}{3}$ cups) ground almonds
1 level tablespoon cinnamon
icing sugar

Beat the whites until stiff. Fold in all the rest of the ingredients. Moisten hands and make the mixture into small balls. Put on a greased flat tin, making sure to leave a space around each. Preheat oven to 175°C (350°F or Gas Mark 3). Bake for twenty-five minutes or just until they are firm to the touch but do not overbake. Roll them in icing sugar when *warm* and again when *cold*.

Ingber

This carrot candy is one of the traditional sweetmeats served during Passover. The quantities given below should make about thirty pieces of ingber:

1kg (2lb) carrots
$\frac{1}{2}$kg (1lb or 2 cups) sugar
$1\frac{1}{2}$ teaspoons ground ginger
3–4 tablespoons lemon juice
180g (6oz or $1\frac{1}{2}$ cups) blanched, chopped almonds
sugar for final sprinkling

Scrape the carrots, rinse, and grate finely. Put in a saucepan with sugar and cook over an asbestos mat on very low heat, stirring frequently. As soon as sugar is dissolved, add ginger and lemon juice and continue to cook gently, stirring, until all moisture evaporates and the mixture is thick. Stir in nuts and remove from heat.

Spread on a board sprinkled with sugar, sprinkle the surface with a little sugar, allow to cool. Then before the candy sets hard, with a knife, mark into squares.

Leave until quite cold and hard, break into marked out pieces.

Passover dishes

Coconut pyramids

180g (6oz or 2½ cups) desiccated coconut
120g (4oz or ½ cup) sugar
30g (1oz or 3 tablespoons) potato flour
3 egg whites

Preheat oven to 177°C (350°F or Gas Mark 3). Combine coconut, sugar, and potato flour.

Whisk the egg whites until very stiff and fold into coconut mixture. Put mixture on a lightly greased baking sheet in spoonfuls, work into pyramid shapes, and bake for thirty-five to forty minutes until crisp and lightly coloured.

Bread, dough, pastry

The Israelis, on returning to Palestine from various parts of the world, encountered dishes which were new to them but must have been known to their ancestors. Foremost among these are the excellent Arab breads. One of the great pleasures of the table in Israel is the breadbasket, which often accommodates both the Jewish cholla, or Sabbath loaf, and the Arab pita. An example of coexistence I particularly enjoy. Here are the recipes for both cholla and pita:

Pita

30g (1oz or 2 cakes) fresh yeast
1 teaspoon sugar
250ml ($\frac{1}{2}$ pint or $1\frac{1}{4}$ cups) warm water
480g (1lb or $4\frac{1}{2}$ cups) flour
$1\frac{1}{2}$ teaspoons salt

Dissolve yeast and sugar in water, which should be lukewarm.
Sift flour and salt, add dissolved yeast, knead until smooth, sprinkling extra flour if needed. Cut into uniform 30-g (1-oz) pieces. The above amount of dough should give twenty-four small pita loaves.

On a lightly floured board, roll each piece into a ball, put in rows on a floured board, cover with a cloth, and leave to rise for thirty minutes.

Roll out each ball into a pancake and leave to rise for another thirty minutes, when the pita should look slightly puffed up.

Heat the oven to 260°C (500°F or Gas Mark 9). Place the loaves puffed side down on a backing sheet. Bake up for two to three minutes, by which time the pita should be gently browned and puffed up in the middle.

Remove and serve at once. The pita are hollow in the centre and, cut in half, provide a marvellous edible container for falafel (page 8).

Bread, dough, pastry

Cholla

This is the traditional Sabbath braided loaf. It is made of white flour and is
glazed with egg. It is easy to make and exquisite to eat with its crisp crust,
sprinkled with poppy or sesame seeds, and delicately soft inside.

In an orthodox household two chollas are placed on the table on Sabbath
eve and are cut only after the blessing. The two loaves are said to
symbolize the double portion of Manna which God sent down on the eve
of a more distant Sabbath. The same cholla dough is used for various
holidays but the loaves are given different shapes.

To conform with tradition, the recipe which follows is calculated for two
loaves. Don't cut down on the quantity, even if you feel that two loaves may
be too much for your weekend needs. Cholla keeps well and remains
delicious for days.

30g (1oz or 2 cakes) yeast
2 tablespoons castor sugar
0·5 litre (1 pint or $2\frac{1}{4}$ cups) lukewarm water
1kg (2lb or 8 cups) flour
2 teaspoons salt
3 eggs
oil for greasing baking sheet
1 raw yolk
poppy seeds

Put yeast and sugar in a bowl, dilute with 120ml (4oz or $\frac{1}{2}$ cup) lukewarm
water, and leave to stand.

Sift flour and salt into a large mixing bowl. Lightly beat the eggs. Add
yeast mixture, eggs, and the rest of the water to flour and mix well. Knead
into a firm smooth dough, adding more warm water, if required. Cover with
a tea cloth and leave in a warm place to rise for forty-five to fifty minutes.
Knead for six to seven minutes, cover again, and leave to rise once more
until the dough has doubled in volume.

Divide the dough in halves and cut each half into three pieces. With your
hands, roll each piece into a long, thin sausage. You will need three of
these to make each braid. Starting with three rolls, attach them by pinching
together at one end, then plait and taper off and pinch the other end. This
completes one cholla. Repeat the procedure with the remaining dough.

Bread, dough, pastry

Grease the baking sheet, or sheets, lightly with oil. Put the chollas on them, cover, and leave in a warm place for twenty minutes until the loaves rise and double their size. Preheat the oven to 235°C (450°F or Gas Mark 7).

Dilute the egg yolk with a tablespoon of water, beat lightly, and paint the loaves with this glaze. Sprinkle with poppy seeds and put in the upper part of the oven.

Bake for fifteen minutes, then reduce heat to 190°C (375°F or Gas Mark 4) and continue to bake for another twenty to twenty-five minutes until the cholla loaves look golden.

Dough for knishes and pirozhki

240g (8oz or 2 cups) self-raising flour
½ teaspoon salt
2 eggs
100 ml (4fl oz or ½ cup) oil
2–3 tablespoons water

Sift flour into a mixing bowl, sprinkle in salt. Make a well in the middle, add eggs, oil, and water. Mix well, then knead and roll out as required.

Bread, dough, pastry

Strudel dough

240g (8oz or 2 cups) plain flour
½ teaspoon salt
1 beaten egg
1dl (1 gill or ½ cup) warm water
melted butter

Sift the flour and salt into a bowl four or five times. Make a well in the centre, add egg and water, and mix with a fork to a very soft dough, adding a little more warm water, if necessary. Beat vigorously until dough pulls away from the side of the bowl. Turn out onto pastry-board and, with your fingers, lift, stretch, throw it against the board or pound with a rolling pin until it grows smooth and elastic, is not sticky and begins to 'blister' (about fifteen to twenty minutes). This 'maltreatment' of the strudel dough is essential to ensure its elasticity for the stretching it has to do.

Divide in two, roll into a ball, dust with flour, cover, and leave to 'rest' in a warm place for forty-five to fifty minutes. Prepare the filling, for this must be ready before you start stretching the dough.

Put a clean cloth on a table, dust lightly with flour, put a ball of dough in centre, brush with melted butter, and roll out slightly. Start to stretch the dough, pulling it with your hands. Gently stretch the dough in all directions, towards the edge of the table, working your way around until you have a dough that is tissue-paper thin, easing it carefully to prevent breaks. Tear off thick dough around edge. Let it 'rest' again for ten minutes. Brush with melted butter and spread with filling, keeping the dough on the cloth. Roll up into shape by lifting the cloth, pinch the edges to seal filling, trim off ends.

Place, sealed side down, on a baking sheet, brush with melted butter. Put in a moderately hot oven 205°C (400°F or Gas Mark 5) for twenty minutes, reduce heat to 175°C (350°F or Gas Mark 3) and continue to bake for a further fifteen to twenty minutes, until crisp and pale golden.

Bread, dough, pastry

Filo dough

360g (12oz or 3 cups) flour
½ teaspoon salt
2 teaspoons olive oil
about 0·25 litre (½ pint or 1 cup) cold water
cornflour

Sift flour and salt into a bowl, add oil and enough water to make a stiff
dough. Turn out on to a floured board and knead for twenty-five to thirty
minutes to make the dough smooth and malleable. Dust with cornflour,
cover with a cloth, and leave to rest for thirty minutes. Divide into twelve
pieces. Cover the table with a cloth and dust lightly with flour.

Taking pieces of dough, pat with fingers, roll out as thinly as possible, then
dust with cornflour and, working from the centre, stretch the dough
towards the edges. (See strudel dough page 188). Continue until all twelve
sheets are stretched paper thin. Leave sheets of dough to dry slightly, for
about thirty to forty minutes. If you need to break off work at this stage,
the sheets of filo can be wrapped in waxed paper and kept in the
refrigerator for a few hours.

Quick puff pastry

120g (4oz or ½ cup) butter or margarine
240g (8oz or 2 cups) flour
½ teaspoon salt
4 raw yolks
7 tablespoons cold water
1 tablespoon lemon juice

If pastry is required for use with a meat filling, use vegetable margarine
instead of butter.

Using a palette knife, cut the fat into the flour, add salt, continue to mix,
incorporate yolks, water, and lemon juice, work with the knife until the
paste is smooth, then put on a lightly folded board. Roll out to a thickness
of 5mm (¼ inch) fold, and leave to rest for ten minutes. Repeat the rolling
and folding process three times.

Bread, dough, pastry

Bagels

Bagels originate in Eastern Europe. The Russians call them *bubliki* and make up songs about them. At fairs in Russian towns bagels used to be sold like quoits on a string. The bagel, being circular, is credited with all sorts of magical properties, 'having no beginning and no end'. They are supposed to bring luck – as if they needed a justification beyond their taste!

Bagels and hard boiled eggs were part of a traditional Jewish meal after a funeral, symbolizing by their round shape the cycle of life without end.

To make 12 bagels:
360g (12oz or 3 cups) flour
1½ teaspoons salt
5 tablespoons castor sugar
15g (½oz or 2½ teaspoons) dried yeast
150ml (6fl oz or ⅔ cup) lukewarm water
1 egg
4 litres (4 quarts) boiling water
1 raw yolk
1 tablespoon cold water
poppy seeds, or caraway seeds or sea salt crystals.

Sift flour, salt, and two tablespoons sugar into a large mixing bowl. Dissolve yeast in half the lukewarm water, stir well. Add oil and the rest of the lukewarm water to the yeast.

Beat the egg and add to yeast mixture. Make a well in the centre of the flour. Pour the yeast and egg mixture into the well, mix and knead to a firm smooth dough. This should take only three to four minutes.

Cover with a cloth and leave in a warm place to rise for one hour. Turn out onto a floured board, knead well until the dough acquires elasticity.

Divide into twelve equal portions and shape each into a roll about 12·5cm (5 inches) long and 15mm (¾ inch) thick. Shape these rolls into rings, pinch the ends and even them out, to make as perfect a circle as possible.

Leave on a floured board, covered, for ten to fifteen minutes until they begin to rise.

Add remaining three tablespoons of sugar to boiling water and drop bagels into it one by one, allowing the water to come to the boil before adding any

Bread, dough, pastry

bagels. Use the widest saucepan you have to give bagels enough room. When all are in the water and boiling has been re-established, reduce heat and allow the bagels to simmer gently for ten to fifteen minutes, until they become light enough to float up to the surface

Preheat oven to 205°C (400°F or Gas Mark 5).

Remove bagels from water with a perforated spoon, drain on kitchen paper, and place on lightly oiled baking sheets. Beat yolk with cold water and brush the bagels with the mixture to glaze them.

Sprinkle with poppy seeds, caraway seeds or salt and bake in the oven for twenty-five to thirty minutes, until the bagels are smooth, crisp, and golden brown.

Tart pastry

240gr ($\frac{1}{2}$lb or 2 cups) plain flour
pinch salt
120gr (4oz or $\frac{1}{2}$ cup) margarine or butter
iced water (or beaten egg and water)

Sift flour and salt together – this puts air into them. Rub margarine or butter into flour with fingertips, lifting mixture over the mixing bowl for further aeration, until it looks like fine crumbs. Stir in enough water (or egg and water) to bind and, using a knife, mix to a stiff paste.

For sweetened tart pastry, above ingredients allow 30gr (1oz or 2 tablespoonsful) sugar.

Orange tree from an eighteenth century Viennese Megillah
in the Jewish Museum, London

Puddings and desserts

Puddings and desserts

Blinzes

This is one of the traditional delicacies for the festival of *Shavuot*. Both the dish and the word are of Ukrainian origin – *blinz* is a diminutive of *blin*, which means 'pancake' – but they are firmly entrenched in the affections and summer menus of all Jewish communities. Real traditional honest to God blinzes must have a filling of cottage cheese and be served with lashings of sour cream. Filling them with jam, however good, reduces them to the status of mere jam pancakes. Blinzes are traditional for *Shavuot* and I have a particular tenderness for this festival – the Feast of Weeks, because it provided me with a mystical culinary experience.

Last summer I stayed in a marvellously isolated house in the south of Italy, where I divided my time between swimming and studying Hebrew. Somehow these two occupations so filled my days that I had no time to do anything else. My hair was full of salt and badly needed washing, but I kept on setting myself a few more pages until it would be too late.

After about five days of such bargaining with myself, I finally decided to break off my studies in the middle of the afternoon so that I could wash my hair and still have a couple of hours' sunshine to dry it.

I went into the house with my head ringing with Hebrew sentences, saying out loud to myself words which captured my fancy that day. I was still doing this as I turned on the shower with one hand and a radio set with the other. When I heard Hebrew speech, I still thought it was in my head and it took me a few seconds to stop in my tracks. What I heard was a beautifully modulated man's voice, suddenly saying things which had only recently become familiar to me.

It didn't sound like Naples Light Programme ... could I have by some quirk of the radio waves hooked on to Kol-Israel? Dripping with water and shampoo, I waited for the station identification. The Italian announcer said: 'You've just heard the Rabbi of Florence, explaining the festival of of *Shavuot* ...'

I put my head back under the shower and as the black water streamed away from hair, I heard the Rabbi's voice again, saying: 'As the water washes away the dirt from your body, so the law of the Lord cleanses your spirit . . . .'

It was obvious what I had to do. I walked to the village three kilometres away, bought some cottage cheese and made blinzes. Here is the recipe:

Puddings and desserts

8 Servings

0·5kg (1lb or 2 cups) cottage cheese
2 raw yolks
0·5 litre (1 pint or 2 cups) sour cream
60g (2oz or 4 tablespoons) sugar
2 teaspoons salt
½ teaspoon powdered cinnamon
3 eggs
120g (4oz or 1 cup) flour
100ml (4fl oz or ½ cup) water
150ml (6fl oz or ¾ cup) milk
120g (4oz or ½ cup) melted butter
1 tablespoon oil

Combine cottage cheese, yolks, three tablespoons sour cream, sugar, one teaspoon salt, and cinnamon. Mix well and set the filling aside. Beat eggs until fluffy. Blend water with milk. Add flour to eggs and gradually stir in milk and water. Season with remaining salt and blend in half the melted butter.

A heavy pan or skillet is best for pancakes of all kinds and one of about 15cm (6 inches) diameter is ideal. Grease the pan with butter very, very lightly and heat. Spoon a little batter into the pan, tilt to spread the batter in an even layer over the entire bottom of the pan. Fry gently until golden on one side only. Turn out on to a cloth, cooked side up. Continue in this manner until all batter is used up. Take care to keep the blinzes very thin and cook only long enough for them to set.

Put a tablespoon of the filling in the centre of each pancake, fold over into a triangle and press the edges. (Or fold the edges towards the centre and roll up.) The preparations up to this point can be done well in advance as the filled blinzes may be safely left in the refrigerator.

Before serving, fry blinzes in hot butter to brown and top with sour cream.

Puddings and desserts

Vareniki

6–8 Servings

noodle paste as for kreplach (page 126)
0·5kg (1lb or 2 cups) cream cheese
2 eggs
1–2 tablespoons sugar
½ teaspoon salt
0·5 litre (1 pint or 2 cups) sour cream
pinch cinnamon

Prepare noodle paste as described. Combine cream cheese, eggs, sugar, salt, four tablespoons sour cream, and cinnamon and mix well.

Roll out dough, as for kreplach, cut into small squares. Fill each square with a spoonful of cream cheese, fold into triangles, and seal up the edges, then bring corners together and pinch (or cut dough with a round pastry cutter into small circles, fill with cheese, fold and shape into semi-circles).

Drop a few at a time into boiling salted water, allowing boiling to be re-established before adding any more. Boil for ten minutes or until the vareniki rise to the surface.

Remove with a perforated spoon and serve piping hot with sour cream and sugar. Vareniki can also be served with melted butter.

Vareniki with cherries

6–8 Servings

noodle paste (page 126)
1kg (2lb) cherries
180g (6oz or ¾ cup) sugar
sour cream

Prepare dough as described. Stone the cherries, preserving all the juice, add sugar, and leave for three to four hours.

Crush five to six cherry stones into fine powder, add to cherries, and put them into a saucepan with 2·5dl (½ pint or 1 cup) water. Bring to the boil, cook for two minutes, and strain through muslin, keeping all the liquid. Roll out the dough, cut, fill vareniki with two to three cherries each, and boil as described in the previous recipe.

Puddings and desserts

Remove with a perforated spoon, put in a heated serving dish, and keep warm. Boil down the strained juice left from cooking the cherries until it thickens and becomes syrupy. Serve this sauce and sour cream with vareniki.

Purim vareniki

Follow above recipes but fill the vareniki with full fruit cherry or strawberry jam. Cook and serve as described.

Persian rice pudding

This is a traditional sweet for the festival of *Shavuot* among Persian Jews. See note on rose petal jam (page 285):

6–8 Servings

1 litre (2 pints or 4 cups) milk
1½ teaspoons rose-water
120g (4oz or 9 tablespoons) rice
30g (1oz or 2 tablespoons) butter
75g (2½oz or 5 tablespoons) sugar
¼ teaspoon salt
90g (3oz or ½ cup) sultanas or chopped dates
3 eggs
rose petal jam
2–3 red roses

Bring the milk gently to the boil with rose-water. Remove from heat. Wash rice, bring to the boil in enough water to cover, drain at once, rinse with cold water, and drain again thoroughly. Preheat oven to 175°C (350°F or Gas Mark 3).

Butter a fluted baking form lightly. Strain milk, add rice, sugar, butter, salt, and sultanas or dates. Beat eggs and stir into pudding mixture. Pour into prepared pudding mould, put in the oven. As soon as the pudding reaches boiling point, reduce heat to 150°C (300°F or Gas Mark 2) and bake for one to one and a quarter hours.

Remove from oven, cool, and chill. Turn out on to a serving dish, decorate with roses, and serve with rose petal jam.

Puddings and desserts

Armut (Persian pear and macaroon dessert)

6 Servings

6 pears
0·25 litre (½ pint or 1 cup) water
60g (2oz or ¼ cup) castor sugar
¼ teaspoon vanilla
100ml (4fl oz or ½ cup) blackcurrant liqueur
0·5 kilo (1lb) macaroons
500ml (1 pint or 2 cups) sour cream
6 large eggs
180g (6oz or ¾ cup) icing sugar
pinch salt
½ teaspoon oil
1 carton cream, for whipping
1 dozen toasted, slivered almonds

Peel, halve, and core the pears. Put water, castor sugar, and vanilla in a saucepan, slowly bring to the boil, and cook gently until the sugar melts completely. Flavour with one tablespoon blackcurrant liqueur. Put the pears in a pan large enough to take them all. Pour the syrup over them, cover, and poach very gently until tender. Remove from heat, leave to cool, and drain.

Crush the macaroons in a bowl, sprinkle with liqueur, reserving one tablespoon for tinting whipped cream. Add sour cream, mix well, and either rub through a sieve or put through a blender. Preheat oven to 190°C (375°F or Gas Mark 4).

Separate the eggs. Beat the yolks with icing sugar and salt until creamy and pale coloured, add to macaroons, and stir well. Oil a 1-litre (1-quart) mould lightly.

Whisk the egg whites until very stiff, fold into the macaroon mixture. Pour the mixture into the prepared mould. Put the mould in a shallow pan of hot water and cook for forty minutes. Remove from oven and allow to stand while you whip the cream, adding the remaining liqueur to it, little by little.

Unmould the baked macaroon mixture onto a serving dish. Surround with well-drained pears. Pipe or spoon a whorl of pink-tinted whipped cream into each halved pear, stud with slivered almonds, and serve.

Puddings and desserts

Sahalab

This is a Yemenite milk dessert which resembles junket, except that cornflour is used instead of rennet:

4 Servings

1 litre (1 quart) milk
4 tablespoons sugar
4 tablespoons cornflour
3 tablespoons cold water
4 tablespoons ground coconut
cinnamon

Gently heat milk with sugar, stirring until the sugar dissolves completely. Dilute cornflour with cold water, blend into milk, and continue to heat on low flame. As soon as milk comes to the boil, remove from heat. Pour into individual serving bowls, allow to cool then chill. Just before serving, top each bowl with ground coconut and sprinkle with ground cinnamon.

Citrus custard

6 Servings

4 oranges
6 eggs
240g (8oz or 1 cup) sugar
juice of 1 grapefruit
juice of 1 lemon
4 tablespoons sugar for caramel

Grate the rind of one orange. Squeeze all oranges. Beat eggs and sugar until smooth, add orange rind and all the fruit juices. Mix well.

Preheat oven to slow: 150°C (300°F or Gas Mark 2).

Caramelize a metal mould: heat four tablespoons sugar with two tablespoons water in the mould. As soon as the sugar turns light brown, tilt the mould so as to coat with it the bottom and the sides evenly.

Pour the custard mixture into the mould, stand in a pan of hot water or a *bain-marie*, and bake in the oven until set.

Puddings and desserts

Iraqi dried fruit and nut salad

6 Servings

180g (6oz or ¾ cup) prunes
180g (6oz or 1 cup) dried apricots
120g (4oz or 1¼ cup) dried apple slices
1 dozen dried figs
60g (2oz or 6 tablespoons) seedless raisins
4 tablespoons sugar
60g (2oz or 5 tablespoons) blanched, peeled almonds
3 tablespoons shelled pine kernels
3 tablespoons rose-water
chipped ice

Wash all dried fruit, put in a bowl, cover with water, and leave to soak overnight. The fruit should be cold and can, therefore, be left in a refrigerator.

Strain and put the liquid in which the fruit was soaked into a pan with sugar. Heat gently, stir to dissolve sugar, cook until the liquid boils down and becomes syrupy. Remove, allow to cool, and chill.

Put fruit in a dish, add almonds and pine kernels, pour syrup and rose-water over them, stir in crushed ice, and serve.

Strawberry froth

6 Servings

480g (1lb or 3 cups) strawberries
300g (10oz or 1¼ cups) sugar
1 tablespoon brandy
300ml (12fl oz or 1¼ cups) water
3 egg whites

Wash strawberries, cut in half lengthways, sprinkle with six tablespoons sugar and the brandy, and leave for two hours. Over moderate heat dissolve remaining sugar with water to make a syrup. Rub strawberries and their juice through a sieve or purée them in a blender, adding all the syrup. Whisk egg whites until stiff, fold into strawberry purée, and freeze.

Puddings and desserts

Sabra dessert (prickly pear compote)

This is a truly Israeli national dessert. The Hebrew word for prickly pear is *sabra* and this is the name which the children of the one time immigrants, native Israelis, have adopted. Thus an Israeli born girl is called *sabra*, because like her namesake, the fruit of the cactus, she is 'prickly on the outside and sweet inside'.

4 Servings

8 prickly pears
120g (4oz or ½ cup) sugar
0·5 litre (14fl oz or 1¾ cups) water
1 tablespoon lemon juice

Peel the prickly pears and leave them whole. Heat the sugar with water, slowly bring to the boil, simmer for five minutes. Add prickly pears, cook for two to three minutes, and remove from heat. Sprinkle in lemon juice. Serve hot or cold.

Meringued melon

This luxurious dessert can be made in advance and left until required, as it can be served warm or cold:

4 Servings

2 medium-sized melons
240g (8oz or 1½ cups) strawberries
4 peaches
4 tablespoons maraschino
2 egg whites
2 tablespoons sugar

Cut melons in half. Scoop out and discard seeds. Cut the strawberries in half lengthways. Peel and slice peaches. Put strawberries and peaches into melon cups, sprinkle with maraschino or other liqueur, and leave in the refrigerator for an hour. Preheat oven to 235°C (450°F or Gas Mark 7).

Beat the egg whites until stiff, gradually work in sugar. Top each melon cup with a portion of meringue. Put in the oven just to brown lightly for about three or four minutes.

Puddings and desserts

Apricot or plum fritters stuffed with almonds

150g (5oz or 1¼ cups) flour
1 raw yolk
¼ teaspoon salt
100ml (4fl oz or ½ cup) beer
1 teaspoon brandy
1kg (2lb) apricots (or plums)
120g (4oz or ½ cup) castor sugar
blanched almonds
fat for deep frying
vanilla sugar*

Make a light batter using flour, yolk, salt, beer, and brandy.
Stir until smooth and allow to stand for two to three hours. Wash
apricots but do not cut. Heat the castor sugar in a pan with a tablespoon
water. As soon as sugar dissolves into syrup, put in apricots, simmer gently
for seven to eight minutes, and remove from heat. Drain apricots and leave
to cool. Taking care not to break them, extract stones, fill each apricot
with as many almonds as it will take comfortably.

Put fat to heat. Dip each apricot in batter, deep fry until golden brown,
and drain on absorbent paper.

Sprinkle with vanilla sugar and serve hot.

* To have vanilla sugar always on hand, keep one or two vanilla beans in a 500-g (1-lb) jar of
sugar. Top up as you take out vanilla flavoured sugar and make sure the jar has a well-fitting lid.

Canadian lemon meringue pie

flan case baked 'blind' (page 225)
30g (1oz or 3 tablespoons) cornflour
2·5dl (½ pint or 1 cup) water
juice and grated rind of 2 lemons
240g (8oz or 1 cup) sugar
15g (½oz or 1 tablespoon) butter
2 raw egg yolks
2 stiffly beaten egg whites
glacé cherries and angelica for decoration

Puddings and desserts

Mix cornflour with enough water to make a thin cream. Bring the rest of the water to the boil, pour on the cornflour, and stir. Return mixture to saucepan, add lemon juice, and boil for five minutes, stirring constantly. Add half the sugar, butter, and grated lemon rind, cool slightly; one by one, beat in the yolks and pour the mixture into the flan case.

Gradually whisk sugar into the egg whites, pile on top of the lemon mixture, and bake in a slow oven 150°C (300°F or Gas Mark 2) for about half an hour, until the filling is set and the meringue crisp and a rich creamy colour.

Decorate with cherries and angelica and serve cold.

Jaffa strawberry salad

4 Servings

720g (1½lb or 4½ cups) strawberries
4 large Jaffa oranges
1 tablespoon curacao (optional)
90g (3oz or 6 tablespoons) sugar

Hull strawberries and wash quickly in cold water, without allowing them to soak. Pile in a pyramid in a serving dish.

Squeeze two oranges and heat the juice with curacao and sugar. As soon as sugar dissolves and the liquid becomes syrupy, remove from heat and while still hot pour over strawberries. Peel and slice remaining two oranges and garnish the dish. Serve chilled.

Puddings and desserts

Zabaione

Zabaione is a luxurious dessert which is easily accessible in Israel. Israel's poultry and egg production is very great. She also produces an abundance of sweet wines which can do for zabaione all that Marsala or sweet sherry can.

Made as described in the first recipe for hot zabaione, without cream, it is acceptable after a meat or poultry dish. Zabaione is also good as a sauce for a cake which is intended as dessert. As an accompaniment for *compôtes* or fruit salads, it beats custard any day! It is a most rewarding preparation to make and only overcooking can ruin it.

Zabaione (hot)

4 Servings

210g (7oz or 1 cup) castor sugar
6 egg yolks
2·5dl (2 gills or 1 cup) Marsala
flavouring

Beat sugar and yolks until the mixture turns light and begins to form a ribbon. Add Marsala and, whisking all the time, heat in a double boiler over very low heat until the zabaione becomes frothy and stiff, but *do not allow to boil*, or your zabaione will curdle. Whisk in flavouring of your choice (vanilla, orange or lemon sugar, chocolate, Kirsch, Kummel, Maraschino, Grand-Marnier, etc.) and serve at once in warmed goblets. Dry white wine, Madeira, port, sherry or champagne can be used instead of Marsala.

Zabaione (cold)

Prepare as above, flavour to taste, and as soon as the sauce acquires its characteristic velvety and frothy consistency, remove from heat, decant into a chilled bowl whisking all the time. When the zabaione cools down, whisk into 1dl (1 gill or ½ cup) whipped cream and keep in refrigerator, but do not freeze. It will remain unimpaired for several days.

Delicious with fresh, soft fruit.

Puddings and desserts

Grapefruit mousse

4 Servings

5 raw yolks
180g (6oz or ¾ cup) sugar
juice of 1 grapefruit
2 tablespoons lemon juice
5 egg whites

Beat yolks with sugar until light and pale. Transfer to a double boiler, add fruit juices, and heat over simmering water until the mixture becomes thick and creamy, stirring all the time. Remove from heat and allow to cool.

Beat egg whites until very stiff, fold into the grapefruit mixture, pour into a serving dish, and chill.

Plum brandy iced soufflé

In the original recipe Carmel plum brandy was used, but apricot brandy or any other liqueur would make good flavouring for this dessert:

75g (2½oz or 5 tablespoonsful) sugar
water
4 egg yolks
7·5g (¼oz or 1 tablespoonful) gelatine
1 glass plum brandy
4 whites of egg
2·5dl (½ pint or 1 cup) cream
3 tablespoonsful crushed macaroons
preserved cherries for decoration

Put sugar in a pan, add enough water to moisten, make a syrup, pour it on the yolks, stir constantly until the mixture is cold. Dissolve gelatine in a little warm water, blend into mixture, pour in plum brandy, and stir well. Beat whites of egg with cream, fold into mixture. Pour into a soufflé mould with a collar of paper extending about 5cm (2 inches) from the top. Chill. Before serving, remove paper collar, sprinkle the top with crushed macaroons, and decorate with cherries.

Puddings and desserts

Honeyed grapes

4 Servings

0·5kg (1lb or 2½ cups) seedless grapes
1 teaspoon lemon juice
90g (3oz or 4 tablespoons) honey
2 tablespoons sherry (or brandy)
carton sour cream (optional)

Wash grapes and remove stems. Combine lemon juice, honey, and sherry and pour over the grapes. Chill for several hours or preferably overnight. Decant into dessert glasses, top with sour cream, and serve.

Mint and melon jelly

4 Servings

1 honey dew melon
120g (4oz or ½ cup) sugar
4 tablespoons fresh, chopped mint
30g (1oz) gelatine
4 tablespoons lemon juice
1–2 tablespoons crème de menthe liqueur
4–5 ice cubes
mint leaves for garnish

Cut melon, discard seeds, and scoop out the flesh with a ball scoop. Keep the juice which comes out of the melon. Put sugar in a pan with 240ml (8oz or 1 cup) water, heat gently, bring to the boil, simmer syrup for five to six minutes. Put chopped mint in a bowl, pour hot syrup over it, and leave to infuse. When the minty syrup is cold, strain.

Dissolve gelatine in 180ml (6oz or ¾ cup) cold water and stir into syrup. Add lemon juice and crème de menthe, to intensify colour. Add ice cubes and stir until they melt and cool down the mixture. Reserve a dozen melon balls for garnishing, add the rest, together with any melon juice to the jelly liquid. Rinse a mould with cold water, pour the mixture into it, and chill to set.

To serve: turn out, garnish with mint leaves and melon balls. The melon shell makes a good container for orange and lemon sorbet (page 214).

Puddings and desserts

White wine dessert

4 Servings

4 eggs
180g (6oz or ¾ cup) castor sugar
100ml (4fl oz or ½ cup) white wine
1 tablespoon (or 3 leaves) gelatine
2 tablespoons warm water
1–2 teaspoon almond oil

Separate eggs and blend yolks with sugar and wine. Cook mixture in a a double saucepan over simmering water to heat and amalgamate it. On no account allow the mixture to boil. Remove from heat. Dissolve gelatine in water and blend into the wine mixture. Keep stirring the mixture from time to time as it cools, to prevent formation of skin on the surface.

Leave until it begins to set. Whisk egg whites until very stiff, fold into the mixture, and pour into a mould lightly greased with almond oil. Chill to set. To serve, dip the mould into a bowl of warm water for an instant and turn out.

Oeufs à la neige

4–6 Servings

4 egg whites
180g (6oz or 12 tablespoons) castor sugar
1 litre (2 pints or 4 cups) heated milk
0·5kg (1lb or 2½ cups) fresh, sliced strawberries (or other fruit)
vanilla custard (page 265)
1–2 tablespoons toasted, slivered almonds

Beat egg whites until they are stiff, gradually adding sugar. Using a wet tablespoon, form the meringue into egg shapes and slip them off into simmering milk. Poach the meringues two minutes on each side, turning them once. Remove the eggs with a perforated spoon and dry on kitchen paper. Heap the strawberries in a dish, put the eggs on them, pour cold vanilla custard around the eggs, sprinkle with toasted slivered almonds, and serve.

Puddings and desserts

Baked alaska (Norwegian omelette or surprise omelette)

This is a most rewarding dessert to make, it can be prepared in the morning and safely left in the freezer until the evening. A ten egg-white baked alaska will only need five minutes' cooking.

The culinary column of the *Liberté*, printed on 6 June 1866, credited the chef of the Chinese Mission with the authorship of this dessert. The column says: 'The chefs of the Celestial Empire have exchanged civilities and information with the chefs of the Grand-Hôtel.' The Grand-Hôtel was opened in 1862 and its first chef's name was Balzac.

The report goes on to describe how delighted the French chef in charge of sweet courses was to have learnt from his Chinese colleague 'the method of baking vanilla and ginger ices in the oven', and gives the following instructions: 'Chill the ice until hard, wrap each in a very light pastry crust and put in the oven. The pastry is baked before the ice, protected by the pastry shell, can melt. The gourmets can thus give themselves the double pleasure of biting through piping hot crust and cooling the palate with the fragrant ices.'

Oval-shaped Genoese cake

1 tablespoon liqueur (Kirsch, Maraschino, etc.) (optional)
0·75 litre (1½ pint or 3 cups) ice-cream
180g (6oz or 1 cup) soft fruit (strawberries, raspberries, etc.)
ordinary meringue (page 227) using 10 egg whites and 180g (6oz or ¾ cup) sugar and icing sugar
½ teaspoon cream of tartar
1½ tablespoons chopped almonds

Put the cake on a board covered with foil, scoop out the centre, leaving a shell 2·5cm (1 inch) thick, and sprinkle with liqueur. Pack the ice-cream and fruit in the centre, freeze until very firm. Cover completely with meringue, to which cream of tartar has been added during beating, smooth over the surface to a thickness of 1·5cm (⅔ inch). Decorate the omelette by piping some of the meringue mixture through a forcing bag, sprinkle with almonds, and leave in the freezer on the board until required.

When you are ready for it, preheat the oven to 245°C (475°F or Gas Mark

Puddings and desserts

8), dust the omelette with icing sugar, bake on the board for five minutes, which is enough to cook and colour the meringue without melting the ice-cream, and serve at once.

Alternatively, instead of using a foil-covered board, you can put the piece of cake on a long dish, place the ice-cream and fruit on top, then cover with meringue and continue as described, but hollowing out the cake into a shell helps the omelette to keep its shape for several hours.

Avocado b'kazefet (avocado salad with coffee cream)

4 Servings

2–3 tablespoons cream cheese
1–2 tablespoons sugar
2 tablespoons grated coconut
2 avocado pears
1–2 sliced bananas
pinch ground cinnamon
2·5dl (2 gills or 1 cup) whipped cream
strong black coffee

Mash the cream cheese, sweeten with half the sugar, shape into small balls, roll in coconut. Stone the avocados and scoop out flesh with a ball scoop. Arrange cream cheese and avocado balls in a glass dish with bananas, sprinkle with rest of sugar and cinnamon and chill. Before serving, flavour whipped cream with freshly made strong black coffee (cold) to taste, about one to two tablespoons. Mask the salad with it and serve.

Whipped avocado

6 Servings

3 avocados
240g (8oz or 1 cup) sugar
4 tablespoons fresh lemon juice and 1 lemon cut in wedges
2–3 tablespoons crème de menthe liqueur

Cut avocados, remove pulp, taking care not to damage skin. These will be used as shells for serving. Mash the pulp, or better still, put through a blender, with sugar, lemon juice, and liqueur, until the mixture is creamy. Pile into shells and chill. Serve garnished with wedges of lemon.

Ice-creams, water-ices, and non-dairy ice-cream

Figure based on an eighteenth century Derby Ware Jewish Pedlar
in the Jewish Museum, London

Ice-cream custard

6 Servings

300ml (12fl oz or 1½ cups) very fresh cream
flavouring (vanilla bean, thinly cut lemon or orange peel, etc.)
4 yolks
120g (4oz or 8 tablespoons) icing sugar (or pounded castor sugar)

Put cream and flavouring into a double boiler, stir in yolks, heat, stirring all the time over simmering water until the mixture thickens. Remove from heat but continue to stir for a few minutes. Add sugar, stir to dissolve and blend in, allow to cool, strain, and use as required.

Half and half ice-cream custard

0·25 litre (½ pint or 1 cup) milk
0·25 litre (½ pint or 1 cup) single cream
6 yolks
thinly sliced lemon peel, without pith
90–120g (3–4oz or 7–8 tablespoons) sugar

Using above ingredients, proceed as described in recipe above.

Vanilla ice-cream

6 yolks
0·75 litre (1½ pints or 3 cups) milk
1 teaspoon vanilla
pinch salt
300g (10oz or 1¼ cups) sugar
2·5dl (½ pint or 1 cup) whipped cream

Beat the yolks and dilute with a little milk. Scald the rest of the milk with vanilla, salt, and sugar and heat to dissolve stirring all the time. Remove from heat, one by one stir in yolks, pour mixture into a double saucepan, cook until the mixture thickens over simmering water (eight or ten minutes), stirring constantly.

When the mixture coats the back of a wooden spoon, remove from heat. (i.e. take the pan with the custard mixture out of hot water), stir to cool . Strain, add whipped cream, and freeze.

Ice-creams

Almond ice-cream

Make vanilla ice-cream mixture (page 211), add 120g (4oz or $\frac{2}{3}$ cup) almonds and four bitter almonds, blanched and pounded with two to three tablespoons water. Mix well and freeze.

Hazel nut ice-cream

As almond ice-cream, substituting 180g (6oz or 1 cup) blanched and pounded hazel nuts for almonds.

Walnut ice-cream

Vanilla, coffee or chocolate ice-cream (pages 211, 212–13). 150g (5oz or $1\frac{2}{3}$ cups) peeled, ground walnuts.

Prepare ice-cream, adding the walnuts with the whipped cream.

Strawberry or raspberry ice-cream

Prepare ice-cream mixture as described and add the sieved pulp from 0·5kg (1lb or 2 cups) of fresh strawberries or raspberries and proceed as described.

(Redcurrants and other soft fruit can also be used for ice-cream.)

Coffee ice-cream

Add 120g (4oz or 9 tablespoons) freshly roasted coffee beans to the uncooked custard mixture (page 211).

Cook as described. When the custard thickens to the desired consistency, remove from heat and leave to infuse for two to three hours. Strain and freeze as described.

Ice-creams

Chocolate ice-cream

Dissolve 180g (6oz or 1½ cups) grated chocolate in the milk intended for ice-cream custard (see vanilla ice-cream). Make the custard as usual and freeze.

Avocado sorbet in lime or lemon cups

6 Servings

juice and shells of 4 limes (or lemons)
2 avocados
small pinch salt
1 teaspoon grated lime rind
240g (8oz or ⅔ cup) honey

You will only need six half lime shells for freezing and serving the sorbet, but an extra lime or two may be needed to make up the right amount of juice. Squeeze out the juice and strain, measuring out 100ml (4oz or ½ cup). Then take the squeezed halved limes, carefully pare away all pith and membranes to enlarge the cups, and cut a little slice off the end of each to make them stable. Peel and dice the avocados, put through a blender with salt, lime juice, grated lime rind, and honey. When the blended mixture is smooth, pour into refrigerator tray and freeze until just firm. Stir and return to refrigerator. Pile into lime cups and serve.

Ice-creams

Jaffa ice

6 Servings

6 large Jaffa oranges
240g (8oz or 1 cup) sugar

Slice off the top of the oranges, scoop out all pulp. Press out and keep the juice and the shells.

Put sugar to heat with two tablespoons water and simmer the syrup until it reaches thread degree. Test by tapping with a spoon. If the syrup forms a fibrous thread, it is ready. If you use a sugar thermometer, this degree is reached at 105°C (220°F).

Remove pan from heat and add orange juice. Return to heat and cook until the syrup reaches thread degree once more.

Freeze in ice-cream freezer. Tidy up the orange shells, carefully cutting away filaments. Fill with iced mixture, chill, and serve.

Orange and lemon sorbet in melon shell

4 Servings

1 melon shell
500g (1lb or 2 cups) sugar
150ml (6fl oz or ¾ cup) water
juice of 2 oranges and 2 lemons
2 egg whites

Save the melon shell when using the flesh for a fruit salad or other dessert (see recipe for mint and melon jelly, page 206).

Cut the top off the melon, remove seeds with a spoon, then carefully scoop out flesh without damaging the shell. Keep the shell in refrigerator. Boil sugar with water to make syrup. Add orange and lemon juice. Cool, chill in ice tray in refrigerator. When the mixture is almost set, stir it, put back in refrigerator, and leave until it begins to thicken.

Beat the egg whites until stiff. Add to sorbet mixture, stir, and chill until firm.

Fill melon shells with sorbet and keep in refrigerator until ready to serve.

Ice-creams

Chocolate praline pareve (non-dairy ice-cream)

This section includes many recipes for ice-creams made with eggs and cream, as well as water-ices, but it would not be complete without the mention of this Israeli invention of *pareve glidah* – ice-cream made without resorting to powders, or any other 'instant' products, yet not using any dairy products, which makes it acceptable at kosher meat meals.

Personally, I feel that a far superior non-dairy ice-cream can be made by using coconut cream (page 262) for the basic ice-cream custard. It has a finer flavour and texture and is much easier to make. Just substitute coconut cream for ordinary cream or milk and follow the recipe for the ice-cream of your choice.

Pareve glidah is based on best quality vegetable margarine, egg yolks, and sugar and can be flavoured with chocolate, coffee, chopped nuts or fruit.

The actual preparation is a matter of minutes, but you do need an efficient blender. Unlike most ice-creams made in a refrigerator freezer, *pareve glidah* must not be stirred after freezing.

8 Servings

120g (4oz or $\frac{1}{2}$ cups) cooking chocolate
5 yolks
120g (4oz or $\frac{1}{2}$ cup) sugar
90g (3oz or 1 cup) crushed, burnt almonds
360g (12oz or 1$\frac{1}{2}$ cups) margarine
250ml ($\frac{1}{2}$ pint or 1 cup) water
1 egg

Put chocolate to melt over simmering water.

Whisk yolks and sugar until light and fluffy. Put in a double saucepan with chocolate and almonds, keep over gently simmering water whisking vigorously for four to five minutes. Remove from heat. Put margarine in a blender and whisk incorporating water little by little.

When the mixture is well emulsified, add contents of double saucepan and egg and blend well. Pour into trays and freeze.

Cakes and biscuits

Decorative panel from a seventeenth century Italian Megillah
in the Jewish Museum, London

Slivovitz lemon cake with grape sauce

8 Servings

360g (12oz or $1\frac{1}{2}$ cups) butter
180g (6oz or $\frac{3}{4}$ cup) castor sugar
4 eggs
$\frac{1}{2}$ tablespoon lemon juice
100ml (4fl oz or $\frac{1}{2}$ cup) slivovitz (plum brandy)
180g (6oz or $1\frac{1}{2}$ cups) flour
1 teaspoon baking powder
90g (3oz or $\frac{2}{3}$ cup) icing sugar
pinch cinnamon
$\frac{3}{4}$ teaspoon cornflour
240g (8oz or 1 cup) seedless grapes

Preheat oven to 180°C (350°F or Gas Mark 3). Grease and lightly flour a 20-cm ($8\frac{1}{2}$-inch) ring mould.

Stir all but two tablespoons butter and castor sugar until creamy. Separate eggs, add yolks to butter and sugar, and whisk well. Add half the lemon juice and one and a half to two tablespoons slivovitz.

Sift flour and baking powder and stir into the butter and sugar mixture. Beat egg whites until stiff and gradually fold into the dough. Pour the dough into the prepared mould and bake in the oven for forty minutes. Start testing after thirty-five minutes, by inserting a wooden cocktail stick. If it comes out clean without any batter sticking to it, the cake is done.

Turn out on to a cooling rack, sprinkle with two tablespoons icing sugar, and leave to cool completely.

To make the sauce, put the remaining butter, icing sugar, lemon juice, slivovitz, and cinnamon into a saucepan. Heat gently and simmer on lowest possible heat for a few minutes just to amalgamate the ingredients. Dilute cornflour with a tablespoon of cold water, blend into sauce, simmer stirring until the sauce thickens. Add grapes, simmer for thirty seconds, and remove from heat.

To serve: cut the cake into portions and spoon the sauce over it.

Cakes and biscuits

Poppy seed roll

Dough
30g (1oz or 2 cakes) fresh yeast
90g (3oz or 6 tablespoons) sugar
250ml ($\frac{1}{2}$ pint or 1 cup) milk
120g (4oz or $\frac{1}{2}$ cup) melted margarine
480g (1lb or 4 cups) flour
pinch salt
3 beaten eggs

Filling
360g (12oz or 2$\frac{1}{4}$ cups) poppy seeds
250ml ($\frac{1}{2}$ pint or 1 cup) milk
3 tablespoons honey
2 tablespoons sugar
2 tablespoons chopped, candied peel
$\frac{1}{2}$ teaspoon vanilla flavouring
1 teaspoon powdered cinnamon
1 tablespoon melted margarine

Cream the yeast with half a tablespoon sugar in a basin. Warm the milk gently with the margarine until the margarine melts. Pour milk and margarine mixture on the yeast and blend well. Take care not to overheat the milk; it should be lukewarm.

Warm a mixing bowl big enough to take all dough ingredients and to allow for rising. Sift flour and salt into it, make a well in the centre, and pour in the yeast and milk mixture. Work in the flour from the sides and knead until you get a smooth dough.

Cover with a lightly floured cloth and leave to rise in a warm place until the dough doubles in bulk. This may take from one and a half to two hours. Sprinkle in remaining sugar and work in beaten eggs. Knead well and dough is ready for rolling out.

Prepare filling while the dough is rising, i.e. before you add sugar and eggs to it, to allow filling time to cool.

Rinse the poppy seeds with hot water, drain well (this is best done in a muslin bag), grind finely.

Cakes and biscuits

Bring the milk to the boil gently, with honey and sugar. Add poppy seeds, cook, stirring frequently, until the mixture becomes thick. Add candied peel, vanilla flavouring, and cinnamon, stir, and remove from heat. Leave to cool.

Roll out the dough on a floured board into a rectangle 5mm ($\frac{1}{4}$ inch) thick. Moisten the edges and spread the filling thickly over the rectangle of dough almost to the edges. Roll up lightly and seal the edges. Put the roll in a baking tin, greased with melted margarine, cover with a cloth, and leave again in a warm place to rise for another one and a half to two hours.

Preheat oven to 190°C (375°F or Gas Mark 4). Brush the top of the poppy seed roll with melted margarine and bake for about one hour.

If desired, mixed chopped dried fruit and/or chopped nuts may be added to the filling.

Plava cake

8 Servings

5 large eggs
300g (10oz or $1\frac{1}{4}$ cups) castor sugar
1 tablespoon lemon juice
180g (6oz or $1\frac{1}{2}$ cups) plain flour
butter or margarine
1–2 tablespoons extra sugar

Separate the egg yolks from the whites. Divide the sugar into two equal parts. Put one lot into a bowl with the egg yolks and whisk well until thick and white. Add lemon juice.

Whisk the egg whites until very stiff. Add remaining sugar and beat well until you have a firm meringue. Add this to the whisked yolks and sugar. Add the flour and mix well. Use a 24cm (9 inch) diameter cake tin with a loose bottom. Grease well with butter or margarine and sprinkle with sugar. Preheat oven to 175°C (350°F or Gas Mark 3). Spoon cake mixture into prepared tin, sprinkle the top with sugar.

Bake for sixty-five to seventy minutes. Allow the cake to cool before removing from tin.

Cakes and biscuits

Honey cake

120g (4oz or 1 cup) sifted flour
1 teaspoon baking powder
pinch salt
4 eggs
120g (4oz or ½ cup) sugar
200ml (8fl oz or 1 cup) yoghourt
½ tablespoon grated orange rind
1 tablespoon butter
360g (12oz or 1 cup) honey
250ml (½ pint or 1 cup) sour cream or whipped cream

Combine flour, baking powder, and salt. Beat eggs until fluffy, add sugar little by little, beating all the time. Add two tablespoons yoghourt and a pinch of orange rind and continue to whisk. Repeat this until all yoghourt and orange rind have been used up and the batter is smooth.

Grease a 20cm (8 inch) square baking tin. Preheat oven to 190°C (375°F or Gas Mark 4). Pour batter into tin and bake until done. Start testing after twenty-five to thirty minutes (see slivovitz lemon cake, page 217).

Remove from oven. Warm the honey to melt it and pour evenly over the cake. Leave to stand for three to four hours to let the cake become impregnated with honey, spooning over the cake any honey which runs off it.

Cut into portions, top each with sweetened sour cream or whipped cream.

Oriental rice cake

120g (4oz or 1 cup) sifted, self-raising flour
pinch salt
90g (3oz or 6 tablespoons) butter
120g (4oz or 10 tablespoons) ground rice
60g (2oz or 6 tablespoons) sultanas
60g (2oz or 6 tablespoons) seedless raisins
30g (1oz or 3 tablespoons) currants
1 tablespoon lemon rind
90g (3oz or 9 tablespoons) soft brown sugar

Cakes and biscuits

2 beaten eggs
100ml (4fl oz or ½ cup) milk

Preheat oven to 190°C (375°F or Gas Mark 4). Lightly grease a 17·5-cm (7-inch) cake tin.

Put flour in a mixing bowl, add salt, and rub in butter. Add all ingredients, except eggs and milk. Stir well.

Whisk eggs with milk, add to dry cake mixture, mix thoroughly, put into the prepared tin, and bake. Start testing for readiness after one hour.

Cheesecake

As a guaranteed topic for instant controversy this is only rivalled by gefilte fish and chopped liver. It is said that if there are twenty-five Jewish women present at some gathering, there will be twenty-five distinct points of view on the correct composition of the basic cheesecake!

3 tablespoons butter
60g (2oz or 1 cup) wholewheat biscuit crumbs
4 yolks
180g (6oz or ¾ cup) sugar
480g (1lb or 2 cups) cottage cheese
1 tablespoon flour
1 tablespoon semolina
100ml (4fl oz or ½ cup) sour cream
grated rind of 1 lemon
2 tablespoons chopped peel or
white raisins (optional)
4 egg whites

Butter a hinged flan (pie) tin. Mix biscuit crumbs with butter and use to line the tin, pressing down to make an even, well-packed crust. Preheat oven to 190°C (375°F or Gas Mark 4). Beat yolks with sugar until light and creamy. Rub cheese through a sieve, add to yolks with all the rest of the ingredients, except egg whites. Mix throughly.

Beat egg whites until very stiff, fold into the cheese mixture, put into the prepared flan tin, and bake for forty to forty-five minutes. Turn off heat and leave the cake in the oven for fifteen to twenty minutes before taking it out.

Cakes and biscuits

Prize pineapple cheesecake

This prize-winning recipe was sent in by Mrs Toby Veinish of Montreal Women's ORT:

23-cm (9-inch) spring form pan is recommended
480g (1lb or 2 cups) cream cheese
480g (1lb or 2 cups) cottage cheese
6 eggs
210g (7oz or 1½ cups) sifted icing sugar
1 small tin (180g or 6oz) evaporated milk
1½ teaspoons lemon juice
2 tablespoons flour
¼ teaspoon salt
13–14 Graham wafers

Topping
1 tin crushed pineapple
3 tablespoons icing sugar
2 tablespoons cornstarch

Beat cheese together. One by one, add eggs, then sugar, milk, lemon juice, flour, and salt, ensuring that each ingredient is well blended in before adding the next. Preheat oven to 150°C (300°F or Gas Mark 2).

Using Graham wafers make crust according to directions on box. Line pan with Graham wafer mixture. Pour in cheese mixture. Bake in the oven for about two hours until top is golden brown and firm. *Allow to cool with oven door open*. Refrigerate.

Cakes and biscuits

Drain the pineapple. Using 240ml (8oz or 1cm) of the juice, bring it to the boil with sugar. Cook until sugar dissolves. Blend cornflour with two to three tablespoons pineapple juice, blend into syrup, and continue to cook, stirring constantly until the syrup thickens. Add drained, crushed pineapple. Remove from heat, cool, and put on cold cheesecake.

Cheese strudel

strudel dough (page 188)
melted butter
120g (4oz or ½ cup) sugar
60g (2oz or ½ cup) fine breadcrumbs
pinch cinnamon
90g (3oz or 9 tablespoons) raisins
2 tablespoons butter
6 egg yolks
0·5 kilo (1lb or 2 cups) well-drained cream cheese
0·25 litre (½ pint or 1 cup) sour cream
6 egg whites, beaten stiff

Brush stretched strudel dough with melted butter, sprinkle with four tablespoons sugar, breadcrumbs, cinnamon, and raisins. Blend butter with egg yolks, add cheese, and mix well. Add sour cream, the rest of the sugar, and stir. Fold in egg whites and spread the mixture over strudel. Roll up, put on a greased baking sheet, and bake in a moderately hot oven, 205°C (400°F or Gas Mark 5) for twenty minutes, then lower to 175°C (350°F or Gas Mark 3) and bake for thirty-five to forty minutes, brushing with melted butter a couple of times during baking.

Other suggestions for strudel fillings
1   Sliced apples and chopped walnuts or almonds
2   Almonds blended with egg yolks and sugar
3   Mixed dried fruit and shredded coconut
4   Turkish delight, chopped, mixed with raisins and walnuts, and flavoured with nutmeg
5   Buttered breadcrumbs, hazelnuts, and stoned cherries

If the strudel is intended as a dessert for a meal including a meat or poultry dish, substitute margarine for butter throughout.

Cakes and biscuits

Haman's pockets

Purim is the Feast of Lots, which commemorates the escape of the Jews from total extermination planned by Haman in Persia. The symbolic foods for *Purim* include hamantaschen, or Haman's pockets, crisp pastries made of honey, poppy seeds, and almonds, and the *Purim* candy, or mohnlach (page 237).

Traditionally, these are triangular little cakes with a poppy seed filling, though both prune jelly and cream cheese fillings are also popular. They are good to eat and keep well:

Pastry
240g (8oz or 2 cups) flour
2 teaspoons baking powder
90g (3oz or 6 tablespoons) castor sugar
pinch salt
60g (2oz or ¼ cup) melted margarine or oil
1 teaspoon finely grated lemon rind
2 eggs

Filling
60g (2oz or 4 tablespoons) margarine
90g (3oz or ¼ cup) honey or golden syrup
240g (½lb) poppy seeds
30g (1oz or ¼ cup) chopped nuts
30g (1oz or ¼ cup) chopped, seedless raisins
1 tablespoon lemon juice
1 tablespoon melted margarine or oil for sealing edges
2 tablespoons melted honey

To make dough, sift flour, baking powder, sugar, and salt into a mixing bowl. Add melted margarine and lemon rind. Beat the eggs and work into the dough. Mix thoroughly and leave covered with a lightly floured cloth, while you prepare the filling.

Gently heat margarine, add honey and poppy seeds, cook for two to three minutes, stirring. Add nuts, raisins, and lemon juice. Cook, stirring for a couple of minutes, and remove from heat. Allow filling to cool.

Turn on the oven to 205°C (400°F or Gas Mark 5).

Cakes and biscuits

Roll out the pastry on a lightly floured board to a thickness of 5mm
($\frac{1}{4}$ inch). With a round pastry cutter cut out circles about 10cm (4 inches)
in diameter, brush the edges with melted margarine, put a spoonful of
filling on each circlet, pinch the edges together into a triangle, leaving a
small opening on the top so that the filling just shows.

Warm the two tablespoons of honey and brush the tops of the
hamantaschen with it. Bake in the oven for about twenty minutes until
golden brown.

Hamantaschen are also made with yeast dough (see recipe for poppy seed
roll, page 218). Proceed as described above, but after filling and brushing
the cakes with honey, leave them to stand in a warm place until the dough
rises and the cakes double in size, then bake as directed.

Cases baked 'blind'

Roll out tart pastry, line a flan tin, press down gently, to make it fit and
prevent formation of bubbles underneath, and crimp the edges. Prick the
bottom of the flan all over with a fork, cover with a circle of greaseproof
paper, cut to fit the bottom, and fill with dried beans or rice. Bake in a hot
oven 204°C (400°F or Gas Mark 6) for about thirty minutes or until the
flan case becomes lightly browned. (The beans can be stored and used
again and again for the same purpose.)

Cakes and biscuits

Russian doughnuts

The advantage of these doughnuts over the ring type doughnut is that instead of having a mere hole in the middle, these have a filling of delicious home-made jam:

To make two dozen doughnuts
30g (2oz or 2 cakes) yeast
0·25 litre ($\frac{1}{2}$ pint or $1\frac{1}{4}$ cups) lukewarm milk
120g (4oz or $\frac{1}{2}$ cup) castor sugar
60g (2oz or 4 tablespoons) butter or margarine
2 eggs
1 teaspoon salt
1 teaspoon vanilla
$\frac{1}{4}$ teaspoon nutmeg
480g (1lb or 4 cups) flour
jam or povidl (pages 277–84)
oil for deep frying
icing sugar
cinnamon

Mix yeast with milk and stir to dissolve. In a big mixing bowl blend castor sugar and butter until light and creamy. Stir in eggs. Add salt, vanilla, and nutmeg and beat well. Add flour and little by little work in milk with yeast.

Knead until the dough is smooth. Cover with a cloth and leave in a warm place to rise, which should take from two to two and a half hours.

Turn out on to a lightly floured board, knead lightly for five to six minutes. Divide dough into twenty-four pieces, roll each into a small ball, flatten, and put half a teaspoon of jam in the middle. Enclose the jam and reshape the dough into a ball again. Leave on a floured board for fifteen to twenty minutes.

Heat oil and deep fry doughnuts a few at a time, turning them once until golden brown all over. Drain on kitchen paper.

Mix icing sugar with cinnamon and dust the doughnuts with the mixture. Serve with lemon tea.

Cakes and biscuits

Meringue shells

4 stiffly beaten egg whites
240g ($\frac{1}{2}$lb or 1 cup) castor sugar
1 tablespoon lemon juice
extra castor sugar for dredging

Add sugar to beaten whites a tablespoonful at a time, whisking back into a stiff foam after each addition. Beat in lemon juice. Shape with two spoons dipped in cold water or, better still, using a forcing bag, pipe into small rounds or ovals on to a baking sheet lined with oiled kitchen paper. Dredge with castor sugar and dry on the lowest shelf of a very slow oven 135°C (275°F or Gas Mark 1) for one to one and a quarter hours until the meringues are thoroughly dried and creamy in colour.

If you wish to keep the meringues white, reduce heat after fifty to sixty minutes to 120°C (250°F or Gas Mark $\frac{1}{2}$) and continue to dry very, very slowly. When meringues have to be kept, slow down the drying process. If dried in a gas oven, with the tap set at its lowest and the oven door left ajar, the meringues can be left up to ten to twelve hours. This greatly enhances both their crispness and keeping qualities. After taking out of the oven, press base of each lightly to make a little hollow. Store in an air-tight tin.

Italian meringue zephirs

Bake small meringues, sandwich together with rum-flavoured vanilla ice-cream, arrange in a pyramid, chill, and serve with chocolate-flavoured zabaione (page 204).

Canadian meringues

Small almond-flavoured biscuit-coloured meringues, with a blanched almond trapped in each one.

Meringue chantilly

Bake meringues as described and sandwich together with sweetened, whipped cream.

Cakes and biscuits

Date meringue tart

6 Servings

tart pastry (page 191)
120g (4oz or $\frac{1}{2}$ cup) large, stoned dates
1 tablespoon brandy
3 egg whites
60g (2oz or $\frac{2}{3}$ cup) ground almonds
120g (4oz or $\frac{1}{2}$ cup) castor sugar

Line a 20-cm (8-inch) tart tin with pastry. Cut each date into four, sprinkle with brandy, and leave to macerate for twenty minutes, then drain. Beat the egg whites to a stiff froth and add almonds, sugar, and dates. Fill the tart shell with the mixture, bake in a hot oven 235°C (450°F or Gas Mark 7) for twenty-five to thirty minutes, sprinkle with castor sugar, and serve hot.

Iced walnut gateau

6 Servings

360g (12oz or 3 cups) walnuts
6 egg yolks
300g (10oz or $1\frac{1}{4}$ cups) sugar
1 teaspoon butter
6 stiffly beaten whites of egg
vanilla custard cream (pages 211 and 265)

Grind the nuts into coarse flour, mix three quarters of it with yolks. Beat until the mixture is well blended. Add sugar and repeat beating to amalgamate the ingredients.

Preheat oven to 220°C (400°F or Gas Mark 5). Butter two layer cake tins. Fold stiffly beaten egg whites into the walnut mixture, lifting gently to keep it as light as possible. Divide the gateau mixture equally between the two tins and bake for thirty minutes. Cool before removing from tins.

Mix reserved ground walnuts with vanilla custard cream to make filling. Spread filling on one of the cakes and set the other on top, to make a two-tier sandwich. Chill for several hours before serving.

Cakes and biscuits

Honey and hazelnut cake

6 Servings

a little butter
5 eggs
120g (4oz or $\frac{1}{3}$ cup) honey
60g (2oz or $\frac{2}{3}$ cup) ground hazelnut
2 tablespoons sugar
75g (2$\frac{1}{2}$oz or $\frac{3}{4}$ cup) sifted cake flour
4 tablespoons double cream

Preheat oven to 150°C (300°F or Gas Mark 2). Butter the cake tin. Separate eggs. Mix yolks with honey, stirring with a wooden spoon, blend thoroughly.

Pound hazelnuts and sugar in a mortar or put through a grinder to reduce to powder. Little by little stir flour into the honey and yolk mixture. Equally gradually add hazelnuts, stir well. Blend in cream.

Beat the whites until stiff, fold into the cake mixture, gently lifting with a palate knife as you mix. Pour into prepared cake tin, bake for thirty minutes. Cool before removing from tin.

Oogiot sumsum (sesame biscuits)

240g (8oz or 2$\frac{1}{4}$ cups) flour
1 teaspoon salt
90g (3oz or 9 tablespoons) toasted sesame seeds
180g (6oz or $\frac{3}{4}$ cup) shortening
50ml (2floz or 4 tablespoons) strained orange juice

Combine flour, salt, and sesame seeds in a mixing bowl. Add shortening. First cut it into the flour, then rub lightly with fingertips until the mixture begins to look like fine breadcrumbs. Little by little mix in orange juice and knead lightly. Roll out pastry to a thickness of 5mm ($\frac{1}{4}$ inch).

Cut into oblongs 6cm (2 inches) long and 2·5cm (1 inch) wide. Put the cut biscuits on ungreased baking sheet. Bake in a moderately hot oven, preheated to 205°C (400°F or Gas Mark 5) for about fifteen minutes, until the biscuits are golden brown. Take off baking sheet, and leave on a wire rack to cool.

Cakes and biscuits

Hazelnut fingers

360g (12oz or 1½ cups) sugar
90g (3oz or 1 cup) ground hazelnuts
2 eggs
1½ tablespoons sherry
180g (6oz or 1¾ cups) pastry flour
60g (2oz or 4 tablespoons) melted butter
90g (3oz or ½ cup) semi-sweet chocolate

Put sugar and hazelnuts into a bowl, add eggs and sherry, and mix well.
Add flour, then stir in butter, which should be melted but not hot. Tear
off small pieces of pastry, roll into little fingers.

Preheat oven to 175°C (350°F or Gas Mark 3).

Lightly grease a baking sheet, put hazelnut fingers on it, and bake for
about fifteen minutes. Remove and leave on a rack to cool. Melt
chocolate in a bowl over hot water. Dip one end of each finger in it and
stand upside down to dry.

Walnut macaroons

This recipe originates in Ukraine. Unlike other macaroons the mixture for
these is first cooked in a double saucepan, then baked.

2 egg whites
180g (6oz or ¾ cup) sugar
½ tablespoon lemon juice
240g (8oz or 2 cups) chopped walnuts
3 tablespoons shelled pine kernels

Put egg whites with sugar and lemon juice in the top of a double saucepan
and start cooking over simmering water, whisking all the time. Cook in this
manner for ten minutes. Add walnuts, stir well, cook for five minutes, and
remove.

Preheat oven to 175°C (350°F or Gas Mark 3). Lightly grease a baking
sheet. Take a spoonful of the walnut mixture at a time and drop onto
baking sheet without allowing the macaroons to touch. Stud each with a
few pine kernels and bake until the macaroons set and turn pale golden.

Cakes and biscuits

Iraqi peppery macaroons

240g (8oz or 2 cups) plain flour
1 teaspoon baking powder
240g (8oz or 1 cup) sugar
pinch freshly grated black pepper
1 teaspoon ground cinnamon
½ teaspoon ground cloves
½ teaspoon ground nutmeg
4 tablespoons candied peel
1 teaspoon grated lemon rind
3 eggs
1–2 tablespoons butter
icing sugar

Combine flour, baking powder, sugar, pepper, cinnamon, cloves, and nutmeg in a mixing bowl.

Chop candied peel and add to dry ingredients together with lemon rind. Beat eggs, put in mixing bowl, and mix well. Grease a baking sheet with butter and rub some in the palms of your hands. Pinch off pieces of dough, roll into balls the size of a walnut, place on baking sheet, and leave to dry overnight.

Preheat oven to 150°C (300°F or Gas Mark 2). Bake the macaroons for twenty-five to thirty minutes, until they brown. Sprinkle with icing sugar, cool, and store in an air-tight tin for ten to fifteen days for the macaroons to mellow.

Sweetmeats, candies, and nibblers

Figure based on an eighteenth century Derby Ware Jewish Pedlar
in the Jewish Museum, London

Sweetmeats, candies, and nibblers

Almond crunch

Many of the sweetmeats included in this section are intended for various religious festivals, when it is important to be sure that all the ingredients used are in accordance with the laws of purity. That is why they are made at home, rather than bought in shops.

480g (1lb or 2½ cups) blanched almonds
240g (8oz or ⅔ cups) honey
240g (8oz or 1 cup) castor sugar
1 teaspoon ground cinnamon

Make sure the almonds are thoroughly dry. In a heavy skillet gently heat honey and sugar. Add almonds, sprinkle in cinnamon, and cook on low heat until the almonds turn a pale brown and the sugar reaches the hard ball degree (page 237). Stir, remove from heat, spread out to cool in an even layer, cut into uniform square pieces, and store in air-tight tins.

Coconut delight

These are typically oriental sweetmeats, served as a special dinner dessert or as something for the ladies to nibble at tea-time. In the Middle East they are often decorated with blanched slivered almonds, crushed cardamom seeds, silver balls, silver hundreds and thousands; in India, for a festive occasion, they are wrapped in silver leaf:

0·75 litre (1½ pints or 3¼ cups) milk
120g (4oz or 1¼ cups) finely grated coconut
2–3 tablespoons shredded coconut
120g (8oz or ½ cup) sugar
butter
nutmeg
edible silver leaf (optional)

Slowly bring the milk to the boil, add both kinds of coconut, and simmer for twenty-five to thirty minutes. Add sugar and continue to simmer until all surplus moisture is evaporated and the mixture is thick. Spread it evenly in a lightly buttered shallow dish, sprinkle with freshly grated nutmeg, and leave until cold. Cut into lozenges and cover with a film of silver leaf.

Sweetmeats, candies, and nibblers

Spiced almonds

This is an Iraqi Jewish recipe. What makes these almonds different is the blend of sweetness and spiciness. The traditional Iraqi recipe calls for greatly increased amount of chilli:

240g (8oz or 1¼ cups) icing sugar
2½ tablespoons cornflour
1 teaspoon cinnamon
¼ teaspoon ground cloves
¼ teaspoon ground allspice
¼ teaspoon ground chilli
½ teaspoon salt
2 egg whites
3 tablespoons water
375g (12oz or 2 cups) blanched almonds

Combine sugar, cornflour, all the spices, and salt. Beat egg whites with water. Heat oven to 120°C (250°F or Gas Mark ½). Dip a few almonds at a time in egg white and roll in spiced sugar making sure it adheres in an even coating.

Put almonds on a baking sheet without allowing them to touch, bake for one and a half to one and three-quarter hours. When cold, put in air-tight tin until required.

Dates stuffed with almond paste

480g (1lb or 2 cups) wiped, pitted dates
240g (8oz or 1⅓ cups) shelled almonds
240g (8oz or 1 cup) castor sugar
135g (4½oz or 1 cup) icing sugar
1 tablespoon vanilla sugar
1 raw egg yolk
1 tablespoon Marie Brizard or other liqueur
a few drops colouring matter (optional)

Wipe the dates, slit with a knife down one side, and remove the pit. Blanch the almonds, i.e. scald them with boiling water and slip off the skins. Dry on a cloth.

Sweetmeats, candies, and nibblers

Mince the almonds with castor sugar, pound in a mortar or pass through a blender, to make a smooth paste.

Blend the yolk with half the icing sugar and the vanilla sugar, stirring well until creamy. (By hand this operation takes fifteen minutes.) Add liqueur, stir well, and blend this cream into the almond paste. Add colouring, if desired.

Using a little of the paste at a time, roll into pellets about twice the size of the pits, and stuff the dates. Roll in remaining icing sugar and decorate with a pattern traced with a knife.

Kirsch or rum are also excellent as flavouring for the almond paste.

Loukoum (Turkish delight)

0·75 kilo (1½lb or 3 cups) castor sugar
0·5 litre (1 pint or 1 cup) water
4 tablespoons cornflour
6 tablespoons white grape juice
1 teaspoon cream of tartar
1 tablespoon rose-water
3 tablespoons shelled pistachio nuts
a few drops cochineal
1 tablespoon almond oil
90g (3oz or 1 cup) ground coconut
120g (4oz or $\frac{7}{8}$ cup) icing sugar

Put castor sugar and water in a pan and slowly bring to the boil, then simmer gently until the sugar is dissolved.

Dilute cornflour with grape juice and gradually blend into the syrup. Add cream of tartar and continue to cook slowly, stirring all the time, until the mixture thickens. Remove from heat, add rose-water and pistachio nuts. Divide the mixture in two; leave one half plain and colour the second with a few drops of cochineal.

Grease a couple of shallow tins with almond oil. Pour the white mixture into one tin and the pink into the other. Leave to set and cool completely.

With a sharp knife cut into squares. Dip white loukoum in ground coconut, making it adhere on all sides. Roll the pink loukoum in icing sugar.

Sweetmeats, candies, and nibblers

Mebos (South African sugared apricots)

480g (1lb or 3 cups) dried apricots
480g (1lb or 2 cups) sugar
¼ teaspoon salt
icing sugar

Soak the apricots overnight. The next morning, strain, mince, and add sugar. Stir over heat until sugar melts. Add salt and continue to cook until the mixture reaches setting point.

Test by dropping a little of the mixture into a glass of cold water. As soon as it sets in the water, it is ready.

Spread the apricot mixture on a sugared board, flattened to a thickness of 1cm (½ inch). Cut into desired shapes and sprinkle with icing sugar.

Quince paste squares

This preserve is served as a sweetmeat at the end of a meal throughout many of the countries of the Middle East:

1kg (2lb) quinces
water
1kg (2lb or 4 cups) sugar
juice of 1 lemon
2–3 tablespoons orange-flower water
90g (3oz or ½ cup) blanched almonds or pistachio nuts
½ teaspoon almond oil
icing sugar

Rub the quinces with a wet towel to clean, put in a large saucepan, cover with cold water, bring to the boil, cover, and simmer for forty-five to fifty minutes or until tender. Drain, peel, and dice or grate. Weigh the quince pulp and add equal amount of sugar. Mix well. Add lemon juice and orange-flower water and stir over steady heat until sugar is dissolved. Then boil fast to evaporate moisture.

Stir in almonds or pistachio nuts, cook until the mixture turns into a paste. Turn out into a shallow tin, lightly greased with almond oil, smooth the top, and chill. Cut into squares, dip in icing sugar, and arrange on a dish.

Sweetmeats, candies, and nibblers

Purim candy

360g (12oz or 1 cup) honey
360g (12oz or 2¼ cups) poppy seeds
1 tablespoon lemon juice
180g (6oz or 1 cup) blanched almonds

Heat honey until it melts, add poppy seeds and lemon juice, and slowly bring to the boil. Add almonds and, stirring from time to time, continue to cook until the syrupy mixture reaches the soft ball stage. To test, drop a spoonful into a cup of cold water. The right degree is reached if the mixture has a consistency which can be moulded into a soft ball with the fingers.

Professional confectioners use a saccharometer and the soft ball is registered at 110°C to 116°C (230°F to 240°F). (Hard ball at 119–122°C or 246–252°F.) Remove from heat and continue to stir for a few minutes. Spread the mixture in an even layer (1cm or ½ inch thick) on a moistened slab or board, cut into diamond shapes, and leave to harden. Store in air-tight jars or tins.
For complete success in making this sweetmeat, it is essential to cook the syrup to the right degree, and to make sure that the almonds are thoroughly dry before they are added to honey and poppy seeds.

Sweetmeats, candies, and nibblers

Moroccan candied chestnuts

Good edible chestnuts flourish in the Mediterranean region and are used in many ways, from soups to desserts. They are eaten raw, boiled, steamed, grilled, and roasted. Chestnuts have a very high food value and innumerable ways of preserving them have been evolved.

There is a good chestnut jam (page 284), but this recipe is perhaps the most satisfying of all. All you need to turn them into marrons glacés is to wrap them in metal foil.

1kg (2lb) chestnuts
1kg (2lb or 4 cups) castor sugar
1 litre (1 quart) water
1 vanilla bean
1 stick cinnamon

Score the chestnuts, bring to the boil, simmer for thirty minutes, remove shell and inner skin as described in recipe for chestnut jam (page 284), and put in a bowl.

Warm sugar, heat gently with water, vanilla, and cinnamon. Simmer and stir to dissolve sugar completely. Pour syrup over chestnuts, cover, and leave overnight.

On the following day, drain off syrup into a pan, bring to the boil, and remove vanilla bean (which can be washed, dried, and used again). Discard cinnamon.

Put chestnuts in a preserving pan, pour syrup over them, and leave to stand for four hours. Place an asbestos mat under the pan, heat gently, and simmer on lowest possible heat for two hours without allowing syrup to boil. Remove chestnuts carefully with a perforated spoon, letting the syrup drip off into the pan, and put nuts in jars.

Reheat syrup and boil it down to concentrate and thicken. Pour over chestnuts, allow to cool in jars, and seal.

Leave for three to four weeks. Drain chestnuts carefully, without breaking them. Bring syrup to the boil, put chestnuts into it, remove from heat, and leave to complete the candying process for fifteen minutes. Drain chestnuts, place on cake rack to dry off, and they are ready for eating or to be given away as treats.

Sweetmeats, candies, and nibblers

The recipe sounds more laborious than it is. After all, the three to four week period while they are proving requires no effort and if you have a well bearing tree and your family is sick and tired of chestnut purée, you've got to do something with them!

Salted pumpkin seeds

The Israelis, in common with other Middle Eastern nations, as well as rural Jewish communities from Eastern Europe, are great nibblers of things sweet and savoury. Poverty has led to great ingenuity in inventing dainties out of the cheapest possible ingredients. Carrots are turned into highly palatable fudge, melon rind makes an excellent preserve.

Chick-peas and seeds of all kinds, from pumpkin and water melon to sunflower, are salted and served much as salted peanuts are at cocktail parties.

Nibbling seeds in many countries at certain seasons amounts almost to a habit forming mania, rather like chewing gum in America, with 'addicts' in all strata of the population. They seem to supply both something to nibble and a soothing occupation. Like peanuts, these salted seeds are also powerful thirst provokers.

In the Orient melon seeds are not only dried but also tinted with edible vegetable dyes for festive occasions. In Russian villages local beauty spots, where relaxation was taken, were easy to find – an unbroken trail of sunflower seed husks would lead you to them.

There are great experts at seed nibbling, who can split them and extract the kernels with impressive speed and flourish.

500g (1lb) washed pumpkin seeds
1 tablespoon salt
water

Put seeds in a pan, add salt and enough water to cover. Bring to the boil, simmer for one hour, and drain thoroughly.

Spread seeds in a roasting dish and put in the oven preheated to 135°C (275°F or Gas Mark 1) to dry out, stirring from time to time. When the seeds are dry, remove and store in air-tight tin.

Sweetmeats, candies, and nibblers

Salted chick-peas

These are easy to make and provide an acceptable alternative to salted peanuts:

Soak chick-peas overnight, boil until tender, drain, spread in a shallow dish, season liberally with salt, cool, and serve.

Copra samosas (coconut samosas)

This recipe is linked in my memory with an unforgettable incident. The dish was cooked for me in India by the mother of a photographer who was doing illustrations for a book I was writing.

I was stunned by the bareness of her kitchen. There was nothing there to show it was a kitchen: no shelves, no sink, no working surfaces, no table, no cooker. The old lady was squatting on her haunches (no chair), arranging a heap of bricks into a stove. To her they represented the acme of convenience.

Her delight with the bricks was pathetic and she felt she was very lucky to have them.

'Do you realize', said she, with an air of making a discovery of the century, 'that bricks are all of the same size and shape? This makes them fit marvellously one on top of another'. There was no denying; they did. And, as she justly pointed out, it wouldn't be nearly so easy to construct a stove out of a heap of any old stones, the way her neighbours had to do.

In no time she produced an excellent four-course meal. Her samosas were delicious. Although I had a recipe, I asked for hers, because by now she had a place in my heart and I wanted to tell her story.

When it came to quantities, she said she didn't hold with measuring. If I wanted such precise details, I should ask her daughter, who, being a modern young woman, went in for this new-fangled idea of measuring ingredients. The next evening, I met her daughter. She believed in measuring because 'that way you always get the same results'. I asked to see her kitchen and was completely unprepared to find it as bare as her mother's, without a hint of any equipment, which in the poorest kitchen in a Western slum would be taken for granted.

Sweetmeats, candies, and nibblers

It was a heart-breaking and humbling experience. This pretty young woman's pride and joy was an old petrol drum, placed on its side, lined with bricks, with two holes cut out to make *two* burners. Now, that was what she called a stove! Could I not appreciate its obvious advantages? Why, her poor mother could only cook one dish at a time. 'She has to wrap them up to keep them warm while she cooks the next one. I can cook two dishes at once.' More, if she put a bamboo lattice on top of the saucepans.

Swallowing hard, I asked about the recipe. How much flour and milk did she use. I shall never forget her reply: 'A cigarette tin of flour to a cigarette tin lid of milk . . .' That was her only measuring device, much envied by her friends, who would walk a couple of miles to borrow it for special occasions. Now that cigarettes are sold in utterly useless plastic wrappers, cigarette tins are at a premium.

These are made in the same ways as savoury samosas (pages 126–7) but the pastry is filled with a sweet filling and these samosas are served as sweetmeats. One of the favourite fillings is freshly made mint chutney (page 264):

dough for samosas (page 126)
syrup for jalebis (page 242)
slivered pistachio nuts
480g (1lb or 6 cups) shredded coconut
6 crushed cardamom seeds
90g (3oz or 1 cup) ground almonds
60g (2oz or 6 tablespoons) raisins
120g (4oz or ½ cup) sugar
a few tablespoons milk
ghee or oil for deep frying

Prepare the dough as described. Make the syrup and keep warm in a pan of hot water. Combine coconut, cardamom, almonds, raisins, and sugar. Mix well, bind with a little milk.

Roll out the dough and make the samosas as described (pages 126–7), putting a teaspoon of coconut filling in each. Deep fry, drain, dip each samosa in syrup, decorate with a sprinkling of pistachio slivers, and arrange on a dish.

Sweetmeats, candies, and nibblers

Jalebis

Jalebis are sometimes sprinkled with ground pistachio nuts, after soaking in syrup, and can be served either hot or cold. Jalebi powder is used as colouring and can be bought in shops specializing in Indian ingredients. If not available, use saffron or turmeric.

I recall friends of mine being surprised at the inclusion of jalebi among Jewish recipes. To begin with, I felt the fact that the recipe reached me through an Indian ORT member was good enough. Later I came across a fascinating description of a mural inside the tomb of Rameses III, which must have been one of the earliest strip recipes in existence, for it depicts stage by stage the preparation of *jalebies*: the pouring of batter into hot fat and twirling it into a spiral, draining it, and plunging it to be bathed in honey. The most astonishing thing of all that jalebi, commonly found not only in India but on the menus of restaurants in London, was known to the Jews in ancient Middle East as *zalebi*.

180g (6oz or $1\frac{1}{2}$ cups) flour
$\frac{3}{4}$ tablespoon baking powder
3 tablespoons curds or yoghourt
water
0·5kg (1lb or 2 cups) sugar
1 teaspoon jalebi powder
a few drops rose or jasmine essence
ghee or oil for deep frying

Sift the flour and baking powder into a bowl, gradually dilute by adding 2·5dl ($\frac{1}{2}$ pint or 1 cup) warm water, stir in curds, and leave the batter in a warm place to ferment overnight.

Dissolve sugar in 1dl ($\frac{1}{4}$ pint or $\frac{1}{2}$ cup) water, add jalebi colouring and flower essence, boil until the syrup thickens, remove from heat, and keep warm over hot water. Heat ghee or oil until it begins to bubble.

Beat the batter, if necessary add more flour or water to make sure the batter has the consistency of double cream.

Pour the batter into the boiling ghee through a funnel, moving the funnel in such a way as to form rings within rings. As soon as one circle is done, close the funnel with your finger, and repeat the pouring to make the next jalebi.

Sweetmeats, candies, and nibblers

Fry only a few at a time, to prevent sticking, until golden brown on both sides. Remove with a perforated spoon, drain off fat and plunge into warm syrup. Leave in the syrup for fifteen minutes to allow the jalebis to absorb it.

Drain and arrange on a shallow dish.

Tayglach

This is a favourite confection, made of dough, boiled in ginger-flavoured honey or golden syrup, and rolled in chopped nuts or desiccated coconut. The quantities given in this recipe should produce about three dozen tayglach:

240g (8oz or 2 cups) self-raising flour
small pinch salt
2 teaspoons ground ginger
2 large eggs
0·5kg (1lb or 1½ cups) honey
240g (8oz or 2 cups) chopped almonds (or other nuts)

Sift the flour with salt and half a teaspoon ginger. Beat the eggs lightly and add to flour, mix and knead dough until smooth. Roll into thin rolls 1cm (½ inch) in diameter and cut into 1-cm (½-inch) pieces.

Melt honey with remaining one and a half teaspoons ginger and bring to the boil. Drop the pieces of dough into boiling honey, a few at a time, no more than a dozen. As soon as boiling is re-established, reduce heat and boil gently for twenty-five to thirty minutes. The tayglach should be a pale biscuit colour. Do not stir during cooking

Moisten a board, sprinkle with chopped nuts. Remove tayglach from honey with a perforated spoon, put on the board, and spread evenly with a wet wooden spoon.

Cool and cut into uniform pieces or shape into little pyramids and leave to dry.

Sweetmeats, candies, and nibblers

Baklava

Properly made, this is a delicious sweet. It is of Greek origin but it is also
common to Turkey, Iran, Egypt, and other Middle Eastern countries and
very popular among Mediterranean Jewish communities. It is made of filo
pastry (page 189), which is similar to stretched strudel dough (page 188),
but must be absolutely tissue-paper thin. A light dusting with cornflour
helps during stretching. Recipes advocating the use of ordinary puff
pastry for baklava should be ignored.

If you can manage a good stretched dough for strudel, you can safely tackle
filo. If you can't face the work of stretching it tissue-paper thin, buy it
ready made from a Greek shop.

It is well worth making baklava at home, not only because you can control
the ingredients, but because it is at its best eaten the day after it is made –
a far cry from the cardboard concoctions which may have languished for a
week on a restaurant dessert trolley.

Walnuts, almonds, and pine kernels, or any combination of these are
used in the filling.

In Iran, apricots are used for the syrup and fresh apricots are served with
baklava, which is excellent. My favourite, however, is the classical
baklava, with chopped nuts sprinkled between layers of filo and saturated
in a syrup made of honey, sugar, and lemon juice.

To make two dozen baklava pieces
filo dough (page 189)
360g (12oz or 1½ cups) unsalted butter or margarine

Filling
360g (12oz or 3 cups) chopped walnuts
180g (6oz or ¾ cup) sugar

Syrup
360g (12oz or 1 cup) honey
360g (12oz or 1½ cups) sugar
300ml (12fl oz or 1½ cups) water
juice and rind of 1 lemon
2 sticks cinnamon

Have the dough ready, rolled out, and stretched into tissue paper thin
sheets. Gently melt butter. Mix walnuts and sugar for filling.

Sweetmeats, candies, and nibblers

Heat oven to 190°C (375°C or Gas Mark 4). Brush a 20cm (8 inch) square baking tin with butter, cut filo dough to match. Put one sheet of dough to line the bottom of the tin, brush generously with butter, cover with another sheet of filo, sprinkle with a layer of nut and sugar mixture. Continue in this way, putting in layers of filo, brushing with butter and sprinkling with filling until all is used up. Finish with a sheet of filo on top and tuck in the ends to enclose all the filling.

Brush this top layer of dough with plenty of butter. With a sharp knife, score the top into diamond shapes, to determine the size of your baklava pieces. Bake in the oven for forty to forty-five minutes until golden brown and crisp.

To make syrup, boil honey, sugar, and water with lemon juice and cinnamon for five minutes. Remove lemon rind and cinnamon sticks. Take baking tin out of oven, drain off any surplus fat, pour hot syrup over baklava, and leave until cold. Cut into pieces along scored lines, leave in the syrup overnight, or until ready to serve.

Start making syrup about ten minutes before baklava is baked. It is important to have the syrup freshly made and hot.

Sauces, dips,
dressings

Panel on bowl from a nineteenth century Italian Passover Plate
in the Jewish Museum, London

Gravy

To retain the full flavour of the bird and ensure the quality of natural gravy – and no commercial substitute can be considered as anything but a travesty – extract all the goodness from your roasting or dripping pan.

Pour off the excess fat, but do not skim off the fat completely. Dilute the pan juices immediately, using simple clear stock, giblet stock, wine or water.

If you like your gravy slightly thickened, after pouring off the fat, sprinkle in a dessertspoon of flour, cook it in the pan, stirring to brown and cook the flour, then dilute as described, simmer for two to three minutes, and serve.

Always save the fat you pour off. It is excellent for cooking and when it sets the jelly, which forms at the bottom of the jar, is valuable glaze for the bird or for strengthening sauces, soups, aspics, etc.

Mushroom sauce for fish

120g (4oz or $\frac{1}{2}$ cup) sliced mushrooms
3 tablespoons butter
2 tablespoons flour
2·5dl ($\frac{1}{2}$ pint or 1 cup) fish stock or fumet (page 259)
1dl (1 gill or $\frac{1}{2}$ cup) cream
2 tablespoons dry white wine
salt and pepper
1 teaspoon chopped dill (or parsley)

Toss the mushrooms in one tablespoon butter. Melt the rest of the butter, blend in flour, fry this *roux* lightly, without allowing it to colour. Dilute gradually with fish stock, stirring constantly to ensure smoothness. Simmer for seven to eight minutes. Add mushrooms with their pan juices, stir, add cream, heat almost to boiling point, pour in wine, season to taste, sprinkle with dill, simmer without boiling for two minutes, and serve.

To make mushroom sauce for a meat dish, omit cream, substitute margarine for butter, and use beef or chicken stock instead of fish stock.

Sauces, dips, dressings

White sauce for meatless dishes

60g (2oz or $\frac{1}{2}$ cup) butter
60g (2oz or $\frac{1}{4}$ cup) flour
0·5 litre (1 pint or 2 cups) milk (or a mixture of milk and vegetable stock)
salt and pepper

Choose a saucepan which will hold all the ingredients comfortably. Melt the butter over low heat, stir in flour, and cook gently for three minutes, stirring all the time and without allowing the *roux* to colour, if you want your white sauce to be white. Remove from heat, blend in half the liquid, return to heat, and cook, stirring vigorously. When the sauce thickens, add the rest of the liquid. Continue to simmer, and beat the sauce until the desired consistency is reached. Season, stir, and use at once.

White sauce for meat dishes

60g (2oz or $\frac{1}{4}$ cup) chicken fat or margarine
60g (2oz or $\frac{1}{4}$ cup) flour
0·5 litre (1 pint or 2 cups) white stock
salt and pepper

Melt the fat over low heat, stir in flour, and cook gently for three minutes, stirring all the time and without allowing the *roux* to colour. Remove from heat, blend in half the liquid, return to heat, and cook, stirring vigorously. When the sauce thickens, add the rest of the liquid. Continue to simmer, and beat the sauce until the desired consistency is reached. Season, stir, and use at once.

Bread sauce for roast chicken or turkey

1 onion
2 cloves
0·25 litre ($\frac{1}{2}$ pint or 1$\frac{1}{4}$ cups) good stock
pinch mace
60g (2oz or $\frac{1}{2}$ cup) breadcrumbs
salt and pepper
pinch cayenne
2 tablespoons softened margarine

Sauces, dips, dressings

Peel the onion, stick cloves into it, cover with stock, bring to the boil, and simmer gently for twenty-five to thirty minutes.

Remove onion, put breadcrumbs into flavoured stock, add remaining ingredients, except margarine, simmer gently for fifteen to twenty minutes, by which time the sauce will be quite thick. Blend in margarine, adding it in small pieces, transfer to heated sauce-boat, and serve.

Apple sauce

1kg (2lb or 6 medium-sized) cooking apples
60g (2oz or 4 tablespoons) margarine
100ml (4fl oz or ½ cup) water
½ teaspoon lemon rind
few drops lemon juice

Peel, core, and slice the apples. Melt margarine in a pan, add apples, cook gently, then add water and simmer until apples are quite soft. Add lemon rind and a dash of lemon juice, rub through a sieve for perfect smoothness, reheat if necessary, and serve.

When apple sauce is intended to accompany rich meats like goose or duck, sugar is best left out, to preserve the essential sharpness of the sauce.

Gooseberry sauce

480g (1lb or 2 cups) gooseberries
100ml (4fl oz or ½ cup) water
1–1½ tablespoons margarine
3 tablespoons sugar
pinch cinnamon

Top and tail the gooseberries, put in a pan with the water, and simmer until soft. Rub through a sieve or pass through a blender or food mill.

Blend in margarine, adding it in small pieces and stirring well. Add sugar and cinnamon, cook stirring over low heat for a couple of minutes to amalgamate.

Like apple sauce, this can be served hot or cold.

Sauces, dips, dressings

Cranberry sauce for turkey

500g (1lb or 4 cups) cranberries
100ml (4fl oz or $\frac{1}{2}$ cup) water
105g (3$\frac{1}{2}$oz or 7 tablespoons) sugar, or to taste

Cook the cranberries in water, pressing with a spoon to make the juices
flow, until the fruit is soft. Rub through a sieve, return to pan, add sugar,
stir until the sugar dissolves, reheat, and serve.

Mayonnaise

2 egg yolks
0·25 litre ($\frac{1}{2}$ pint or 1 cup) olive oil
$\frac{1}{2}$ teaspoon salt
$\frac{1}{4}$ teaspoon dry mustard
freshly ground black pepper
about 2 dessertspoons vinegar, or lemon juice

Place yolks, seasonings, and one dessertspoon of vinegar (or lemon juice)
in a basin. Whisk well together with a fork. Change to a metal spoon and
start stirring. Slowly add the oil. It is unnecessary to add it drop by drop,
approximate teaspoons will work and help to do the job more quickly.
Keep on stirring. It should take only about four minutes to blend in all the
oil. Adjust seasoning and vinegar to taste.

Red wine sauce (rotev yayin)

1 teaspoon potato flour
100ml (4fl oz or $\frac{1}{2}$ cup) water
100ml (4fl oz or $\frac{1}{2}$ cup) sweet red wine
120g (4oz or $\frac{1}{2}$ cup) sugar
2 raw yolks
lemon juice

Dilute potato flour in two tablespoons cold water. Put the rest of the
water, red wine, and sugar in a pan and gently bring to the boil. Stir to
make sure sugar is completely dissolved. Blend in diluted potato flour.
Have a double saucepan ready on the simmer. Drop the yolks into it,
little by little add the wine sauce to them, whisking all the time. Simmer
in a double saucepan (or *bain-marie*) until the liaison thickens the sauce.

Sauces, dips, dressings

Rum sauce (rotev rom)

2 raw yolks
3 tablespoons sugar
100ml (4fl oz or ½ cup) water
strained juice of 1 lemon
1 wineglass rum

Whisk yolks with sugar, gradually dilute with water, stir well, and pour the mixture into a double saucepan (or cook in a *bain-marie*). Add lemon juice and rum, simmer gently, without allowing to boil, until the sauce thickens.

Egg and lemon sauce for lamb sarmi

grated rind and juice of 2 lemons
2·5dl (½ pint or 1 cup) stock
½ tablespoon cornflour
2 raw yolks
pinch nutmeg
salt and pepper

Add lemon rind to stock and bring to the boil.

Blend cornflour with lemon juice, stir into stock, reduce heat, simmer for four to five minutes, and remove from heat.

Drop yolks into a double saucepan, pour warm (*not hot*) sauce over yolks, and cook, stirring constantly, over gently simmering water, until the sauce thickens. Season with nutmeg, salt, and pepper and serve.

Mornay sauce

2·5dl (½ pint or 1 cup) white sauce (page 248)
1dl (1 gill or ½ cup) fresh cream
60g (2oz or ½ cup) grated Gruyère or Parmesan cheese
30g (1oz or 2 tablespoons) butter

Add cream to béchamel sauce, boiled down to reduce by one-third, stir in cheese, and incorporate butter, stirring it in small pieces.

Sauces, dips, dressings

Mint sauce

4 tablespoons chopped, fresh mint
2 tablespoons sugar
1 dl (1 gill or $\frac{1}{2}$ cup) vinegar

Add sugar and vinegar to finely chopped mint, and stir until dissolved.

Zhug

This is one of a series of Yemeni bread dips. There are many others, including, in order of popularity, hawayij, hilbeh, samneh, etc.
These blends of spices, reminiscent of the Indian garam-masala (see page 262), are splendid for giving flavour to a simple meal. The Yemenites further claim that their immunity to coronary diseases, as well as to high blood pressure and the digestive troubles which afflict the Western world, is due to their use of these spice dips from time immemorial to the present day. The *sabra* cooks have adopted all these dips as seasoning for many dishes.

2 teaspoons black pepper
2 teaspoons caraway seeds
6–7 cardamom peeled seeds
3–4 dried red chillis
1 head garlic
a few coriander leaves
1 teaspoon salt

Grind all ingredients, blend well. Transfer to a jar with a tightly fitting lid and store until required.

Hawayij

2 tablespoons black pepper
1 tablespoon caraway seeds
1 teaspoon cardamom
1 teaspoon saffron
2 teaspoons turmeric

Using the above ingredients, follow instructions for zhug (above).

Sauces, dips, dressings

Hilbeh

2 tablespoons fenugreek seeds
125g (4½oz or ¾ cup) peeled, quartered tomatoes
½ teaspoon zhug (page 252)

Pound fenugreek seeds very finely or put through a grinder. Cover with water and leave to stand for three hours. Sieve the tomatoes or put through a blender to make a paste.

Pour the water off the fenugreek seeds carefully. Mix fenugreek with tomato purée and zhug. Blend well, cool, and serve.

Samneh

90g (3oz or 6 tablespoons) margarine
½ tablespoon fenugreek seed

Melt the margarine, add fenugreek seed, simmer over lowest possible heat for twenty-five to thirty minutes. Remove from heat, allow to cool, decant into a small preserving jar, seal well, and keep in refrigerator.

Salad dressings

Oil and vinegar dressing (basic salad dressing)

May be applied to all salads, and is made up of three parts oil to 1 part vinegar, with salt and pepper. Lemon juice may be used instead of vinegar.

With chives: Mix two tablespoons salad dressing with one tablespoon chopped chives. Good with vegetable salads.

With herbs: Mix two tablespoons salad dressing with one tablespoon chopped parsley, half a teaspoon powdered marjoram, and a pinch of powdered thyme. Good with vegetable or meat salads.

With pickles: Mix two tablespoons salad dressing with two tablespoons pickle relish or chopped dill pickle. Good with vegetable, meat or fish salads.

With olives: Mix two tablespoons salad dressing with a few sliced stuffed olives or a few chopped, ripe olives. Good with vegetables, fruit or fish salads.

Sauces, dips, dressings

Egg dressing

Crushed hard-boiled yolks of egg, mixed in the salad bowl with oil, vinegar, salt, and pepper. The whites of egg, cut into thin strips, are scattered over the salad.

Mustard and cream dressing

Good for beetroot, celeriac, and green salads mixed with beetroot.
Use one dessertspoon mustard, mixed with 2·5dl ($\frac{1}{2}$ pint or 1 cup) single cream, juice of a medium-sized lemon, salt, and pepper.

Gorgonzola salad dressing

60g (2oz or $\frac{1}{2}$ cup) Gorgonzola cheese
1dl (1 gill or $\frac{1}{2}$ cup) olive oil
1$\frac{1}{2}$ tablespoons wine vinegar
1 teaspoon prepared mustard
salt and pepper

Mash Gorgonzola cheese with a fork, combine with other ingredients, season to taste, blend well, and use as required.

Roquefort salad dressing

As above, substituting Roquefort cheese for Gorgonzola.

Sherry salad dressing

In a mortar pound one small clove garlic and two small finely chopped white onions, with one teaspoon each of sugar and salt. Add three tablespoons wine vinegar, one tablespoon sherry, and a pinch of freshly ground black pepper. Beat in eight tablespoons salad oil, a tablespoon at a time, and whisk in a dash of lemon juice.

Cream dressing

Excellent with cos lettuce. Three parts very fresh single cream to one part vinegar.

Sauces, dips, dressings

Sour cream dressing

1·25dl ($\frac{1}{4}$ pint or $\frac{1}{2}$ cup) sour cream
3 tablespoons lemon juice
pinch salt
pinch paprika
$\frac{1}{4}$ tablespoon dry mustard
1 tablespoon finely chopped onion

Whip cream, add other ingredients, mix well.

Lemon and oil dressing

4 tablespoons olive oil
pinch salt and pepper
pinch paprika
2 tablespoons lemon juice

Mix oil and seasoning, drip in lemon juice gradually, stirring all the time
to form an emulsion.

Rum dressing

0·5dl ($\frac{1}{2}$ gill or $\frac{1}{4}$ cup) dark rum
120g (4oz or $\frac{1}{2}$ cup) honey
6 tablespoons salad oil
1 tablespoon chopped, candied ginger
1 tablespoon lime (or lemon) juice
1 teaspoon paprika

Mix all ingredients and pass through a food mill or blender.

White wine dressing

0·5dl ($\frac{1}{2}$ gill or $\frac{1}{3}$ cup) olive oil
0·5dl ($\frac{1}{2}$ gill or $\frac{1}{3}$ cup) white wine
1 teaspoon lemon juice
salt and pepper

Blend oil and wine as for lemon and oil dressing above, stir in lemon
juice, and season to taste.

Aspics, stuffings, and miscellaneous

White wine court-bouillon (for fish)

Add 2·5dl ($\frac{1}{2}$ pint or 1 cup) of mixed vegetables (finely sliced carrot, leek, onion, celery, small sprig thyme, and crushed fragment of bay leaf, gently cooked in vegetable margarine) to 2·5dl ($\frac{1}{2}$ pint or 1 cup) of dry white wine. Bring to the boil and reduce by two-thirds. Enrich, if liked, with 2·5dl (2 gills or 1 cup) fish fumet (page 259) simmer for seven to eight minutes. Use as directed.

Aspic jelly

Any meat or bone stock can be used as a basis for aspic jelly but if the bones do not include calf's foot, it will need strengthening with gelatine. You can even make passable aspic jelly, at a pinch, by adding 15g ($\frac{1}{2}$oz or 1$\frac{1}{2}$ tablespoons) gelatine, diluted in 1$\frac{1}{2}$ tablespoons boiling water, to 2dl ($\frac{1}{2}$ pint or 1 cup) water with a bouillon cube added to it.

But short cuts, though admissible in emergencies, are inevitably undertaken at the expense of quality.

500g (1lb) short ribs of beef
1·5kg (3lb) shin-bone
1 calf's foot
2 sliced onions
2 sliced carrots
3 tablespoons sherry (or port)
2 egg whites and shells
salt

Cut the meat into pieces, chop the bones, and split the calf's foot, put into a large pan of salted cold water, slowly bring to the boil, removing the scum as it rises with a perforated spoon. Add carrot and onions, skim the surface until it is clear, cover, and simmer for three and a half to four hours. Strain, taste for seasoning. Chill, skim off all fat, then reheat, add sherry or port, and clarify, i.e. add slightly beaten egg whites and crushed egg shells to the stock, boil it up, simmer for fifteen minutes, and strain through a cloth. Cool, and use as directed.

Aspics, stuffings, and miscellaneous

Quick aspic jelly

0·5 litre (1 pint or 2 cups) chicken stock
1 teaspoon chopped tarragon
2–3 sprigs parsley
juice of 1 lemon
10 peppercorns
1 chopped shallot (or ½ onion)
½ bay leaf
30g (1oz or ¼ cup) gelatine
3 tablespoons sherry (or Madeira)
salt
1 egg white and shell

Boil the stock with tarragon, parsley, lemon juice, peppercorns, shallot, and bay leaf for ten minutes. Dissolve the gelatine in two tablespoons cold water and add to the stock. Simmer for five minutes, add sherry and salt to taste, and strain. To clarify the jelly, bring the stock to the boil. Beat the egg white and crush the shell and add both to the stock. Simmer for five minutes, strain once again, and use as directed.

Fish aspic jelly

1 litre (2 pints or 4 cups) fish stock (page 259)
30g (1oz or 2 tablespoons) gelatine
2 egg whites and shells
1 glass sherry
4 tablespoons vinegar

Cool and strain the fish stock. If it was cooked with a bouquet garni and vinegar or lemon juice, it will not need any further spicing. If you have only cooked fish heads, bones, skin, and trimmings in salted water, then cool and skim off all fat from the stock, use a little of it to dilute the gelatine, and put stock, gelatine, bouquet garni (sprig of thyme, parsley, and a bay leaf), and a stick of celery into a saucepan. Beat the whites, wash the egg shells, and add both to the fish stock to clarify it. Start heating, whisking all the time. As soon as boiling is established, add sherry (and vinegar or lemon juice, if the stock was not acidulated during original cooking). Simmer for ten minutes, strain, and use as directed in individual recipes.

Aspics, stuffings, and miscellaneous

Fish fumet

Fumet is concentrated stock made from bones and trimmings of fish.

1kg (2lb) bones, head and trimmings of various fish (whiting, sole, haddock, plaice, etc.)
1 chopped onion
60g (2oz or $\frac{1}{4}$ cup) mushroom parings (stalks, etc.)
2 sprigs parsley
1 sprig thyme
$\frac{1}{4}$ bay leaf
$\frac{1}{2}$ teaspoon lemon juice
pinch salt
0·5 litre (1 pint or 2 cups) water
2·5dl ($\frac{1}{2}$ pint or 1 cup) dry white wine

Put onion, mushroom parings, parsley, thyme, bay leaf in a stock pot. Cover with fish bones and trimmings, add lemon juice, season with salt, moisten with wine and water, bring to the boil, skim, then simmer gently for thirty minutes. Strain through a muslin bag.

Garlic butter

4 cloves garlic
water
(180g (6oz or $\frac{3}{4}$ cup) butter or margarine

Boil garlic in just enough water to cover for five minutes. Drain, and pound, adding butter little by little. Rub through a sieve and store in a jar with a well-fitting lid.

Tarragon butter

120g (4 tablespoons) fresh tarragon leaves
180g (6oz or $\frac{3}{4}$ cup) butter

Blanch tarragon leaves for two minutes in salted boiling water, drain, dip in cold water, dry. Pound in a mortar with butter and rub through a sieve or pass through a blender. Chill and use as required.

Aspics, stuffings, and miscellaneous

Clarified butter

Melt the butter on a very low heat until it begins to look like olive oil and a
whitish deposit forms on the bottom of the pan. Strain into a clean
container and use as directed.

Tomato fondue

1 medium-sized onion
1½ tablespoons oil
240g (½lb or 1¼ cups) tomatoes, peeled, seeded, and chopped
1 grated clove garlic
salt and pepper
½ tablespoon chopped parsley

Chop the onion and cook in oil until it becomes soft and transparent.
Add tomatoes, garlic, season to taste, simmer gently until all the liquid
yielded by the tomatoes evaporates. At the last moment sprinkle with
chopped parsley.

Chrain (horseradish)

Although the name of this relish is of Russian origin, the preparation itself
is used in all Jewish communities by people who have never been
anywhere near Russia. In the question of condiments there is a world of
difference between say the dill pickles of the European Jews and the fiery
dips of the Yemenites, but horseradish is common to all, because of its
religious significance (see Passover, page 173). It is served invariably with
gefilte fish (pages 5–6). The commercially manufactured horseradish
usually lacks the sharpness and piquancy of the home-made variety and
most self-respecting Jewish housewives grate it themselves, tears
notwithstanding.

The horseradish root should be scrubbed, scraped, and grated finely.
Then it is ready to be made into one of the following variations:

1   *Horseradish with apple*
    Mix horseradish with equal quantity of grated cooking apple, add
    castor sugar and vinegar to taste. Stir well.

Aspics, stuffings, and miscellaneous

2   *Horseradish with beetroot*
    Mix horseradish with cooked grated beetroot. Season with salt and
    pepper, add sugar and vinegar to taste.

3   *Horseradish with mayonnaise*
    Mix freshly grated horseradish with mayonnaise, allowing one
    tablespoon horseradish for 100ml (4fl oz or ½ cup) mayonnaise.

4   *Horseradish with dill pickles*
    Mix horseradish with chopped or sliced dill pickles.

Chestnut stuffing

Sufficient for 4 to 5kg (8 to 10lb) bird:

500g (1lb) shelled, skinned chestnuts (page 284)
240g (8oz or 1 cup) sausage meat or finely chopped turkey giblets
stock
90g (3oz or ¾ cup) fresh breadcrumbs
1–2 tablespoons chopped parsley
60g (2oz or 4 tablespoons) melted margarine
salt and pepper
1–2 beaten eggs

Cook the skinned chestnuts in enough stock to cover until tender. Drain
and rub through a sieve. Add remaining ingredients, season to taste, bind
with one or two eggs, and mix well.

Veal forcemeat

Sufficient for 4 to 5kg (8 to 10lb) turkey:

1 set cooked, chopped turkey liver and gizzard
180g (6oz or 1½ cups) fresh breadcrumbs
grated rind and juice of ½ lemon
2 teaspoons grated onion (optional)
1 tablespoon chopped parsley
90g (3oz or 6 tablespoons) shredded suet
2 beaten eggs
salt and pepper

Mix all ingredients, season to taste, and stuff the bird.

Aspics, stuffings, and miscellaneous

Garam-masala

Garam-masala is an essential ingredient of authentic curry dishes,
a mixture of spices which gives curries their informing flavours. No
oriental cook would be content with buying a tin of commercial curry
powder, they grind and blend their own mixtures, usually fresh daily,
taking it in their stride the way the continental housewife does grinding
coffee.

60g (2oz or $\frac{1}{2}$ cup) coriander seeds
60g (2oz or $\frac{1}{2}$ cup) black peppercorns
45g (1$\frac{1}{2}$oz or 6 tablespoons) caraway seeds
15g ($\frac{1}{2}$oz or 6 teaspoons) cloves
20 peeled cardamom seeds
15g ($\frac{1}{2}$oz or 2 tablespoons) ground cinnamon

Mix all ingredients and grind. A coffee grinder does this job very well and
final product should be fine but not reduced to a dust. Store in a jar with a
well-fitting lid.

Coconut milk

Fresh or desiccated coconut can yield both cream and milk and this can be
used for enriching many preparations, including meat dishes. It lends a
velvety smoothness and mellowness to sauces, is a lighter liaison than
yolks of egg, and is an excellent substitute for dairy milk and cream.

To make coconut cream
1 fresh coconut
100ml (4fl oz or $\frac{1}{2}$–1 cup) boiling water

Have the greengrocer saw the coconut in half, pour out the liquid. (The
natural, and drinkable, liquid inside the coconut is *not* coconut milk.)
Extract the flesh, by scraping it out. Pour boiling water over it and let it
stand for twenty minutes. Squeeze out in a muslin bag or pass through a
fine strainer. (An Indian restaurateur advocates the use of a potato
presser for extracting coconut milk.) This first pressing produces coconut
cream, which after several hours' refrigeration acquires the density of
double cream.

Aspics, stuffings, and miscellaneous

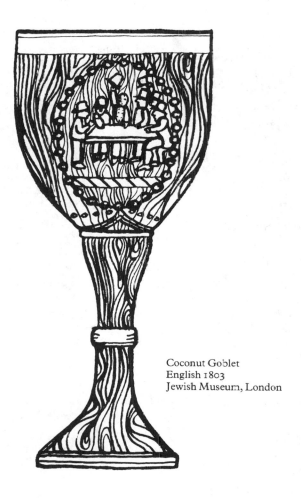

Coconut Goblet
English 1803
Jewish Museum, London

To make coconut milk

Put the husks of the coconut which has been pressed to extract cream into a pan, add the same amount of water as for the first pressing, bring to the boil, and press out again.

Both coconut cream and milk can be made in a liquidizer.

Observe the indicated proportions, and blend a couple of tablespoonsful of grated or shredded coconut and water at a time. Then squeeze through a muslin bag as described. If fresh coconut is not available good quality desiccated coconut may be used.

Aspics, stuffings, and miscellaneous

Mint chutney

This is a pleasant and refreshing chutney. It needs no cooking but it does not keep and should be made fresh on the day on which it is to be used. It is excellent served with curries and makes a pleasant filling for sweet samosas. If mango is not available, use equivalent amount of fresh lime juice. If limes are not available, use lemon juice.

60g (2oz) mint leaves
8 spring onions
2 small, fresh green chillies
pinch salt
1 teaspoon sugar
1 teaspoon garam-masala (page 262)
1 tablespoon pomegranate seeds
1 tablespoon sieved mango pulp

Wash and chop mint leaves. Chop spring onions and chillies. Pound the mint, spring onions, chillies, with salt, sugar, and garam-masala in a mortar. Crush pomegranate seeds, add to mixture, and continue to pound together for a few minutes.

Stir in mango pulp, mix well, decant into a serving dish.

Onion dumplings for pickled (corned) beef

60g (2oz or ¼ cup) suet
180g (6oz or 1½ cups) flour
1 teaspoon baking powder
1 tablespoon chopped parsley
1½ tablespoons finely grated onion
salt and pepper
cold water

Shred the suet finely. Sift the flour into a mixing bowl, reserving a little for rolling the dumplings. Add baking powder, suet, parsley, onion, salt, and pepper to taste. Mix well, then, little by little, stir in enough cold water to make a loose dough.

Taking a little dough at a time, roll into balls with lightly floured hands. Cook as described.

Aspics, stuffings, and miscellaneous

Plain suet dumplings

Follow above recipe but omit onion.

Potato dumplings for sauerbraten

360g (¾lb) potatoes
120g (4oz or 1 cup) flour
1 egg
pinch salt
1 teaspoon grated onion
2–3 tablespoons grated breadcrumbs

Peel potatoes and grate over a bowl of cold water, so that they fall straight into water, to prevent discoloration. Drain well, dry on a cloth, mix with flour and the rest of the ingredients. Taking a dessertspoon at a time, drop into pan of boiling water, poach until the dumplings float up to the surface (eighteen to twenty minutes), drain, and serve.

Vanilla custard cream

500ml (1 pint or 2 cups) milk
120g (4oz or ½ cup) sugar
1 vanilla bean
4 raw yolks

Put milk and sugar in a saucepan. Cut vanilla bean in half and add to milk. Heat to scalding point and leave the vanilla to infuse in the milk. Then remove vanilla. (It can be rinsed, dried, and stored in a screwtop jar for further use.) Keep milk hot but not boiling.

Beat the yolks in a bowl with a wooden spoon. Gradually stir hot milk into yolks.

Pour custard mixture into a double saucepan, stir over gently simmering water until the custard thickens. On no account allow it to boil. Serve cold with fruit salads or use as required.

Vanilla essence can be used as a substitute for vanilla bean, but it should be added as the last ingredient.

Aspics, stuffings, and miscellaneous

Cream cheese filling for pancake pie

360g (12oz or 1½ cups) sieved cream cheese
½ teaspoon salt
1–2 tablespoons softened butter
1 tablespoon chopped spring onions
1 tablespoon chopped parsley
1–2 eggs

Combine all ingredients, mix well, and rub through a sieve or pass through a blender.

Chocolate butter icing

90g (3oz or ¾ cup) grated chocolate
1 tablespoon milk
a few drops vanilla essence
2 tablespoons brandy (optional)
240g (8oz or 1 cup) butter or margarine
180g (6oz or 1¼ cups) icing sugar

Melt chocolate with milk, vanilla, and brandy, stirring it over simmering water. Cream butter, sift the sugar into it, and beat. Cool the chocolate slightly, without allowing it to set, stir into butter and sugar mixture, whisk hard until the icing is smoothly blended, and use as required.

Bedouin coffee

In Israel, as in most of the Middle East, coffee is part of a way of life. All types of coffee are to be found in the cafés and restaurants, from Espresso to Viennese, with a mountain of whipped cream on top. But the coffee which is offered to you in a shop or an office is the Arabic or Turkish coffee.

It is normally made in *jazveh*, those tiny pots, wider at the base and narrowing at the top. One small cup is served per guest. For each small cup of water, allow a dessertspoon of finely ground Mocha coffee and the same amount of sugar, if you like it sweet. The amount of sugar can be reduced to taste.

Aspics, stuffings, and miscellaneous

Bring the water to a fast boil, add coffee and sugar, and remove the pan from the heat as soon as the froth rises up. This takes no time at all. Allow the foam to settle, then put to boil again. Remove from heat as the foam rises again and allow to settle for a few seconds. Repeat the boiling up process for a third time and as soon as it boils up, remove from heat, spoon some of the froth into each cup, then pour the coffee and serve.

For Bedouin coffee, proceed as described but add a split pod of cardamom for each cup of coffee as you start cooking it.

Pickles

Pattern adapted from a manuscript in the Jewish Museum, London

Pickled red cabbage

The splendid Mrs Glasse, in her legendary book *The Art of Cookery Made Plain and Easy*, a bestseller of the eighteenth century, which she wrote 'with the intention of instructing the lower sort', uses almost an identical recipe to the one given below. She has one additional ingredient for the pickling liquor – 'one pennyworth of cochineal, bruised fine', presumably to enhance the colour. She did not have any screw bands or clips for her jars; her final instruction is 'cover jars with a cloth and tie with leather'.

1 red cabbage
salt
1 litre (1 quart) vinegar
1 tablespoon mixed pickling spice

Shred the cabbage as described in recipe for pickled cabbage. Put in a large colander or sieve, sprinkle thickly with salt. Squeeze from time to time to make the dark juice flow out. Leave for three to four hours.

Boil vinegar with spice for a few minutes and leave until quite cold. Drain cabbage, pack into jars as described in the previous recipe, pour vinegar over it so that it comes up 2·5cm (1 inch) above the level of the cabbage. Secure top. The cabbage will be ready in twelve to fourteen days.

Pickled beetroot

12 small beets
375ml ($\frac{3}{4}$ pint or $1\frac{1}{2}$ cups) wine vinegar
1 teaspoon salt
100g ($3\frac{1}{2}$oz or 7 tablespoons) sugar
1 dozen peppercorns
2 bay leaves
1 tablespoon freshly grated horseradish (optional)

Scrub the beets well, bake in their skins in the oven until tender. Slip skins off and slice or dice beets.

Bring vinegar to the boil with the rest of the ingredients and pour over the beets. Bring beets to the boil in the marinade and decant into sterilized jars. They are ready for eating within twenty-four hours.

Really tiny baby beets should be pickled whole.

Pickles

Dill pickles

This name applies first and foremost to dill cucumbers – a favourite Jewish pickle. Many other vegetables and fruit were and are pickled, as can be seen from the recipes in this section, particularly in communities from Russia, Poland, and other East European countries, where in days before refrigeration the only supply of vegetables and fruit in the long winter would be what the housewife had managed to preserve.

There is something special about dill pickles; they are in a class of their own. How else to explain the fact that in our times, in countries where vitamin deficiency is a thing of the past, most gastronomically inclined East European Jews – and rightly – consider a good dill cucumber as a treat?

Good dill cucumbers should be crisp and of a clean olive green colour. They undergo two colour changes in the process of pickling: they first turn yellow, then green again, which proclaims their readiness. In various climates the period of pickling differs. In England it may take two or even three weeks; in Israel they would be ready in seven to eight days.

In Russia 'semi-pickled' cucumbers, made at the end of the summer, kept in brine for three to four days, are particularly popular. In addition to dill, which is the all important flavour, the container – usually an earthenware crock – is often lined with oak, blackcurrant or cherry leaves. In Israel vine leaves are used for this purpose.

In Israel, where many of the spices grow wild and have been known since the biblical days, cumin and coriander crop up in the recipes. Shavings of horseradish are also used in the pickling liquor.

Some authorities advocate soaking the cucumber in water overnight before pickling. I think this is unnecessary. What is essential is to choose young, sound, small to medium-sized, green cucumbers, rejecting any which have turned yellow. Ideally you should be able to pack about a dozen in 1-kg (2-lb) jar.

If you have a pickling crock, make sure the cucumbers are kept under brine by covering with a plate with a weight on top. Keep the crock covered with a piece of muslin and skim off any scum which may rise to the surface.

Only fresh dill should be used, picked in bud, just before it comes into flower.

Pickles

blackcurrant or cherry leaves
3 dozen small cucumbers
2 dozen peppercorns
6 cloves garlic
6 bay leaves
3 red chillis
6 stalks fresh dill in bud
2 litres (2 quarts) water
180g (6oz or $\frac{3}{4}$ cup) coarse salt

Line three 1-kg (2-lb) jars with a few washed and dried blackcurrant or cherry leaves.

Wash cucumbers, dry, and pack into jars in layers, putting them in vertically and fitting them in tightly. Sprinkle each layer with peppercorns and slip a couple of garlic cloves, a bay leaf, and a red chilli between the layers. Insert a couple of good dill stalks in each jar.

Bring water to the boil with salt, allow this brine solution to cool, and pour over cucumbers. There should be enough brine to come to about 2·5cm (1 inch) above the cucumbers.

Cover with a well-fitting lid, if necessary put a weight on top. The cucumbers must not be allowed to float up – hence the weight. But you must also make sure that the lid and weight, or whatever you use for cover, does not press directly on the cucumbers, as this may cause bruising.

Leave in a cool dry place until ready, which can be from one to three weeks, dependent on climate. Should there be any evaporation of the liquid, make up more brine and top up. Allow six tablespoons coarse salt per litre (quart) of water for the brine solution.

If you like the taste of vinegar in your dill pickles, add two tablespoons of vinegar to 1 litre (1 quart) of brine solution and bring to the boil together. Then cool and use as described.

Pickles

Pickled green tomatoes

In Siberia green tomatoes used to be pickled by the barrel. They are served as an appetizer or an accompaniment to other dishes. Very good with boiled beef.

Choose sound firm green tomatoes and observe all the instructions given for dill pickles.

3 dozen green tomatoes
2 litres (2 quarts) water
180g (6oz or ¾ cup) coarse salt
4–5 cloves garlic
1 dozen peppercorns
3 bay leaves
2 tablespoons sugar
6 fresh dill stalks in bud

Wash dry and put tomatoes into a crock or jar. Bring water to the boil with salt, garlic, peppercorns, bay leaves, and sugar. Cool and pour over tomatoes. Insert dill, cover, and put in a cool dry place. Skim off any scum which may rise to the surface. Tomatoes will be ready in eight to ten days time. Make sure tomatoes are completely covered with brine.

In case of evaporation, top up with more brine.

Pickled mushrooms

1kg (2lb) mushrooms
0·25 litre (½ pint or 1 cup) water
0·25 litre (½ pint or 1 cup) vinegar
1 teaspoon salt
8 peppercorns
1 bay leaf
3 cloves
¼ teaspoon cinnamon
2 tablespoons salad oil

Pick firm sound mushrooms. Pick them over, clean, wash without soaking, and drain thoroughly. Bring water and vinegar to the boil with the rest of the ingredients except oil. Simmer for twenty to twenty-five minutes. Allow to cool.

Pickles

Put peppercorns, bay leaf, and cloves in a small cheesecloth bag. Remove mushrooms with a perforated spoon and pack into jars. Discard spice bag. Pour the liquid over the mushrooms. Top with salad oil. Chill for twenty-four hours before serving.

Pickled lemons

Pickled lemons are good served with fish. The liquid from the pickle is used for fish sauce.

12 lemons
3 tablespoons salt
1·5 litres (1½ quarts or 6 cups) mild vinegar
1 tablespoon paprika
240g (8oz or 1 cup) sugar
1 tablespoon peppercorns
3 bay leaves

Score the rind as if you were cutting the lemons into quarters, but very lightly, without cutting to the pith. Rub salt into the scored cuts and leave lemons in the dish overnight, when they will have yielded their liquid. Pour off and reserve this liquid.

Bring vinegar to the boil with all remaining ingredients and the reserved liquid from the lemons. Skim the surface and leave vinegar until cold. Put lemons into it and allow to stand for twenty-four hours, stirring from time to time. Next day, gently bring to the boil, simmer on low heat for twenty minutes, then bottle as usual.

Pickled grapes

1kg (2lb) grapes
250ml (½ pint or 1 cup) cider vinegar
1 teaspoon salt
240g (8oz or 1 cup) sugar
0·5 litre (1 pint or 2 cups) water

Choose whole bunches of ripe but firm seedless grapes. Wash and put into jars. Combine all other ingredients, bring to the boil, cool, and pour over grapes. Seal and store.

Pickles

Pickled plums

Choose firm plums and follow recipe for pickled grapes. This is especially good with roast goose.

Pickled cabbage (sauerkraut)

Long before anything was known about vitamins, many of the poorer communities realized that eating pickled cabbage during winter months, when fresh vegetables were not available, helped them to maintain their health. The fact that they also liked its pleasantly sharp taste was an added bonus. To this day sauerkraut is important in the diet of the Austrian Jews.

All sorts of legends have grown around the alleged health-giving properties of pickled cabbage. In many works of Russian classical literature, describing rural life where a great deal of drinking went on, one comes across scenes in which some poor serf is running to the cellar to draw off a jug of pickled cabbage liquor to cure the master's hangover. Most early recipes only required shredded cabbage to be packed in layers with salt under weights, the natural juices oozing out of the cabbage provided the liquid to make brine, and fermentation did the rest.

This fermentation, which renders the cabbage more digestible, must have made the dwellings well nigh uninhabitable. Now we can avoid the smells by packing it straight into screw-top jars.

Later, refinements in varying flavours by the addition of dill, apples, carrots, cranberries, juniper berries, caraway seeds, etc. were introduced. It is difficult to lay down extact quantities for pickled cabbage. For small amounts allow two tablespoons salt per kilogramme (2lb) of shredded cabbage.

Choose firm, sound white cabbage, discard all green leaves, and remove stem. Wash well, drain, and the cabbage is ready for pickling. Whether you use a crock or jar, line it with a layer of cabbage leaves or vine leaves. Arrange cabbage in tightly packed layers, press down, sprinkle each layer with coarse salt (sea salt) and some caraway seeds, juniper berries or other flavouring of your choice. Finish with a layer of salt.

Pickles

If you are pickling the cabbage in a wide-necked crock, pound down with a potato masher which will cause moisture to appear. Cover with cabbage or vine leaves, then with a cheese cloth and put a plate and a weight on top. The weight should be heavy enough to force the brine above the level of the cloth and it should be kept up at that level. A non-porous stone makes a good weight.

If you are using jars, proceed as described, add a little brine, and keep topping up daily, so that there is always some liquid above the cabbage.

Leave to stand at room temperature, not higher than 15°C (60°F), otherwise fermentation will develop too quickly and ruin the quality of the cabbage.

In addition to regular topping up with brine, you should also remove all surface scum as soon as it appears. The cloth, lid, and weight should be scrubbed and scalded with boiling water each time you do so.

To ensure the keeping qualities of cabbage pickled in a crock, decant it into sterilized jars as soon as it is fully cured. In the right conditions, this should take twelve to fourteen days. Pack tightly into jars, up to two-thirds, filling with juice to within about 4cm (1¾ inch) from the top. If needs be, make up with fresh brine. Make sure jar caps are correctly adjusted for sterilizing and process for fifteen minutes in boiling water.

Jams, jellies, and preserves

Motif on label from an eighteenth century Viennese Megillah in the Jewish Museum, London

Jams, jellies, and preserves

Jams play an important role in the Jewish scheme of things. It is not something one buys ready made. Oh, no. To a good Jewish housewife jam is something to be made at home, at the right time, in the right frame of mind, and with love.

It is something that makes a most acceptable gift to take along when one is visiting friends or relations, or to be offered as a sign of hospitality.

Certain jams are administered as home cures. Raspberry jam, for example, taken in a glass of scalding hot tea used to be considered more effective than any patent medicine for bringing down temperature when one had a cold. Tastes better, too.

The *kibbutzniks* sometimes like to put jam into their tea, which is what their grandparents did in Russia, at first, perhaps, because sugar was scarce, then because they grew to like their tea that way.

There are several distinct types of jam. The most popular among the East and Central European communities are Russian varenye and Central European povidl. Povidl, for which the fruit is sieved, is excellent for pastries, cakes, and for eating on bread. Varenye is so good that it is served at tea in tiny dishes and eaten with a spoon. Its appearance is important and, therefore, fruit is never pulped for varenye. Varenye must capture and hold all the flavour, colour, and fragrance of the fruit, the syrup should be clear and the fruit whole and in no way squashed or deformed in the cooking.

Jewish housewives from North Africa make a lovely jam of baby aubergines (egg-plants) or marrows (zuchini) with walnuts or pistachio nuts.

Sephardic communities have contributed recipes for Seville orange marmalades; the Middle East has given us fine rose petal jam, which is traditional for Shavuot, quince and guava jelly; Tunis and Algeria coconut and chestnut jam; and Israel herself rejoices in citron jam (page 280).

Citron, the *etrog*, the fruit of the goodly tree of the Bible, is one of the offerings at *Succoth*, the Festival of Tabernacles, which God commanded Moses to observe after the harvest had been gathered in – (*Exodus* 34:22).

Jams, jellies, and preserves

A few words about jam-making utensils

If you haven't a preserving pan, use a good aluminium saucepan. It should be big and wide enough to allow plenty of room for the jam to cook without boiling over. Have it about two-thirds full. If you grease the pan lightly with almond oil, you will make it a bit more non-stick.

Use a long handled wooden spoon for stirring the jam. It is safer to allow a bit of distance between your hand and the boiling syrup. Stir only until the sugar dissolves, then allow to boil fast without any further stirring, unless a particular recipe specifices otherwise.

Have a perforated spoon on a saucer near at hand, for skimming off scum which rises to the surface during cooking.

Jam jars should be absolutely clean and dry and should have well-fitting covers. Warm them before decanting jam to prevent them cracking and fill to about 5mm ($\frac{1}{4}$ inch) from the top. Allow jam to cool in jars before sealing. On the whole jam keeps better in 500-g (1-lb) jars than in larger ones. Always store jam in a cool, dry place, away from light to prevent discoloration.

Sugar thermometer is useful to establish the degree of jelling, when the pan must be removed from heat. If you continue to cook jam beyond its jelling point, it will not set at all. On the sugar thermometer this stage is reached at 330°C (220°F).

To test jelling point without a thermometer, put a few drops of the syrup on a cold saucer, cool quickly, and push with a spoon. If the surface wrinkles, the jam is ready.

General notes on making jam

The first requisite for good jam is fresh, sound, firm fruit, under-ripe rather than over-ripe. The second requisite is the right amount of sugar. The proportion of sugar to fruit, as will be seen from the individual recipes, varies according to the pectin content of the fruit. For fruit with low pectin content, you need more fruit than sugar and some extra lemon juice or redcurrant juice. It is pectin, combined with sugar and acid, which gives the jam its setting quality. If you observe the correct proportions of fruit, sugar, and acid, you will never need to add any commercially marketed pectin. Pectin is naturally present as a constituent in certain

Jams, jellies, and preserves

fruits: quince, apples, oranges, lemons, red and blackcurrants, etc. which causes their pulp, when boiled with sugar and sufficient acid, to set as a jelly.

The peel and pips of the fruit contain a great deal of the pectin and should, therefore, be used in the preparation of jellies, tied in a small muslin bag for easy removal. Use slightly warmed preserving loaf or granulated sugar and prepare your fruit just before cooking the jam. Don't let the fruit wait even several hours. Firm fruit, such as plums, should be washed gently, a few at a time, in one layer in a colander, and dried with a cloth. Never soak fruit (except where indicated for citrus fruit) and use only cold water for washing it.

Particular care should be taken in washing soft fruit, such as strawberries, as soaking causes rapid deterioration and spoils their texture. I use a small watering can for sprinkling soft fruit placed in a colander or sieve. Drain on kitchen paper and use immediately. Cook the jam slowly, stirring until the sugar dissolves completely, then boil fast without stirring until jelling or setting degree is reached (see page 278).

To achieve success, follow the proportions of fruit and sugar as given in the recipes. Cutting down sugar is false economy, as jam with deficient sugar content often goes sour. This necessitates re-boiling with an addition of sugar, which tends to discolour the fruit.

If the jam is left to stand before being put into pots, it must not be covered with a lid. Condensation formed on the inside of the lid trickles into the jam and causes it to go mildewy. If jam has to be covered for hygienic reasons, cover it with a light porous cloth; it will absorb the moisture and prevent it from dripping into the jam.

If jam goes 'sugary', which sometimes happens if it is overcooked, pour one tablespoon of cold water into it and stand the jar in a saucepan of cold water – the level of water reaching to the level of jam. Heat the water to boiling-point and remove from heat. Leave the jam jar in the water until it cools. This process of slow re-melting will reconstitute the jam.

If the jam goes sour, which happens when it is undercooked, it should be re-done as quickly as possible. Put into jam-making pan, sprinkle in sugar, boil gently, removing scum as it forms. Cook until there is no more scum. Store in a cool, dry place, away from light.

Jams, jellies, and preserves

Etrog or citron jam

In my first Hebrew reader there is a reproduction of the first stamp issued by the State of Israel in 1948. The stamp shows an early Jewish coin, the silver *shekel* (left), which was in use in the biblical times. (I have looked up *shekel* in the Concordance to the Bible and found twenty-seven references to it.) On one side of the coin, symbolizing human virtue, is engraved the *etrog*, or rather, two *etrogim*. During *Succoth* special religious services are held and *etrog* is one of the thanksgiving offerings which the men take into the synagogue. It makes a delectable, fragrant jam, which must be the grandmother of all marmalades. For this preserve citrons can be used by themselves or with oranges, in equal proportions:

500g (1lb) citrons, or ½ citrons ½ oranges
1·25kg (2½lb or 5 cups) sugar

Wash the fruit, shred or cut very thinly, remove pips. Put pips in a muslin bag.

Soak fruit overnight with enough water to cover. On the following day, pour off water, add enough fresh water to cover, and bring to the boil. Drain the water off once more, cover with 1·25 litre (1¼ quarts) fresh water, bring to the boil with the pips, simmer slowly until the peel is soft. Discard pips.

Warm sugar and add to pan. Cook, stirring until sugar dissolves completely. Boil fast, uncovered and without any further stirring, until the jam reaches jelling or setting point.

Jams, jellies, and preserves

Israeli five fruit marmalade

With the abundance of citrus fruit grown in Israel it is not surprising
that there are many recipes for citrus preserves. Orange, lemon, and
grapefruit marmalades are all popular. Jaffa jam is, in fact,
indistinguishable from orange marmalade. I find this five fruit combination
a very interesting one, though I always feel reluctant to cook pomelo – it
is such a splendid fruit to eat fresh. Where pomelo is not available, add an
extra grapefruit and two oranges and settle for a four fruit marmalade.

1 bitter (Seville) orange
1 sweet (Jaffa) orange
1 grapefruit and pomelo
2 lemons
2 litres (2 quarts) water
2kg (4lb or 8 cups) sugar

Shred the peel of the fruit discarding pith, mince the pulp, remove and
keep all pips. Tie pips in a muslin bag. Soak peel, pulp, and pips in water
overnight. Transfer everything, including water, to a covered pan and
simmer for one and a quarter to one and a half hours, or until the peel is
quite soft. Test by squeezing a piece between finger and thumb. If it does
not disintegrate, continue to simmer. It is fatal to add sugar before the peel
is done – it will go hard and ruin the marmalade.

Remove pips. Warm sugar and add to fruit. Stir until sugar dissolves,
then boil fast, uncovered, until the marmalade jells. Start testing as
described after ten minutes. Keep testing every few minutes, so as not to
pass the essential jelling point.

Grapefruit marmalade

2 grapefruit
1 litre (1 quart) water
1kg (2lb or 4 cups) sugar
juice of 2 lemons

Follow recipe for Israeli five fruit marmalade and remember, you cook the
pulp and peel slowly and for a long time, until the peel is soft. Add warmed
sugar and lemon juice and stir until it dissolves. Then boil rapidly,
uncovered, and after ten minutes test frequently for setting point.

Jams, jellies, and preserves

Sephardic peach jam

1kg (2lb) peaches
1·5kg (3lb) sugar
0·25 litre ($\frac{1}{2}$ pint or 1 cup) water.

Peel and stone the peaches. Cover with the sugar and leave from three to four hours. Put to heat with water and boil for ten minutes, taking the scum off from time to time. Rub through a sieve and put into sterilized, dry jars immediately. (If for reasons of economy 1kg (2lb) instead of 1·5kg (3lb) of sugar is used, boil for twenty minutes.)

Grape jam

Either black or green grapes can be used. Use seedless grapes, or carefully remove seeds, then weigh the grapes. Allow equal amount of sugar. Sharp green grapes have enough pectin. With black grapes, allow juice of two lemons for every 0·5kg (1lb or 2 cups) fruit.

Simmer the grapes for two to three minutes without any water. Add sugar, stir until it dissolves, boil fast until the jam begins to jell.

Raspberry varenye, Kiev recipe

500g (1lb) raspberries
720g (1$\frac{1}{2}$lb) castor sugar

Layer raspberries with sugar in preserving pan and leave in refrigerator overnight. Heat very gently, stirring to dissolve the sugar. Boil rapidly until the jam sets. Start testing after ten minutes.

Quick strawberry jam

The picking of strawberries in Israel takes place much earlier than in Eastern Central Europe and strawberry preserves, therefore, are becoming traditional for Passover celebration, replacing black radish preserves. Black radishes, cut into strips and cooked with sugar and honey, are still popular in East European Jewish communities.

Jams, jellies, and preserves

1kg (2lb or 6 cups) hulled and washed strawberries
1·5kg (3lb or 6 cups) castor sugar
strained juice of 2 lemons

Put the strawberries in a pan in layers with sugar. Add lemon juice.
Gently bring to the boil, stirring to dissolve sugar. Boil rapidly for five
minutes. Decant into heated jars, cool, and seal.

Povidl

This Central European conserve is a cross between plum jam and plum
cheese. For best results and a perfect flavour use ripe but firm plums. In
this state they don't need any water. If under-ripe plums are used, add
120ml (4oz or ½ cup) water to the quantities given in the recipe.

1kg (2lb or 5 cups) stoned plums
1kg (2lb or 4 cups) sugar

Stew the plums gently until soft. Rub through a sieve, add sugar. Cook,
stirring until sugar dissolves completely. Boil rapidly until povidl
thickens and begins to set.

Moroccan aubergine (egg-plant) jam

Only very young, small aubergines are suitable for this jam. If they are not
available, use baby marrows (zucchini). Young vegetables need no
peeling. If you have to use bigger and older aubergines or marrow
(squash), peel and slice very thinly or cut into small dice just before
cooking.

500g (1lb or 2 cups) sugar
3 tablespoons orange-flower water
500g (1lb) tiny aubergines
60g (2oz or ⅓ cup) shelled pistachio nuts or blanched almonds

Warm the sugar, put in a preserving pan, add orange-flower water, heat
slowly, stirring until the sugar has dissolved completely. Add aubergines,
cook until the jam begins to thicken. Stir in nuts, cook for a few minutes
just to distribute the nuts in the mixture. Decant into warmed jam jars.

Jams, jellies, and preserves

Tunisian coconut jam

This jam makes a very good filling for tartlets and cakes. It does not keep and should be made fresh whenever required:

500g (1lb or 2 cups) sugar
2–3 tablespoons water
500g (1lb or 6 cups) grated coconut
a few drops vanilla essence
2 tablespoons shelled pistachio nuts

Warm sugar, put in a pan with water, heat gently, stirring until sugar dissolves completely. Add coconut and vanilla essence to syrup, cook for ten minutes, stirring constantly. Stir in pistachio nuts, decant into warmed jam jars.

Algerian chestnut jam

1kg (2lb) chestnuts, shelled and skinned
1kg (2lb or 4 cups) sugar
95ml (3½oz or 7 tablespoons) orange-flower water

Make a slit in the chestnuts, put in a baking tin, and bake in the oven preheated to 205°C (400°F or Gas Mark 5) for fifteen minutes. In a hot climate, where lighting an oven would be unpleasant, the chestnuts are scored, put in a pan with water to cover, and boiled for fifteen minutes.

Whichever method you employ, remove shell and inner skin while the chestnuts are still hot, as soon as you can touch them, without burning your fingers.

Put in a pan with enough water to cover and simmer for fifteen to twenty minutes. Drain thoroughly.

Warm sugar, put in a pan with orange-flower water, heat, and stir until sugar dissolves. Add chestnuts, cook until the syrup thickens. Test as for ordinary jam.

Decant into warmed jars.

Jams, jellies, and preserves

Rose petal jam

500g (1lb) fresh, red rose petals
500g (1lb) lemons
500g (1lb or 2 cups) sugar
boiling water
iced water
1–2 drops rose oil (optional)

Pick petals of newly opened roses, trim off white parts and measure out
500g (1lb) petals. Put in colander, scald with boiling water, pressing the
petals gently with a spoon, if they tend to float up. Drain and plunge
colander into iced water, with ice cubes in it. Repeat this operation of
scalding and plunging into iced water once more. This will make the
petals crisp and crunchy in the jam. Drain well.

Peel lemons, cut into quarters and then slice very thinly. Put into pan,
add 100ml (4fl oz or $\frac{1}{2}$ cup) water, bring to the boil, simmer to soften.

Warm sugar, put in a pan with two tablespoons water, simmer, stir to
dissolve. Add lemons and rose petals, boil until the jam begins to set.
Start testing after three minutes. This jam is used for a very special
Persian rice pudding (page 197) which is flavoured with rose water and
decorated with live roses.

Prune jam

500g (1lb or 2$\frac{1}{2}$ cups) dried prunes
500ml (1 pint or 2 cups) water
sugar
lemon juice

Soak prunes overnight in water. Cook in the same water until soft. Remove
stones and weigh prune pulp. Add equal amount of sugar and the juice of
one lemon for every 500g (1lb or 2 cups) of fruit pulp.

Simmer gently, stirring until sugar is dissolved. Boil fast until jam sets.

Jams, jellies, and preserves

Redcurrant jelly

1kg (2lb or 8 cups) redcurrants
0·25 litre ($\frac{1}{2}$ pint or 1 cup) water
sugar

Simmer redcurrants with water until the skins break. Hang in thick muslin or a jelly bag over a bowl to catch the juice and leave to drip overnight.

Measure the juice and pour into preserving pan. For each 500ml (1 pint or 2 cups) of juice add 500g (1lb or 2 cups) sugar. Stir it until dissolved completely. Boil until jelling point is reached. Start testing after six to seven minutes.

Guava jelly

In Israel and throughout the Middle East, where fresh guavas are easily obtainable, their pulp is made into jam and jelly.

1kg (2lb) guava pulp
0·25 litre ($\frac{1}{2}$ pint or 1 cup) water
sugar
juice of 2 limes or 1 lemon

Choose under-ripe guavas. Wash, prick all over with a fork, and simmer in water until very soft. Put through a jelly bag without pressing and measure the juice. Add 500g (1lb or 2 cups) sugar for each 0·5 litre (1 pint or 2 cups) of guava juice. Heat, stirring to dissolve sugar. Add lime juice, boil briskly until set.

Mint jelly

240g (8oz or 1 cup) sugar
250ml ($\frac{1}{2}$ pint or 1 cup) water
100ml ($\frac{1}{4}$ pint or $\frac{1}{2}$ cup) vinegar
15g ($\frac{1}{2}$oz or 4 level teaspoons) powdered gelatine
4 tablespoons finely chopped mint

Gently heat sugar with water, stirring until sugar is completely dissolved. Bring to a boil. Simmer until syrup thickens.

Jams, jellies, and preserves

Dissolve gelatine in two tablespoons vinegar. Add to syrup with remaining vinegar and mint. Stir well.

Decant into heated jars. Seal and store as any other jelly.

Marmalade of eggs the Jews way

'Take the yolks of twenty-four eggs, beat them for an hour. Clarify one pound of the best moist sugar, four spoonfuls of orange-flower water, one ounce of blanched and pounded almonds; stir all together over a very slow charcoal fire, keep stirring it all the while one way, till it comes to a consistence. Then put it into coffee cups and sprinkle with pounded cinnamon on top.

'This marmalade, mixed with pounded almonds, with orange peel and citron, is made into cakes of all shapes, such as birds, fish and fruit.'

Glasse, Mrs Hannah *The Art of Cookery Made Plain and Easy*, London, 1796.

Glossary

Aniseed – large cumin. See cumin seed.

Bagel – a ring shaped bread roll, first boiled then glazed and baked.

Bain-marie – vessel containing hot water in which foods can be poached and various dishes and sauces can be kept hot without contact with direct heat. The water in *bain-marie* should be kept near boiling point.

Baklava – popular Greek/Turkish pastry, made of filo dough, which when rolled out should be thin and transparent enough to read through. Expert baklava cooks put in from twenty to thirty tissue layers of filo, interspersed with walnuts crushed with sugar, before the pastry is baked and steeped in honey or syrup. For special occasions baklava is made of up to 100 layers of filo! For our more modest version of only twelve layers.

Baste – spoon hot fat or liquid over food roasted, baked or poached in the oven.

Beolas – matzo dessert fritters, usually served at Passover.

Blanching – boiling ingredients for two to three minutes, to cleanse and harden them or, as in the case of almonds, to make them easier to peel.

Blind (baked) – method of baking a flan or pie shell or other pastry case empty. For instructions see vol-au-vent.

Blinz, blinzes – from the Russian *blin* – pancake.

Bouchée – a small puff pastry pattie. The case is usually baked 'blind' and filled with various preparations.

Bouquet-garni – a bunch of herbs, usually containing three sprigs of parsley, one of thyme, and a small bay leaf. To facilitate extraction from soups, sauces, stews, etc. tie in a piece of muslin.

Bourekas – type of pastry traditional for Syrian Jews, similar to sambousek. See recipe.

Brunoise – finely shredded or diced vegetables cooked in butter, margarine or other fat.

Buckwheat – a variety of Saracen corn, *blé noir.* See kasha.

Capsicum – sweet or green pepper, pimento. Unrelated to the pepper of the peppercorns.

Cardamon – an aromatic herb which imparts a pleasant flavour to curries, sweets, etc. Remove seed from shell and grind before use.

Glossary

Cayenne pepper – ground seeds of several varieties of capsicum, red and extremely pungent.

Cholla – braided loaf of fine white bread for Sabbath. Two uncut chollas are placed on the table on Friday evening – the Sabbath eve. For other festive occasions, cholla is made in different shapes. See recipe.

Chanukah – The Feast of Dedication, celebrating the victory of the Jews over the Syrians in 167 B.C. in their struggle for freedom of religion. Potato latkes are traditionally served at *Chanukah*. See recipe.

Charoseth – a mixture of minced or chopped fruit and nuts, moistened with wine. An essential part of the Passover table (see pages 175–83) symbolizing the mortar or clay which the Jews used to make bricks during slavery in Egypt.

Chillis – small and very hot variety of capsicum. Can be red or green. The seeds have a fiery pungency and a couple of chillis is quite enough for a curry dish for four to five servings.

Cholent – traditional meat and vegetable stew cooked overnight for the Sabbath.

Chrain – Yiddish word for horseradish; from the Russian *khren*.

Cinnamon – bark of the cinnamon tree. For most oriental dishes cinnamon sticks are used, which should be removed before the dish is served. Powdered cinnamon is often used for desserts.

Clarified butter – butter melted on low heat until it begins to look like olive oil and a whitish deposit begins to form on the bottom of the pan. To remove the sediment, strain into a clean jar. Much used in Indian cookery.

Cloves – highly aromatic dried buds of the clove tree flowers. They have a spicy flavour and should be used sparingly.

Coconut cream and milk – see recipe. This is used in many Eastern dishes. Coconut milk of a thick consistency is called coconut cream. This is usually the result of the first extraction. If the process is repeated and water added, the thinner liquid is coconut milk. Dishes cooked with coconut milk should be simmered gently and must not be allowed to come to the boil, to prevent curdling.

Coriander – fruit of the *Coriandrum Sativum*, used for flavouring a variety of foods, from meat and pickles to chocolates and liqueurs. An essential ingredient in many curries. It is sold in seeds and in powdered

Glossary

form. In the East, fresh coriander leaves are used, in the way the Italians used basil or parsley.

Cornflour – white flour milled from corn (maize), used for thickening soups and sauces and less frequently as a substitute for flour. (See filo dough.) One teaspoon of cornflour mixed with two tablespoons of cold water make a thin paste which is stirred into soup or sauce for thickening.

Coulibiac – a Russian pie, usually made of pastry or dough with various meat or fish fillings.

Court-bouillon – aromatized liquid for cooking fish, meat, vegetables.

Croûtons – bread cut in dice or sliced, fried in oil, butter or other fat, toasted under the grill, or dried in the oven. See recipes.

Cumin – spicy seeds used in the West for flavouring liqueurs, bread, and certain cheeses, in addition to being used in cooking. In the East, it has a great many uses and is an essential ingredient of curries.

Dag filay – Hebrew for fried fish fillets.

Etrog – citron, fruit of the goodley tree mentioned in the Bible. Used in the celebration of *Succoth*. See recipe for citron jam.

Falafel – the most popular snack throughout Israel and many Arab and Mediterranean countries. Chick-peas croquettes, dressed with tehina or humous and served in pita. See recipe.

Farfel – a Jewish pasta product, rather like Italian *pastine*, but rounder, hand-made, and excellent as garnish for soups or meat dishes.

Fennel – aromatic herb the seeds and leaves of which are used as a flavouring. The seeds resemble caraway seeds and the flavour of common fennel is like that of aniseed.

Filo – Greek/Turkish pastry dough, rolled out tissue paper thin.

Fines herbes – equal parts of finely chopped chervil, chives, parsley, and tarragon.

Fold in – combine beaten mixtures, particularly egg white, without diminishing their lightness.

Garam-masala – Indian mixture of ground spices, essential ingredient of curries. See recipe.

Gefilte fish – from the German for 'stuffed fish'. The preparation which is served in the shape of a roll, loaf or little quenelles, is also used to stuff

Glossary

whole fish. One of the traditional Sabbath *hors-d'oeuvre*. Delicious at any time, especially with beetroot tinted chrain.

Ghee – Indian clarified butter.

Ginger – root stock of a tropical plant widely used in the East. Many oriental dishes require the delicacy of fresh ginger. The dry variety, sold ground, is more pungent. Ginger in syrup, an excellent preserve, can be used as a sweet course, but is not suitable for cooking.

Hamantaschen or **Haman's pockets** – triangular pastries with poppy seed filling, served during *Purim*.

Humous – chick-pea butter, flavoured with sesame seeds. Served as an *hors-d'oeuvre* in many Middle East and Mediterranean countries.

Kasha – cooked buckwheat; from the Russian *kasha* – porridge. See recipe.

Kishke – from the Russian *kishka* – intestine. This transformation of the cheapest ingredients into palatable sausages started among the poorest population of Russia and Poland, both Jewish and non-Jewish. The beef intestines have to be washed and scraped, then stuffed with onion-flavoured or other spicy, savoury filling, sewn up, and cooked slowly in the oven. I have had several recipes sent to me, but decided not to include one, because it is not easy to buy fresh intestines and, to be truthful, I did not fancy all that scraping and washing.

Knishes – pirozhki of Ukrainian origin, using dough or pastry and fillings similar to pirozhki, but are sealed in such a way as to allow the filling to show in the centre.

Krupnik – from Russian *krupa* – i.e. 'grain'. Thick barley soup.

Kosher – leaving out the innumerable witticisms inspired by this adjective, as applied to food, it means ritually clean and permissible according to the Dietary Laws. This applies particularly to meat. *Leviticus* and *Deuteronomy* list forty-two animals as unfit to eat. To be safe, the orthodox should and do buy their meat and poultry only from butchers or suppliers displaying the sign of the National Council of Shechita Boards, which guarantees that the butcher does not keep any *treifah* or non-kosher meat.

Only four-footed animals which chew cud and have a cloven hoof and only fish with scales and fins are kosher. All shellfish is forbidden.

Glossary

Meat and milk may not be eaten together. *Exodus* 23 : 19 says : 'Thou shalt not see the a kid in his mother's milk'. *Exodus* 34 : 26 and *Deuteronomy* 14 : 21 repeat this injunction.

Orthodox households keep separate cooking utensils and containers for dairy and meat products and observing Jews do not touch any dairy product for six hours after a meat meal.

Latke – from the Russian *latka* – small patch, pancake. See recipes.

Lime – a thick-skinned, small, green, citrus fruit, much superior to lemon in flavour. Lemons may be used as a substitute but on no account should manufactured lime juice be used.

Lokshen – noodles. See recipes. The word is humorously used to describe someone 'as thin as a lath' and perhaps less kindly, the Italians – I suspect in the same sense as the French use 'macaroni'. On second thoughts, it is not so unkind. The implication is that one may be as skinny as a rake but still good enough to eat.

Lox – from the German *lachs* – salmon.

Mace – dried shell of the nutmeg, used as a flavouring.

Macerate – to leave food in preparation to permeate it in its flavours.

Marinade – a seasoned liquid, cooked or uncooked, in which food is steeped before cooking, to tenderize and improve flavour.

Marinate – steep food in a marinade.

Matzo – unleavened bread eaten during Passover, commemorating the unleavened bread the Jews had to eat during their flight from Egypt in 1300 B.C., when the dangers threatening them made it impossible to wait for the dough to rise. *Exodus* 12 : 15 says : 'Seven days ye shall eat unleavened bread; even the first day ye shall put away leaven out of your house . . .' and *Exodus* 12 : 17 lays down : 'And ye shall observe the feast of unleavened bread; for in this selfsame day have I brought your armies out of the land of Egypt : therefore shall ye observe this day in your generations by an ordinance for ever.'

Nutmeg – The seed of the nutmeg tree. Obtainable in powdered form or as a nut, which is much better. Freshly grated it has a delightful fragrance.

Orange-blossom water – extract much used in oriental confectionery and pastry making for its subtle fragrance.

Glossary

Pareve glidah – Israeli ice-cream, made without any dairy products, to made it acceptable at kosher meat meals. See recipe.

Pepper – peppercorns, either whole or ground, are used in the kitchen. Black and white pepper comes from the same vine; the berries turn black as they dry in the sun. White pepper is black pepper with the skin removed and is used for dishes which have to preserve their white colour.

Pesach – Passover, the Festival of Freedom, celebrating the deliverance from slavery in Egypt. See Passover dishes.

Pirozhki – diminutive of the Russian word *pirog*, i.e. pie. Small pies, pasties or patties.

Pita – Arab bread, known as *pide* in Turkey, *peda* in the Caucasus.

Poppy seeds – aromatic seeds which have been used in cooking for thousands of years. Poppy seeds are used for the filling of Haman's pockets – little cakes which are part of the festive fare for *Purim*.

Povidl – jam made of pulped fruit. See recipe.

Purim – The Feast of Lots, celebrating the Jews' escape from complete extermination plotted by Haman in Persia. The plot and the deliverance from peril are described in the *Book of Esther*.

Quenelies – dumplings made of various kinds of forcemeat: meat, poultry, fish, cheese, etc.

Rose-water – an ingredient in oriental cookery, used to impart fragrance mainly to sweet dishes. The best rose-water is exported by Bulgaria. Keep rose-water in a cool, dark place, to prevent evaporation and to preserve the fragrance.

Rosh hashanah – beginning of the year. *Rosh Hashanah* celebrates the birthday of the world. It is both a joyous and a solemn festival, for it begins the Ten Days of Penitence which culminate with *Yom Kippur* – the Day of Atonement.

Roux – a mixture of butter, margarine or other fat, and flour, cooked for varying periods of time, depending on how dark or light the dish has to be, used for thickening sauces and soups.

Saffron – dried stamens of the saffron or cultivated crocus, contains a volatile oil and a colouring substance. Expensive, because it has to be gathered by hand and the yield per plant is small. Fortunately, a tiny

Glossary

amount, dissolved in water or other liquid, is sufficient to flavour and colour a dish. Saffron is mentioned in the Bible: *Solomon's Song* 4:14.

Sambousek – Lebanese Jewish type of pirozhki, made of yeast dough, with spinach and cheese filling, glazed, sprinkled with sesame seeds, and baked. See recipe.

Schav – from Russian *shchavel* – sorrel. Sorrel soup, served cold. Makes an excellent summer first course and in Israel is traditional for *Shavuot*.

Schmaltz – cooking fat, usually rendered down chicken fat, excellent for cooking and used instead of butter or margarine in many Jewish dishes. Some dishes, chopped liver, for example, won't be the same without schmaltz – no other dressing will do.

The word is firmly established in the English language and is commonly used, by people who may never have tasted schmaltz in their lives, to denote sentimentality or lushness.

Sephardic – from the Hebrew *Sfarad* – Spain. Adjective describing descendants of Jews from Spain, Portugal, and the Middle East.

Sesame oil – available from shops specializing in oriental produce. Used for flavouring and enriching dishes.

Sesame seeds – very popular ingredients of oriental cookery.

Shabat – Sabbath. *Shabat* is Hebrew for 'rest'.

Shavuot – The Festival of Weeks or Pentecost, so named by the Greek Jews, because *Shavuot* comes fifty days after Passover. It commemorates the giving of the *Torah*, or the Law, on Mount Sinai. The part of *Exodus* telling of the covenant between God and Israel on Mount Sinai, as well as the Ten Commandments, are read during *Shavuot*.

It is also the festival of the first fruits. Synagogues and homes are decorated with green branches and flowers and in some communities desserts are decorated with roses. Dairy dishes, particularly cheese blinzes, their whiteness symbolizing the purity of the Law, are traditionally served during *Shavuot*.

Succoth – the plural of the Hebrew word *succah* – a booth. *Succoth* is the Festival of the Tabernacles. It starts on the fifth day after *Yom Kippur* and in Israel lasts seven days. It commemorates the years the Jews spent wandering in the wilderness and the orthodox custom is to eat the meals

Glossary

in a *succah*, out of doors. It is a booth the roof of which is made up of green branches, laid on top in such a way as to allow the family to see the stars.

Leviticus 23 : 33 – 44 tells of God's command to Moses to observe the Feast of the Tabernacles : 'Ye shall dwell in booths seven days . . . that your generations may know that I made the children of Israel to dwell in booths, when I brought them out of the land of Egypt'.

Succoth is also a thanksgiving harvest festival and among the fruit offerings is the *etrog* or citron (page 280).

Succoth ends with a special celebration, called *Simchat Torah* – 'rejoicing in the Law'. On this day the last portion of the *Torah* – the *Five Books of Moses* – i.e. the last chapter of *Deuteronomy*, is read and at once the first chapter of *Genesis* is started again, closing the circle and symbolizing the endless continuity of faith. *Simchat Torah* is a happy festival, celebrated with much rejoicing, as its name implies, with dancing, singing, and good things to eat.

Tabasco – a bottle sauce, made of capsicums matured in sherry. Hot and spicy and to be used literally in drops.

Tehina – spicy sesame seed butter, used as a dip or sauce in Arab countries, as well as in Greece and Israel. It also enters into the composition of various popular dishes.

Turmeric – orangey-yellow coloured rhizomes, widely used in the East to impart flavour and colour to food. Only a small quantity is needed, no more than half a teaspoon for a dish for four people. Turmeric is often used as a substitute for saffron.

Tzimmes – a dish containing mixed vegetables and fruit, often sweetened carrots. See recipes.

Vol-au-vent – puff pastry case filled with meat, fish, mushrooms, or other mixtures.

Index